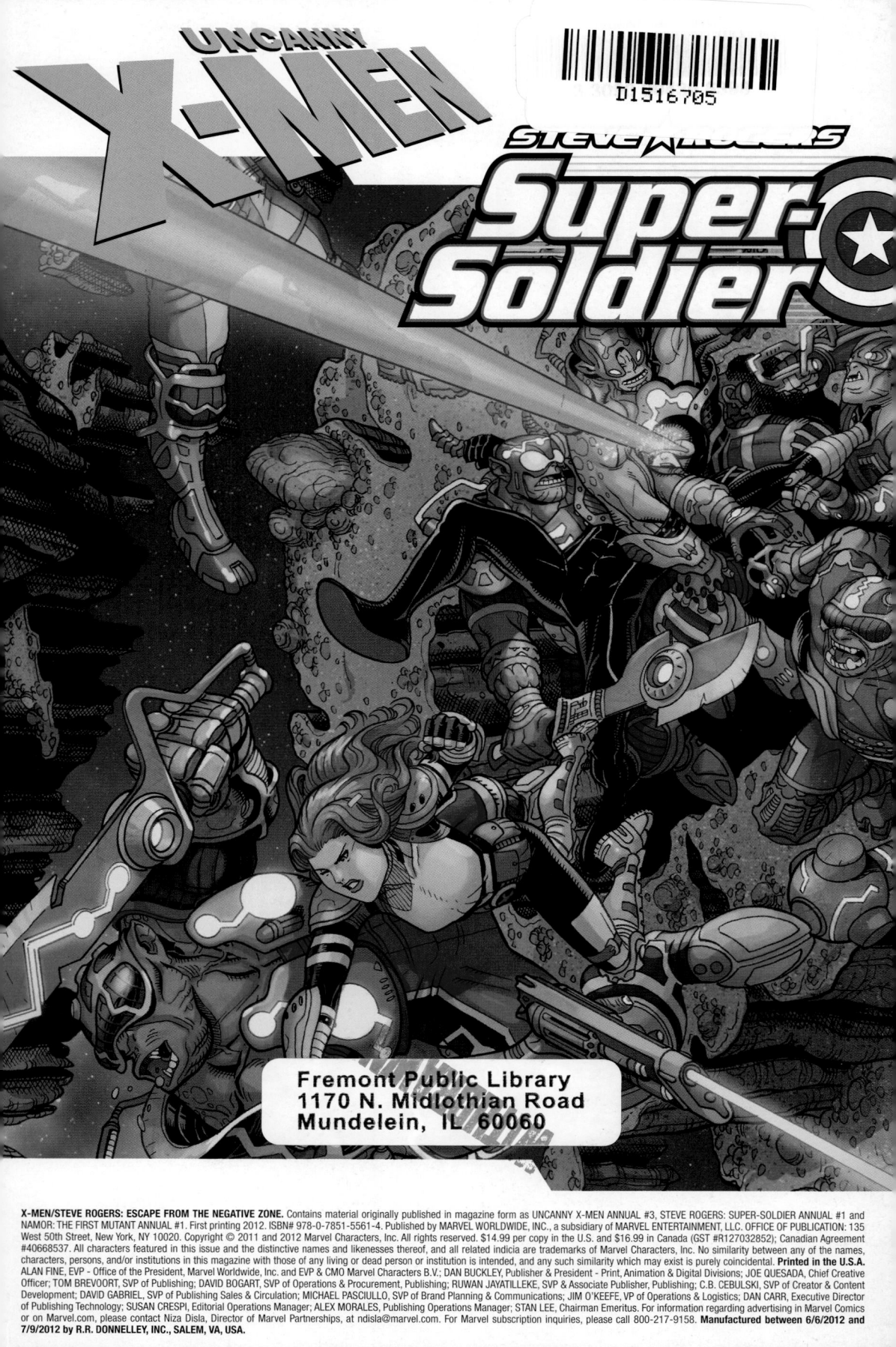

UNCANNY X-MEN

STEVE ROGERS
Super-Soldier

X-MEN/STEVE ROGERS: ESCAPE FROM THE NEGATIVE ZONE. Contains material originally published in magazine form as UNCANNY X-MEN ANNUAL #3, STEVE ROGERS: SUPER-SOLDIER ANNUAL #1 and NAMOR: THE FIRST MUTANT ANNUAL #1. First printing 2012. ISBN# 978-0-7851-5561-4. Published by MARVEL WORLDWIDE, INC., a subsidiary of MARVEL ENTERTAINMENT, LLC. OFFICE OF PUBLICATION: 135 West 50th Street, New York, NY 10020. Copyright © 2011 and 2012 Marvel Characters, Inc. All rights reserved. $14.99 per copy in the U.S. and $16.99 in Canada (GST #R127032852); Canadian Agreement #40668537. All characters featured in this issue and the distinctive names and likenesses thereof, and all related indicia are trademarks of Marvel Characters, Inc. No similarity between any of the names, characters, persons, and/or institutions in this magazine with those of any living or dead person or institution is intended, and any such similarity which may exist is purely coincidental. **Printed in the U.S.A.** ALAN FINE, EVP - Office of the President, Marvel Worldwide, Inc. and EVP & CMO Marvel Characters B.V.; DAN BUCKLEY, Publisher & President - Print, Animation & Digital Divisions; JOE QUESADA, Chief Creative Officer; TOM BREVOORT, SVP of Publishing; DAVID BOGART, SVP of Operations & Procurement, Publishing; RUWAN JAYATILLEKE, SVP & Associate Publisher, Publishing; C.B. CEBULSKI, SVP of Creator & Content Development; DAVID GABRIEL, SVP of Publishing Sales & Circulation; MICHAEL PASCIULLO, SVP of Brand Planning & Communications; JIM O'KEEFE, VP of Operations & Logistics; DAN CARR, Executive Director of Publishing Technology; SUSAN CRESPI, Editorial Operations Manager; ALEX MORALES, Publishing Operations Manager; STAN LEE, Chairman Emeritus. For information regarding advertising in Marvel Comics or on Marvel.com, please contact Niza Disla, Director of Marvel Partnerships, at ndisla@marvel.com. For Marvel subscription inquiries, please call 800-217-9158. **Manufactured between 6/6/2012 and 7/9/2012 by R.R. DONNELLEY, INC., SALEM, VA, USA.**
10 9 8 7 6 5 4 3 2 1

ESCAPE FROM THE NEGATIVE ZONE

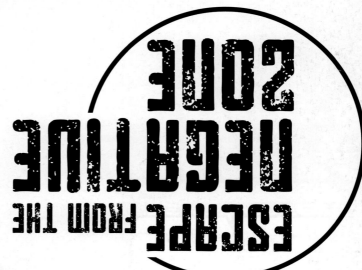

Writer: **James Asmus**
Artist, *Uncanny X-Men Annual #3*: **Nick Bradshaw**
Artist, *Steve Rogers: Super-Soldier Annual #1*: **Ibraim Roberson**
Artist, *Namor: The First Mutant Annual #1*: **Max Fiumara**
with ink assist from **Norman Lee**
Colorist: **Jim Charalampidis**
Letterer: **Jared K. Fletcher**
Cover Artist: **Black Frog**
Assistant Editors: **Jake Thomas** & **Jordan D. White**
Associate Editor: **Daniel Ketchum**
Editor: **Nick Lowe**

Collection Editor & Design: **Cory Levine**
Assistant Editors: **Alex Starbuck** & **Nelson Ribeiro**
Editors, Special Projects: **Jennifer Grünwald** & **Mark D. Beazley**
Senior Editor, Special Projects: **Jeff Youngquist**
Senior Vice President of Sales: **David Gabriel**
SVP of Brand Planning & Communications: **Michael Pasciullo**
Collection Cover Artists: **Nick Bradshaw** & **Jim Charalampidis**

Editor In Chief: **Axel Alonso**
Chief Creative Officer: **Joe Quesada**
Publisher: **Dan Buckley**
Executive Producer: **Alan Fine**

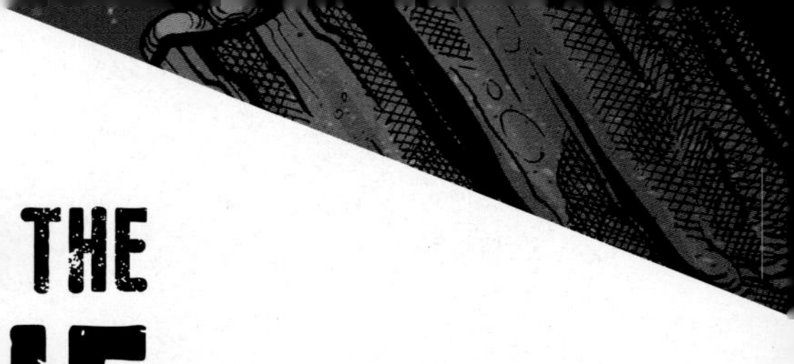

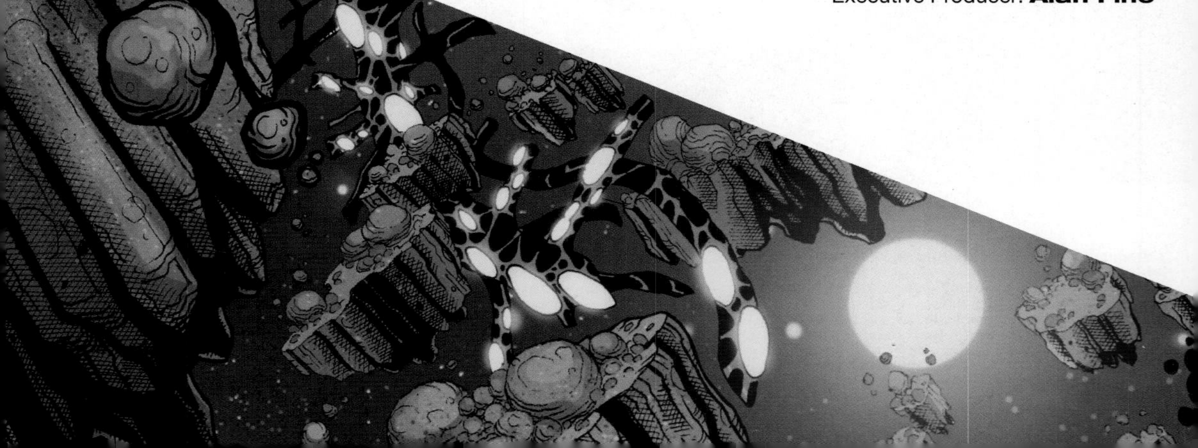

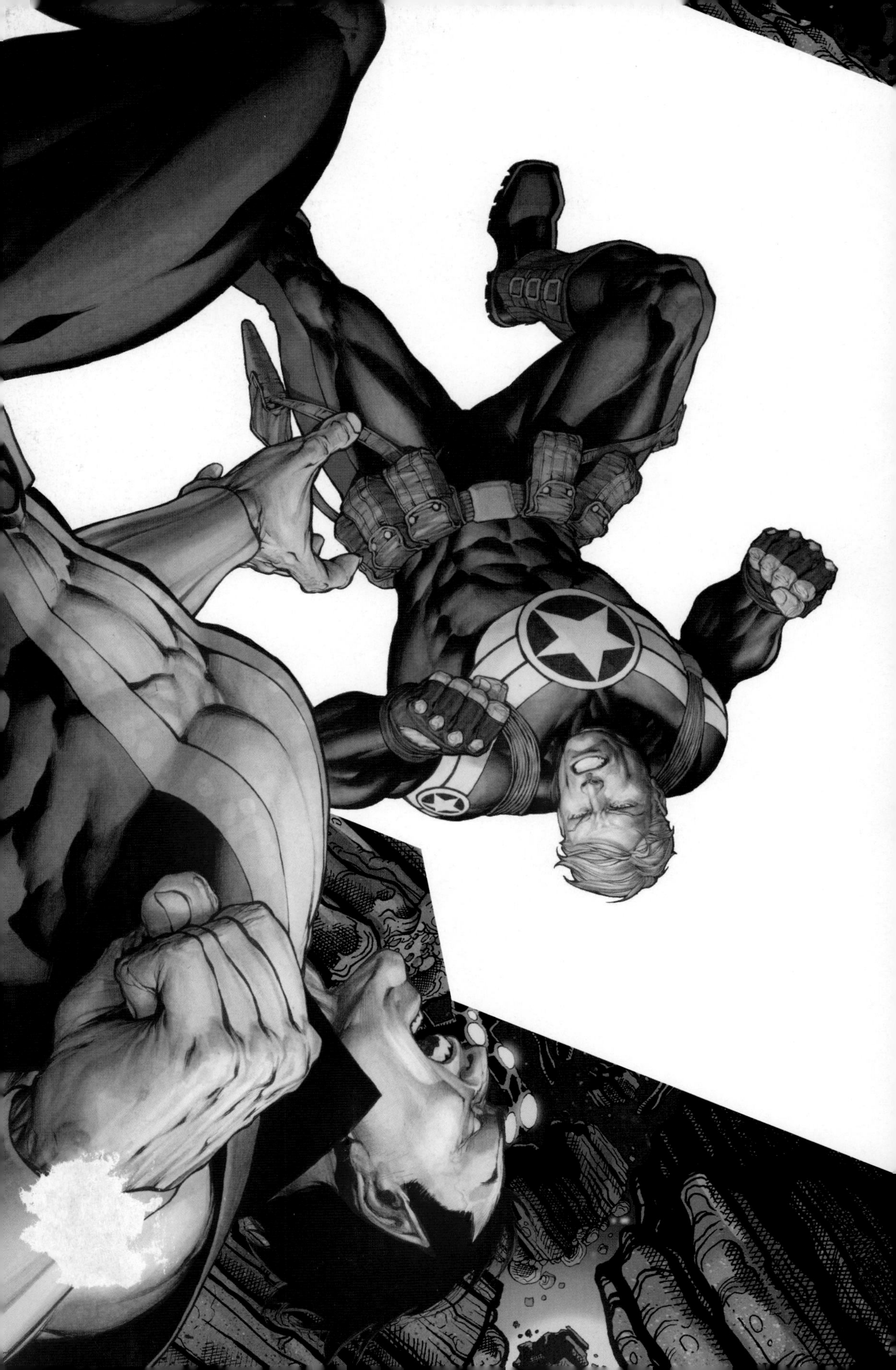

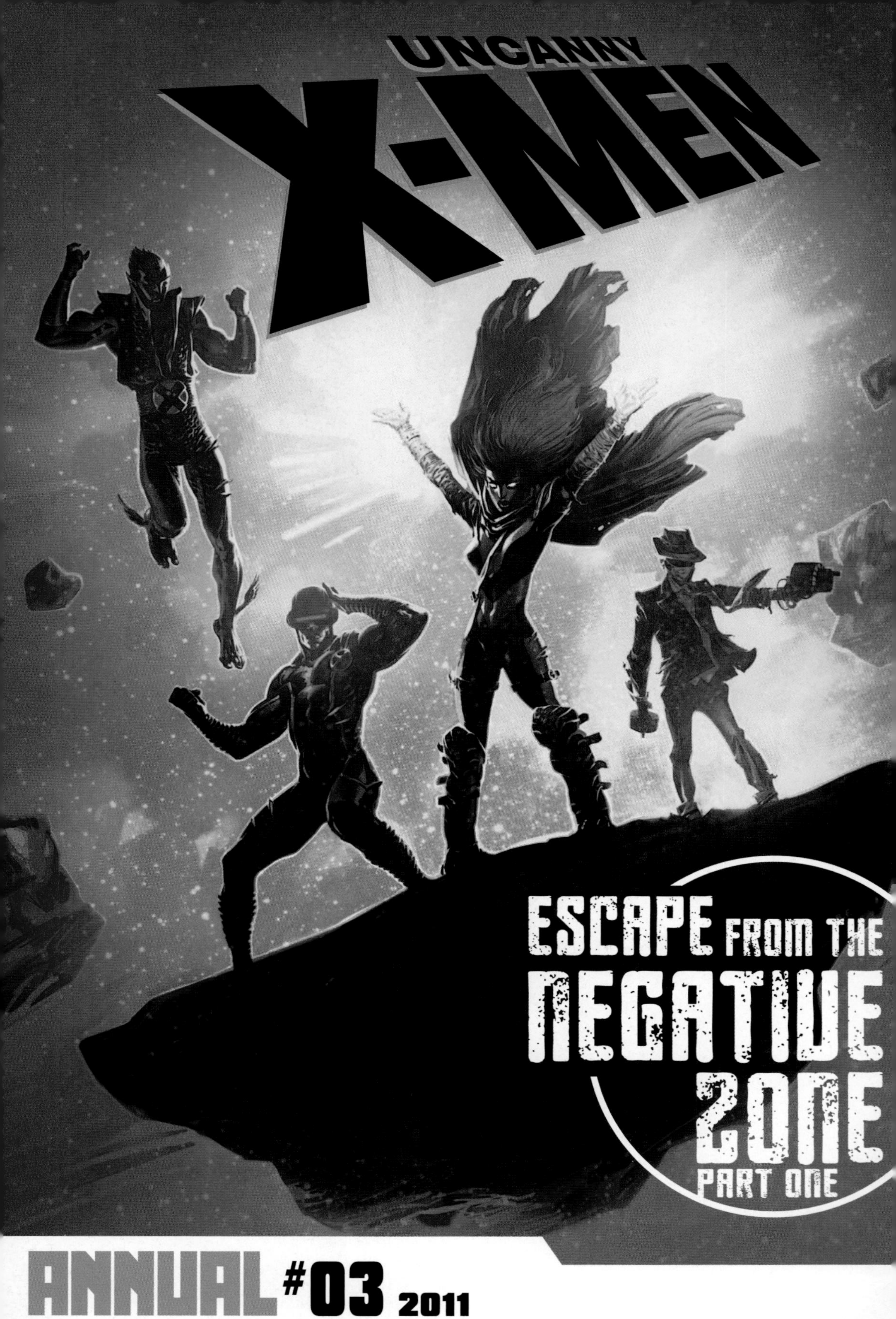
UNCANNY
X-MEN
ESCAPE FROM THE
NEGATIVE
ZONE
PART ONE

ANNUAL #03 2011

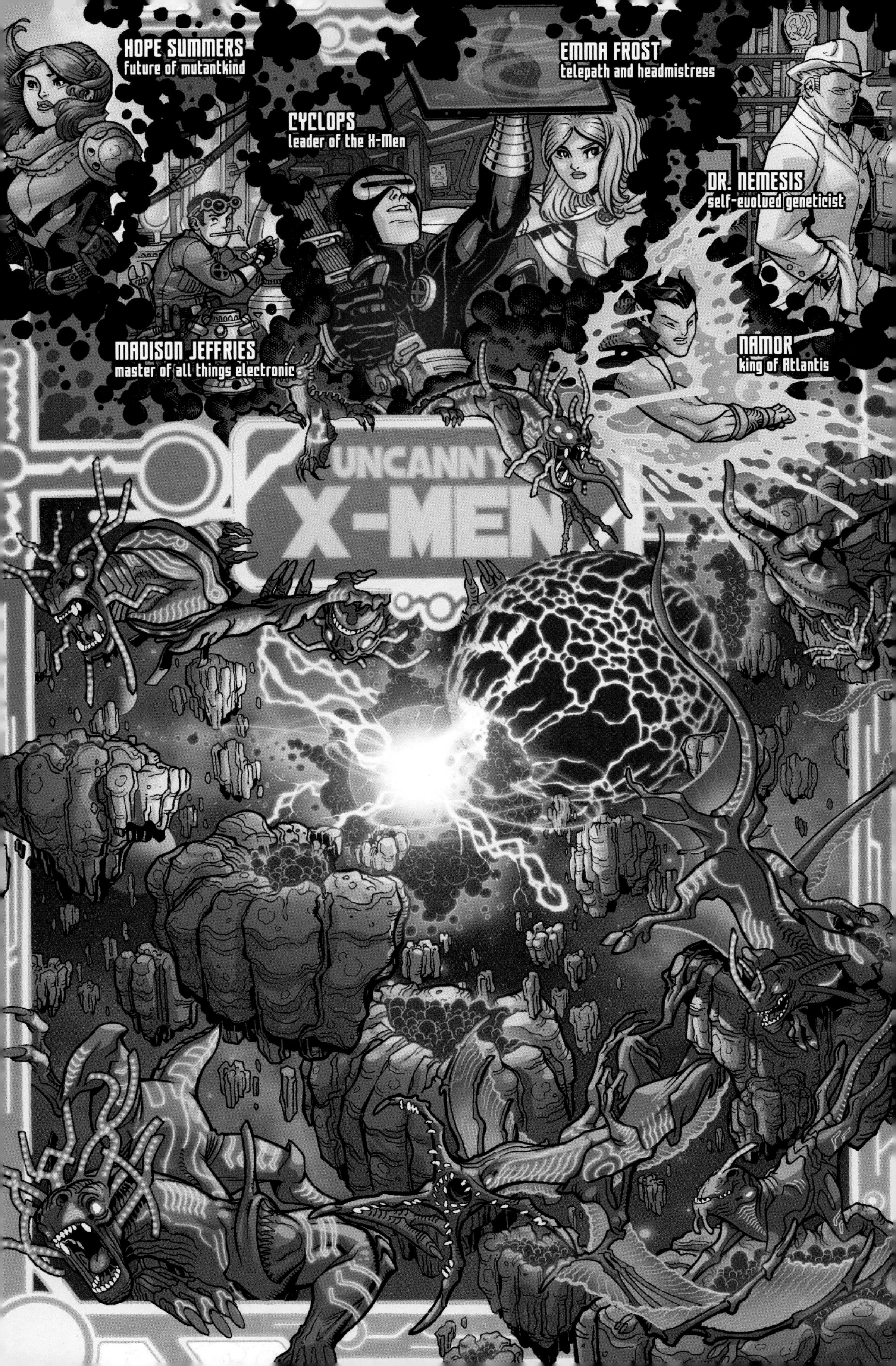
HOPE SUMMERS
future of mutantkind
EMMA FROST
telepath and headmistress
CYCLOPS
leader of the X-Men
DR. NEMESIS
self-evolved geneticist
MADISON JEFFRIES
master of all things electronic
NAMOR
king of Atlantis
UNCANNY
X-MEN

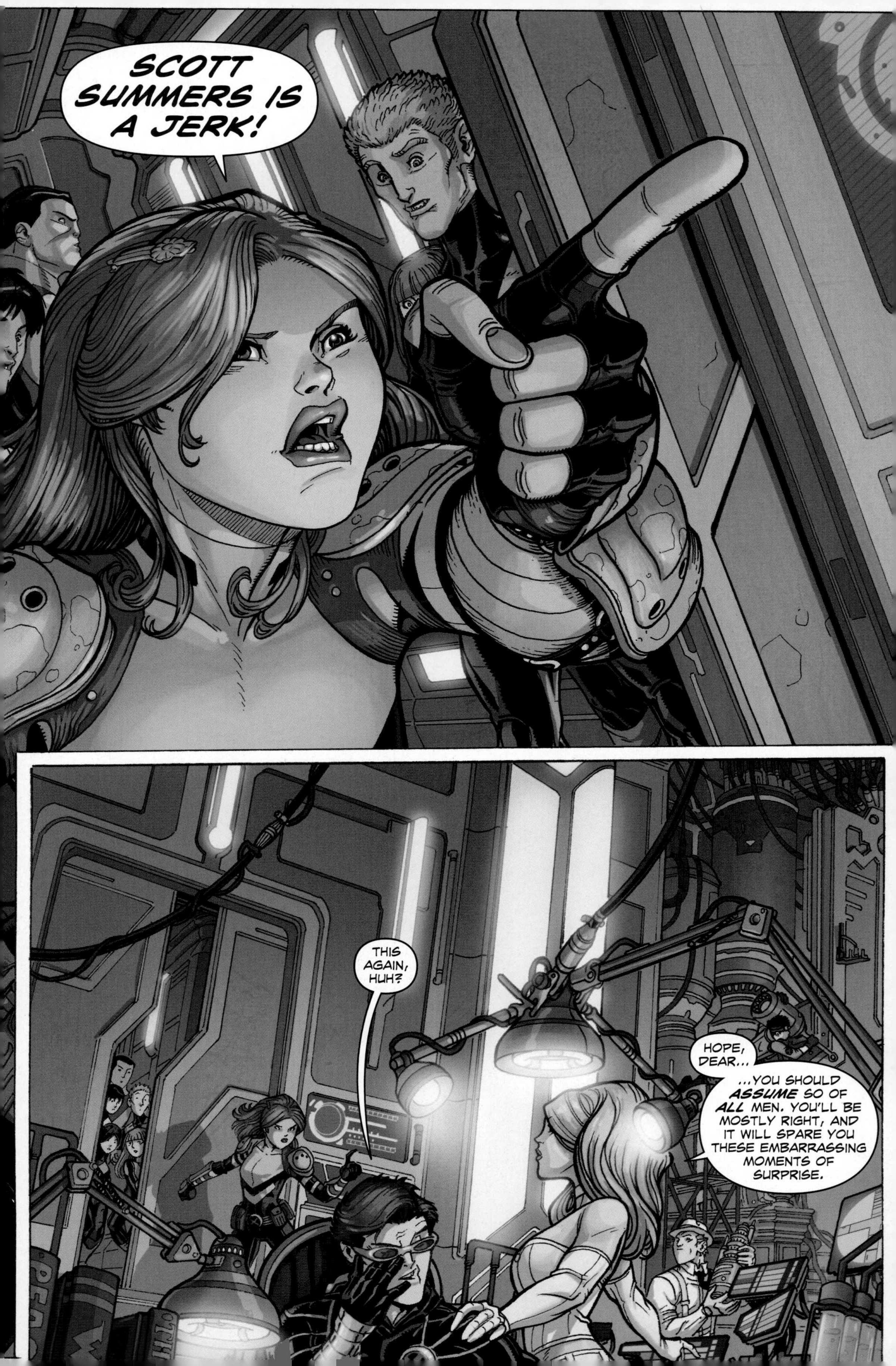
SCOTT SUMMERS IS A JERK!
THIS AGAIN, HUH?
HOPE, DEAR...
...YOU SHOULD *ASSUME* SO OF *ALL* MEN. YOU'LL BE MOSTLY RIGHT, AND IT WILL SPARE YOU THESE EMBARRASSING MOMENTS OF SURPRISE.

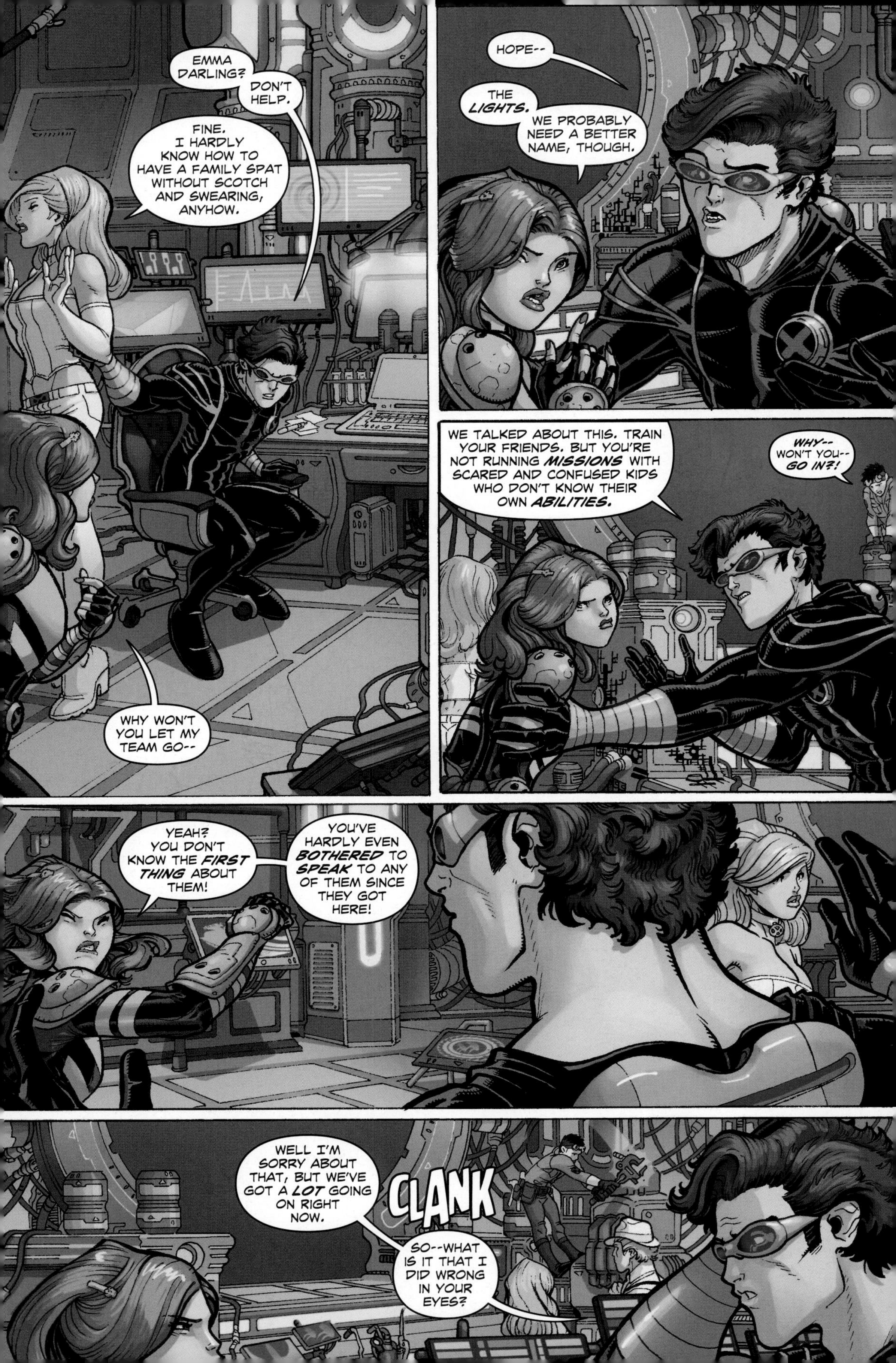
EMMA DARLING?
DON'T HELP.
FINE. I HARDLY KNOW HOW TO HAVE A FAMILY SPAT WITHOUT SCOTCH AND SWEARING, ANYHOW.
WHY WON'T YOU LET MY TEAM GO--
HOPE--
THE *LIGHTS.*
WE PROBABLY NEED A BETTER NAME, THOUGH.
WE TALKED ABOUT THIS. TRAIN YOUR FRIENDS. BUT YOU'RE NOT RUNNING *MISSIONS* WITH SCARED AND CONFUSED KIDS WHO DON'T KNOW THEIR OWN *ABILITIES.*
WHY-- WON'T YOU-- *GO IN?!*
YEAH? YOU DON'T KNOW THE *FIRST THING* ABOUT THEM!
YOU'VE HARDLY EVEN *BOTHERED* TO *SPEAK* TO ANY OF THEM SINCE THEY GOT HERE!
WELL I'M SORRY ABOUT THAT, BUT WE'VE GOT A *LOT* GOING ON RIGHT NOW.
CLANK
SO--WHAT IS IT THAT I DID WRONG IN YOUR EYES?

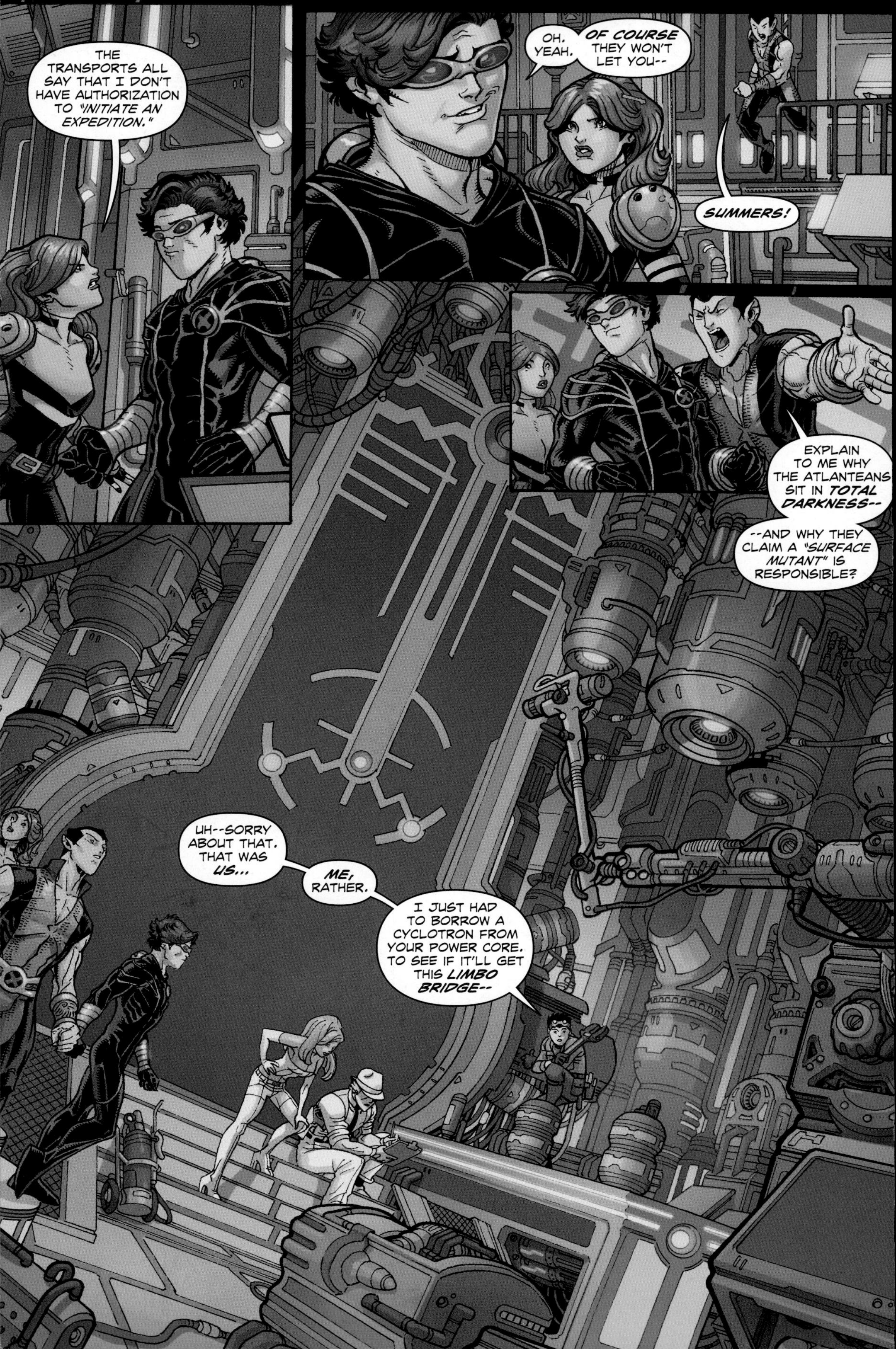
THE TRANSPORTS ALL SAY THAT I DON'T HAVE AUTHORIZATION TO "INITIATE AN EXPEDITION."
OH. YEAH.
OF COURSE THEY WON'T LET YOU--
SUMMERS!
EXPLAIN TO ME WHY THE ATLANTEANS SIT IN TOTAL DARKNESS--
--AND WHY THEY CLAIM A "SURFACE MUTANT" IS RESPONSIBLE?
UH--SORRY ABOUT THAT. THAT WAS US...
ME, RATHER.
I JUST HAD TO BORROW A CYCLOTRON FROM YOUR POWER CORE. TO SEE IF IT'LL GET THIS LIMBO BRIDGE--

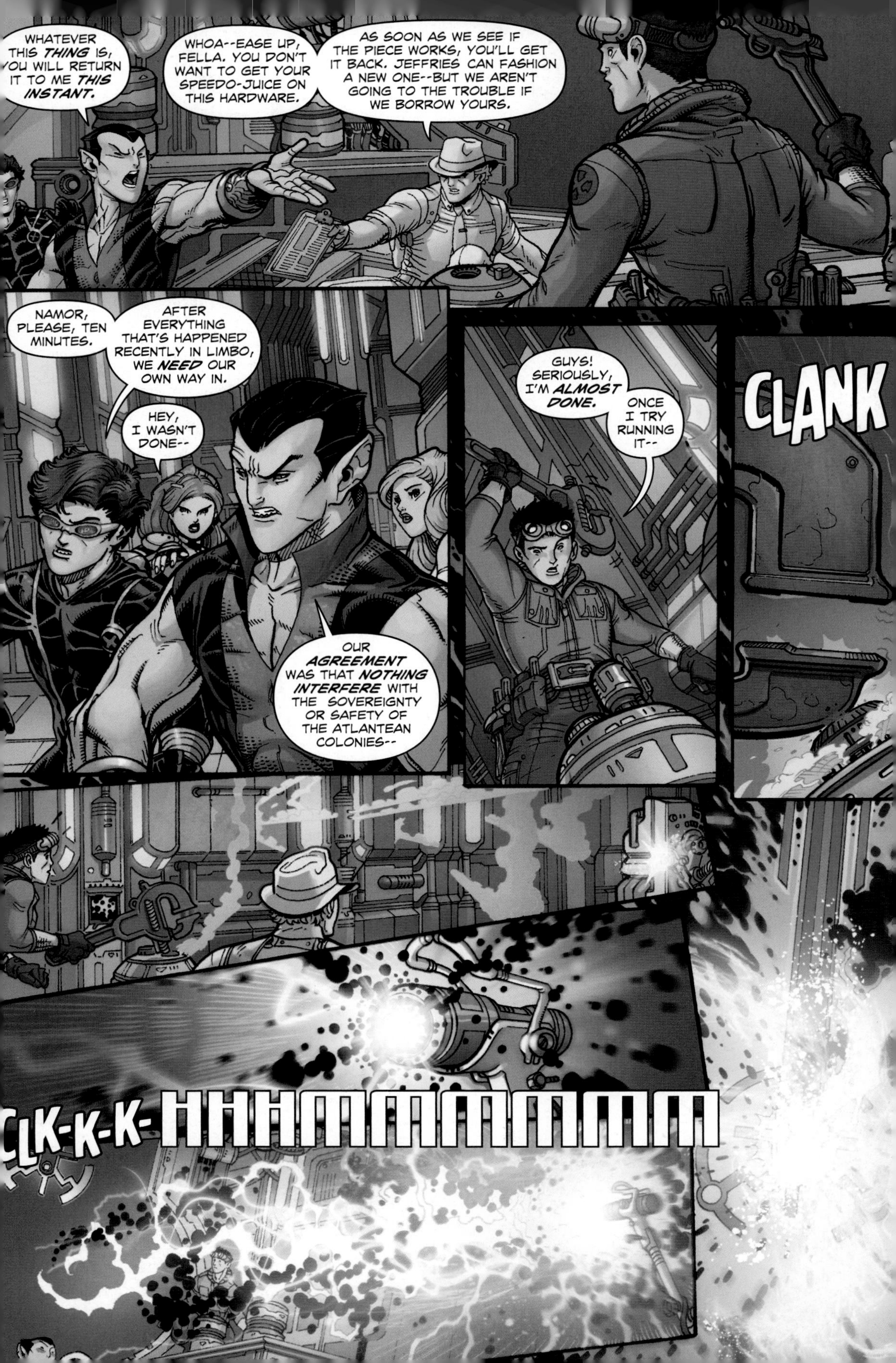
WHATEVER THIS *THING* IS, YOU WILL RETURN IT TO ME *THIS INSTANT.*
WHOA--EASE UP, FELLA. YOU DON'T WANT TO GET YOUR SPEEDO-JUICE ON THIS HARDWARE.
AS SOON AS WE SEE IF THE PIECE WORKS, YOU'LL GET IT BACK. JEFFRIES CAN FASHION A NEW ONE--BUT WE AREN'T GOING TO THE TROUBLE IF WE BORROW YOURS.
NAMOR, PLEASE, TEN MINUTES.
AFTER EVERYTHING THAT'S HAPPENED RECENTLY IN LIMBO, WE *NEED* OUR OWN WAY IN.
HEY, I WASN'T DONE--
OUR *AGREEMENT* WAS THAT *NOTHING INTERFERE* WITH THE SOVEREIGNTY OR SAFETY OF THE ATLANTEAN COLONIES--
GUYS! SERIOUSLY, I'M *ALMOST DONE.*
ONCE I TRY RUNNING IT--
CLANK
CLK-K-K-HHHMMMMMMMM

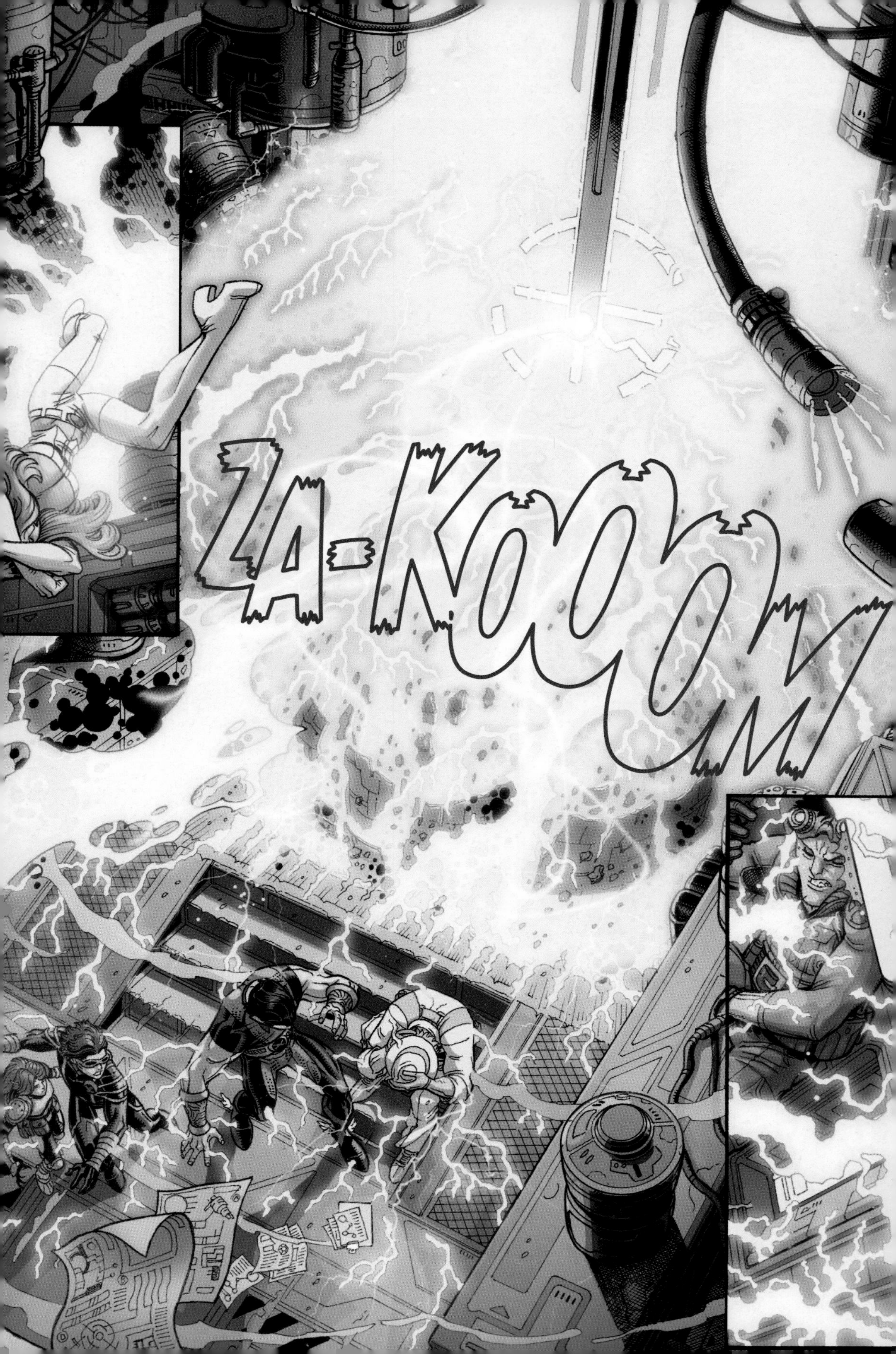
ZA-KOOOOOM

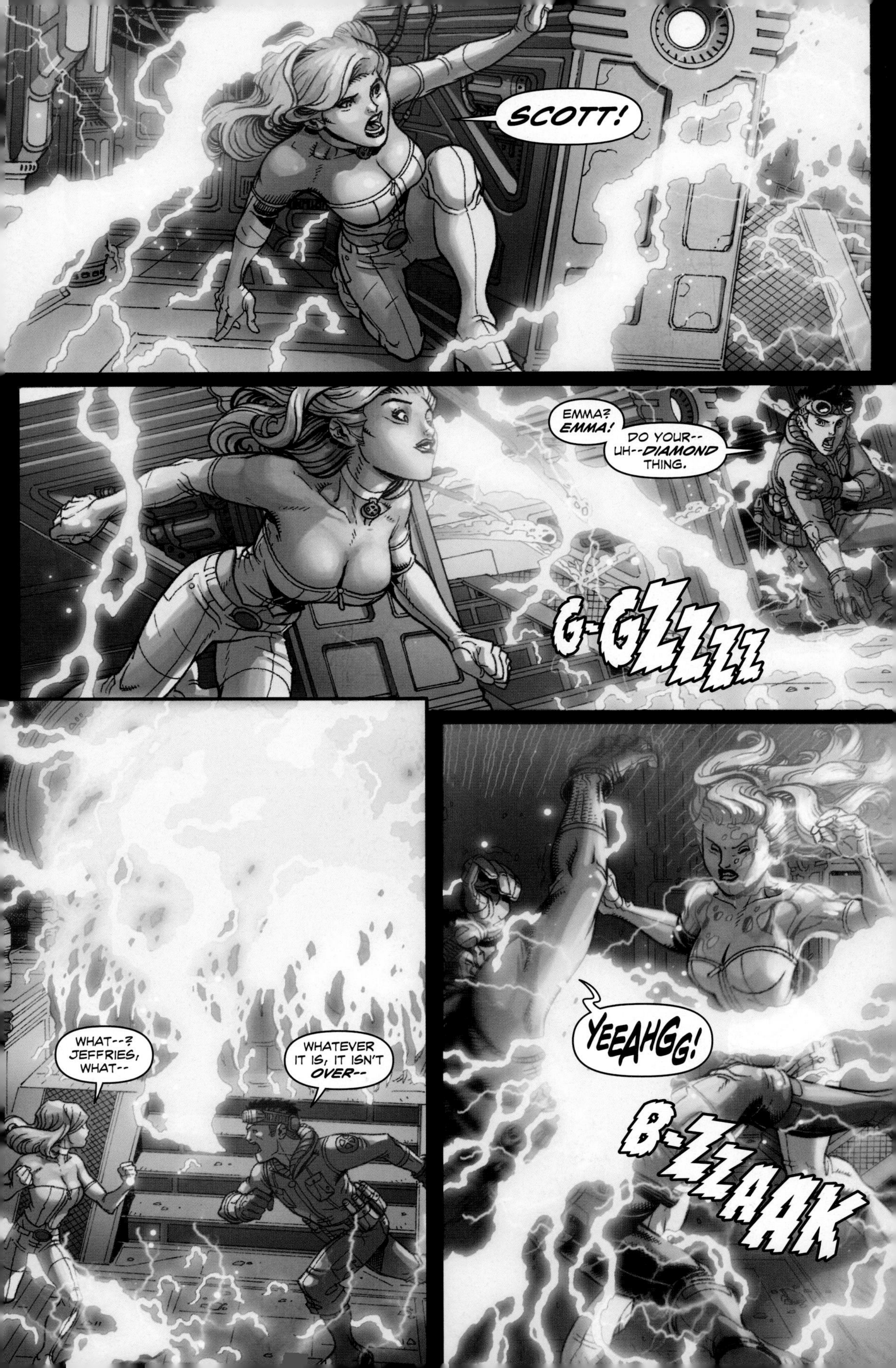
SCOTT!
EMMA? EMMA!
DO YOUR-- UH--DIAMOND THING.
G-GZZZZZ
WHAT--? JEFFRIES, WHAT--
WHATEVER IT IS, IT ISN'T OVER--
YEEAHGG!
B-ZZAAK

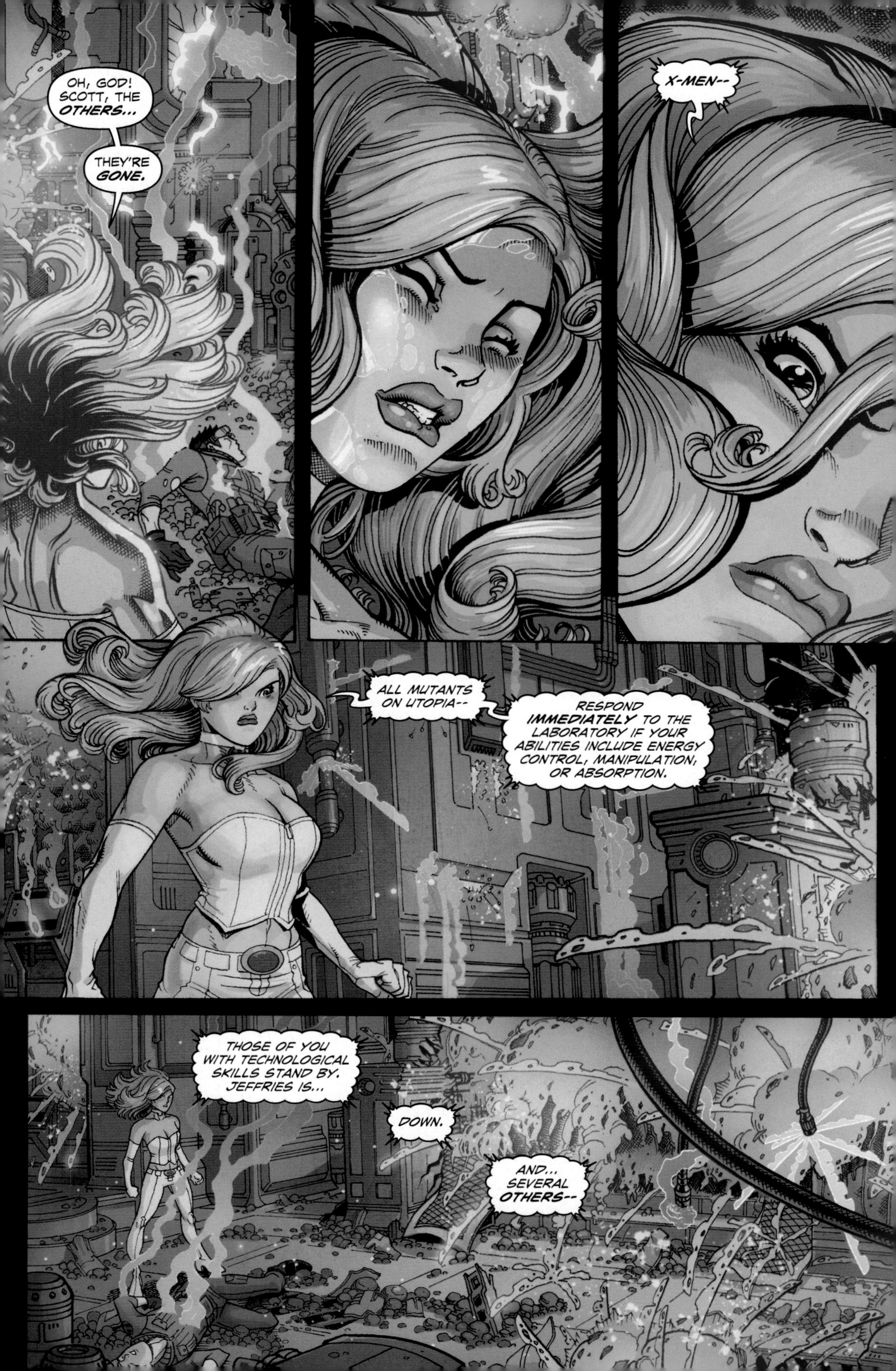
OH, GOD! SCOTT, THE OTHERS...
THEY'RE GONE.
X-MEN--
ALL MUTANTS ON UTOPIA--
RESPOND IMMEDIATELY TO THE LABORATORY IF YOUR ABILITIES INCLUDE ENERGY CONTROL, MANIPULATION, OR ABSORPTION.
THOSE OF YOU WITH TECHNOLOGICAL SKILLS STAND BY. JEFFRIES IS...
DOWN.
AND... SEVERAL OTHERS--

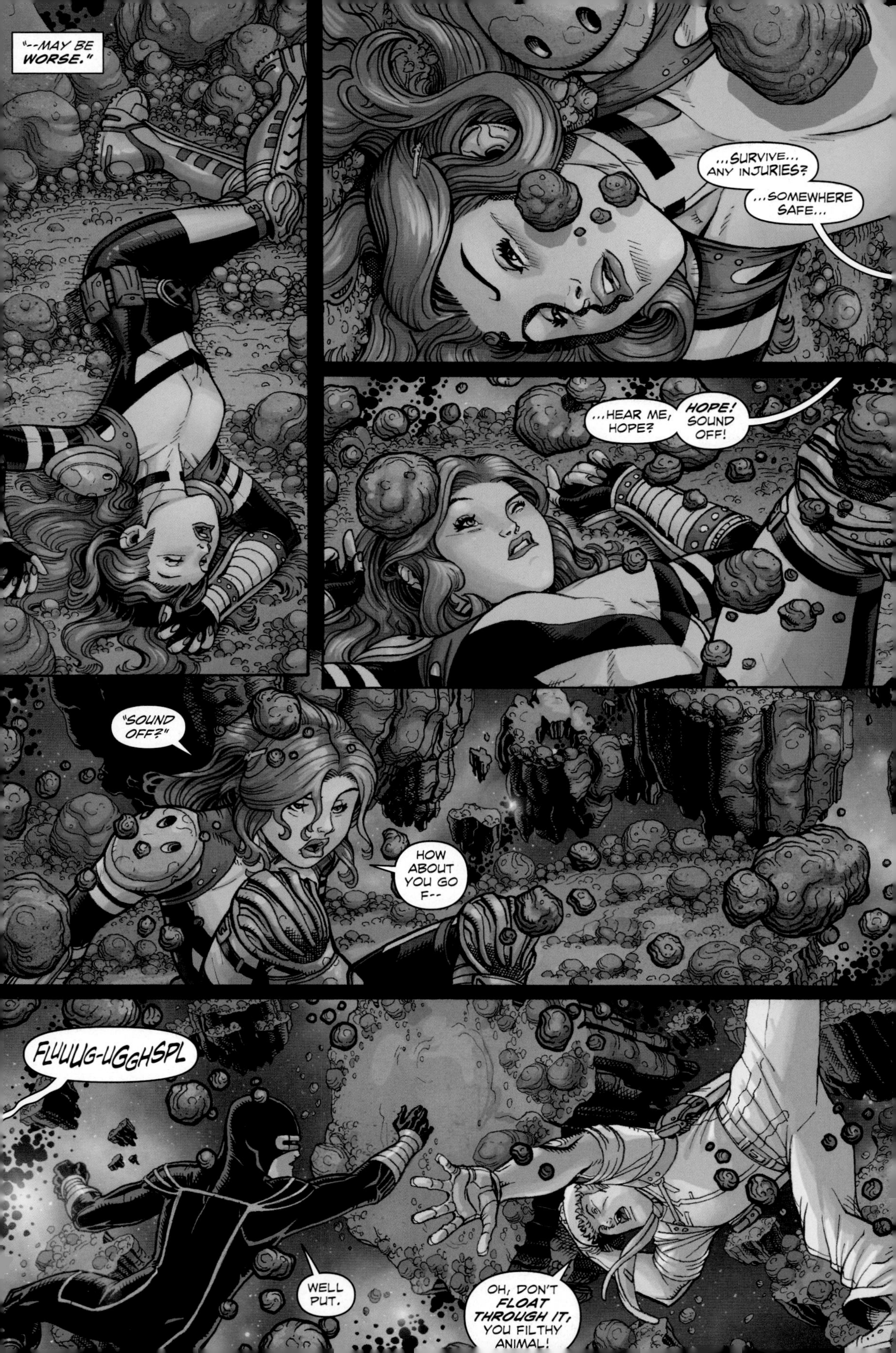
"--MAY BE WORSE."
...SURVIVE... ANY INJURIES?
...SOMEWHERE SAFE...
...HEAR ME, HOPE?
HOPE! SOUND OFF!
"SOUND OFF?"
HOW ABOUT YOU GO F--
FLUUUG-UGGHSPL
WELL PUT.
OH, DON'T FLOAT THROUGH IT, YOU FILTHY ANIMAL!

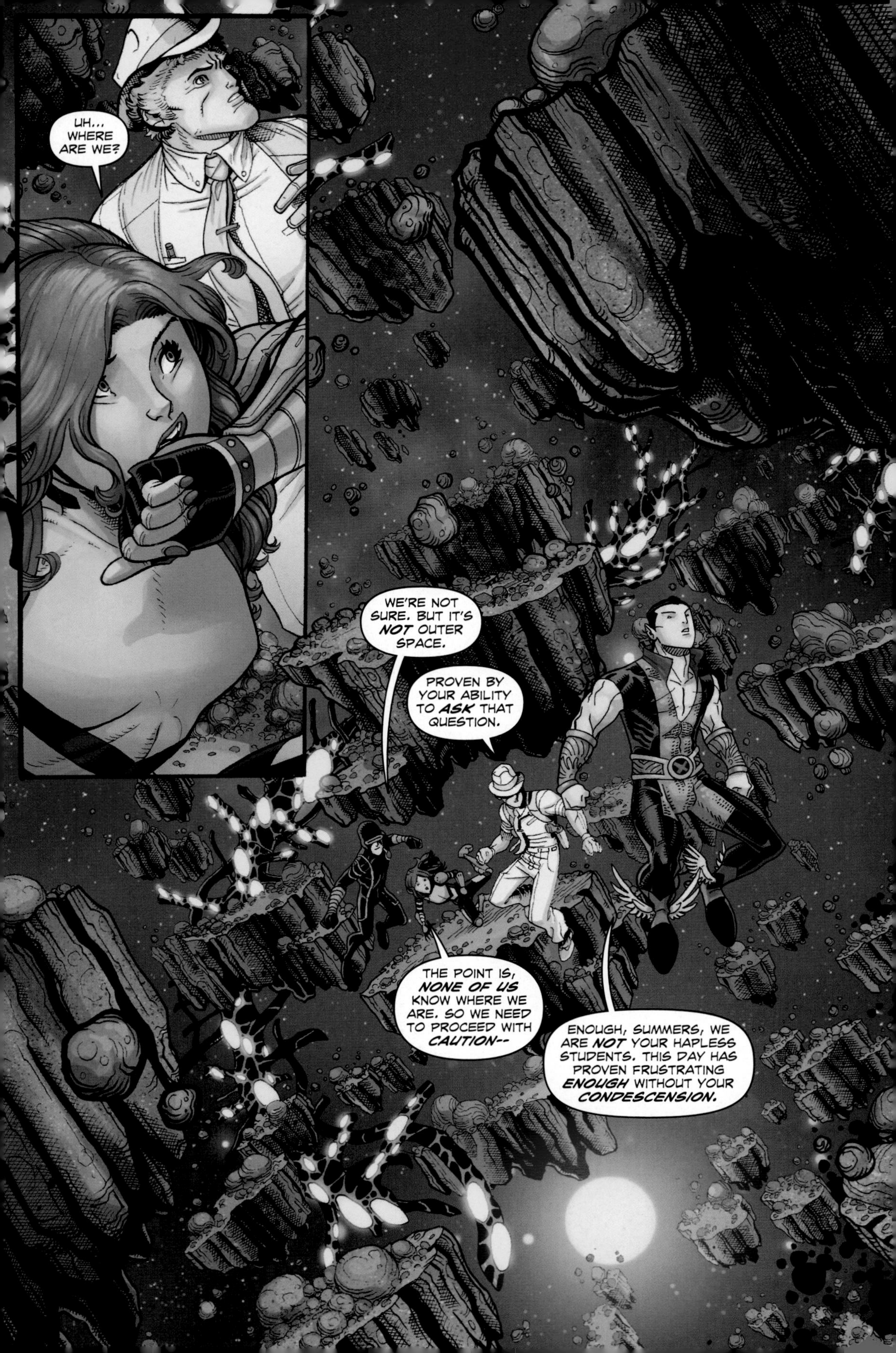
UH... WHERE ARE WE?
WE'RE NOT SURE. BUT IT'S *NOT* OUTER SPACE.
PROVEN BY YOUR ABILITY TO *ASK* THAT QUESTION.
THE POINT IS, *NONE OF US* KNOW WHERE WE ARE. SO WE NEED TO PROCEED WITH *CAUTION--*
ENOUGH, SUMMERS, WE ARE *NOT* YOUR HAPLESS STUDENTS. THIS DAY HAS PROVEN FRUSTRATING *ENOUGH* WITHOUT YOUR *CONDESCENSION.*

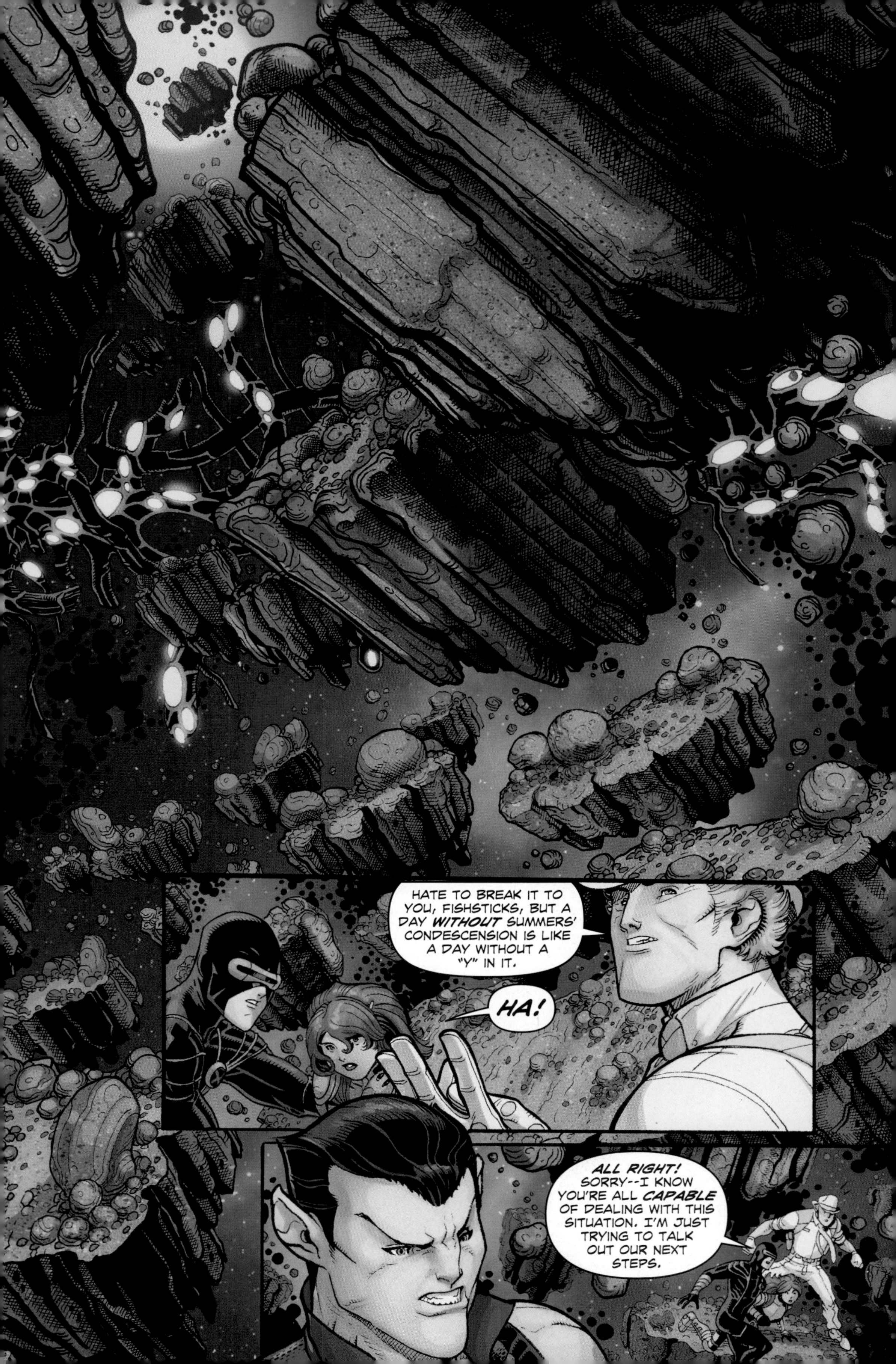
HATE TO BREAK IT TO YOU, FISHSTICKS, BUT A DAY *WITHOUT* SUMMERS' CONDESCENSION IS LIKE A DAY WITHOUT A "Y" IN IT.
HA!
ALL RIGHT! SORRY--I KNOW YOU'RE ALL *CAPABLE* OF DEALING WITH THIS SITUATION. I'M JUST TRYING TO TALK OUT OUR NEXT STEPS.

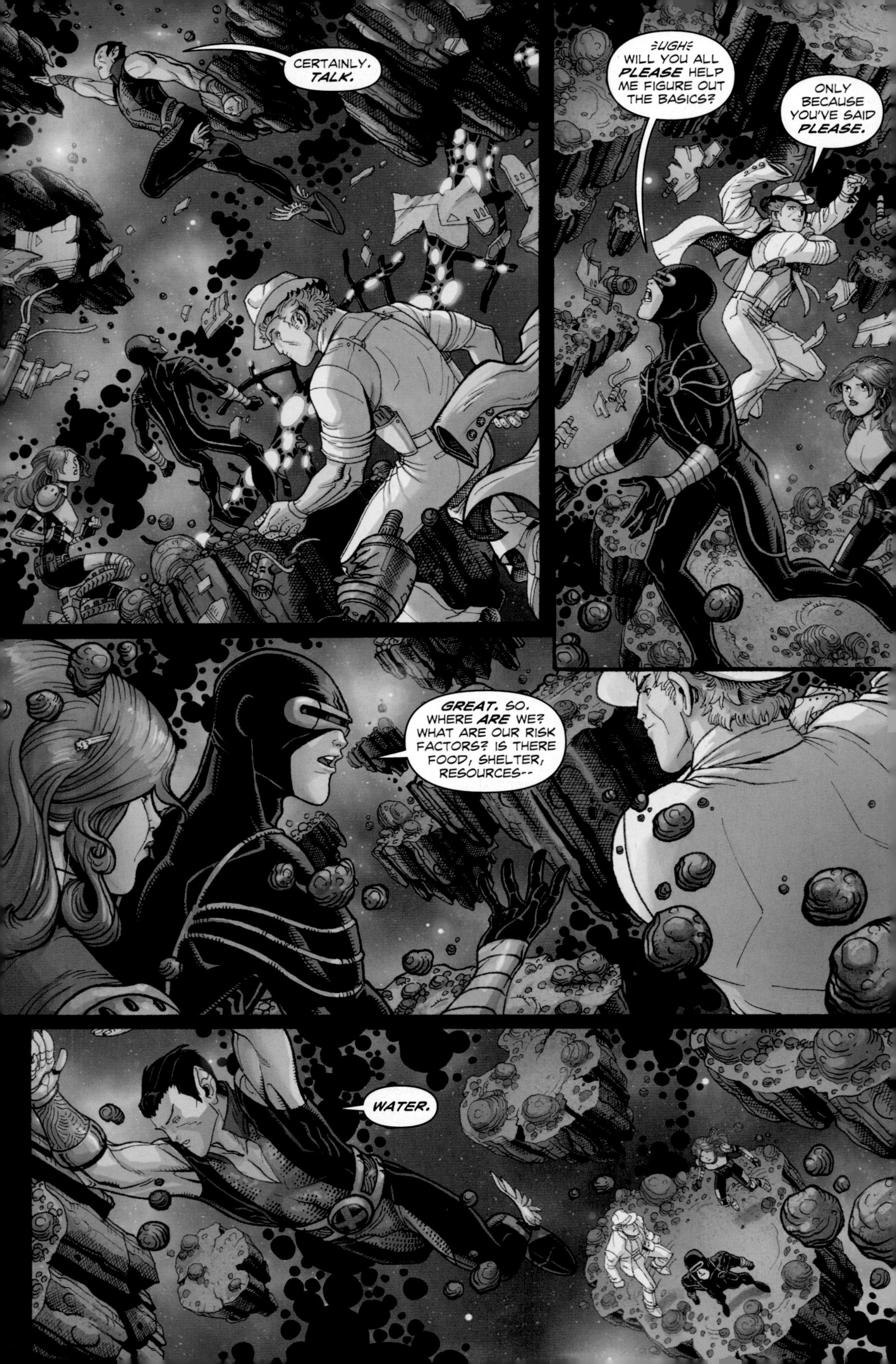
CERTAINLY. TALK.
UGH WILL YOU ALL PLEASE HELP ME FIGURE OUT THE BASICS?
ONLY BECAUSE YOU'VE SAID PLEASE.
GREAT. SO. WHERE ARE WE? WHAT ARE OUR RISK FACTORS? IS THERE FOOD, SHELTER, RESOURCES--
WATER.

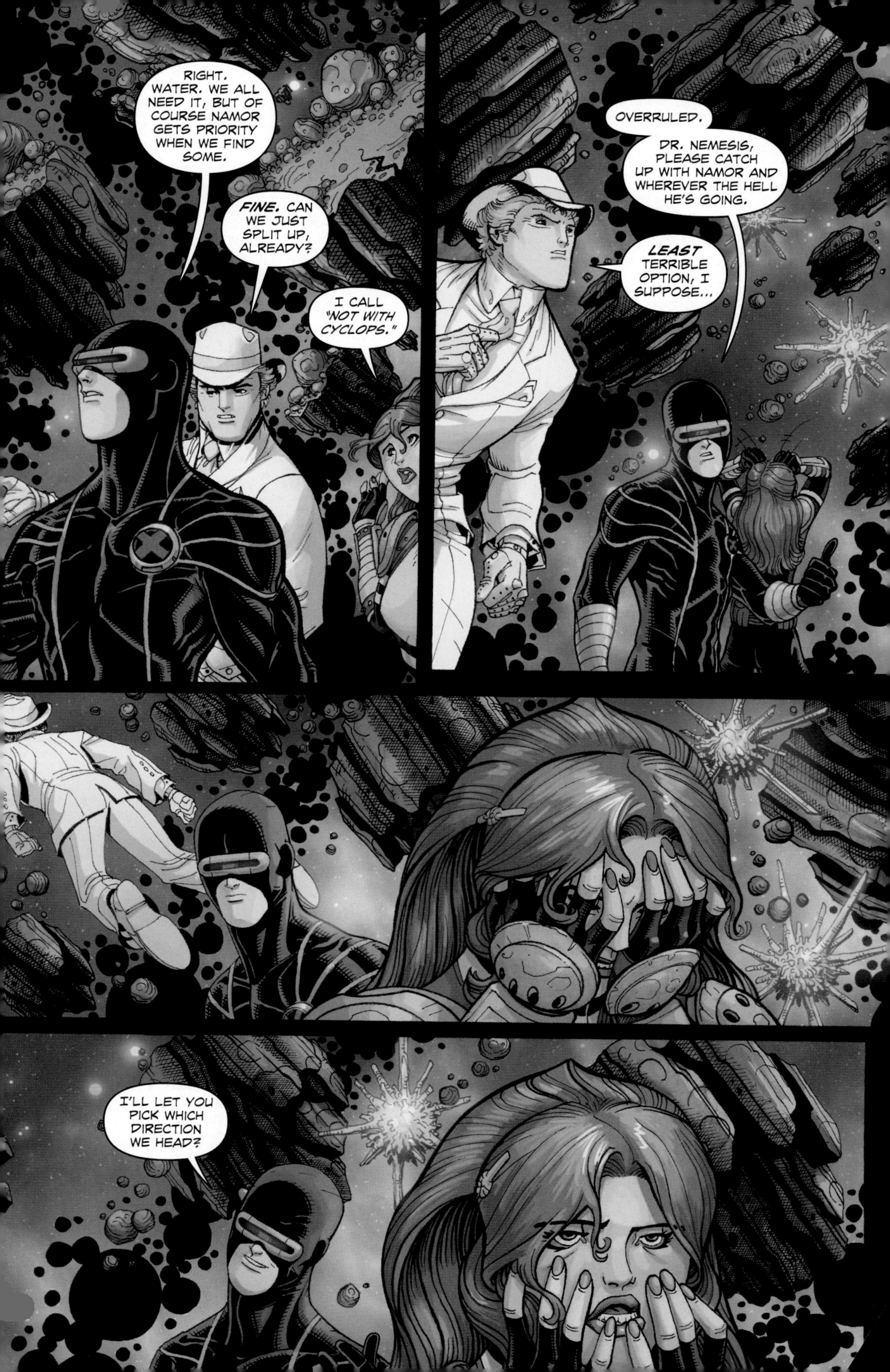
RIGHT. WATER. WE ALL NEED IT, BUT OF COURSE NAMOR GETS PRIORITY WHEN WE FIND SOME.
FINE. CAN WE JUST SPLIT UP, ALREADY?
I CALL "NOT WITH CYCLOPS."
OVERRULED.
DR. NEMESIS, PLEASE CATCH UP WITH NAMOR AND WHEREVER THE HELL HE'S GOING.
LEAST TERRIBLE OPTION, I SUPPOSE...
I'LL LET YOU PICK WHICH DIRECTION WE HEAD?

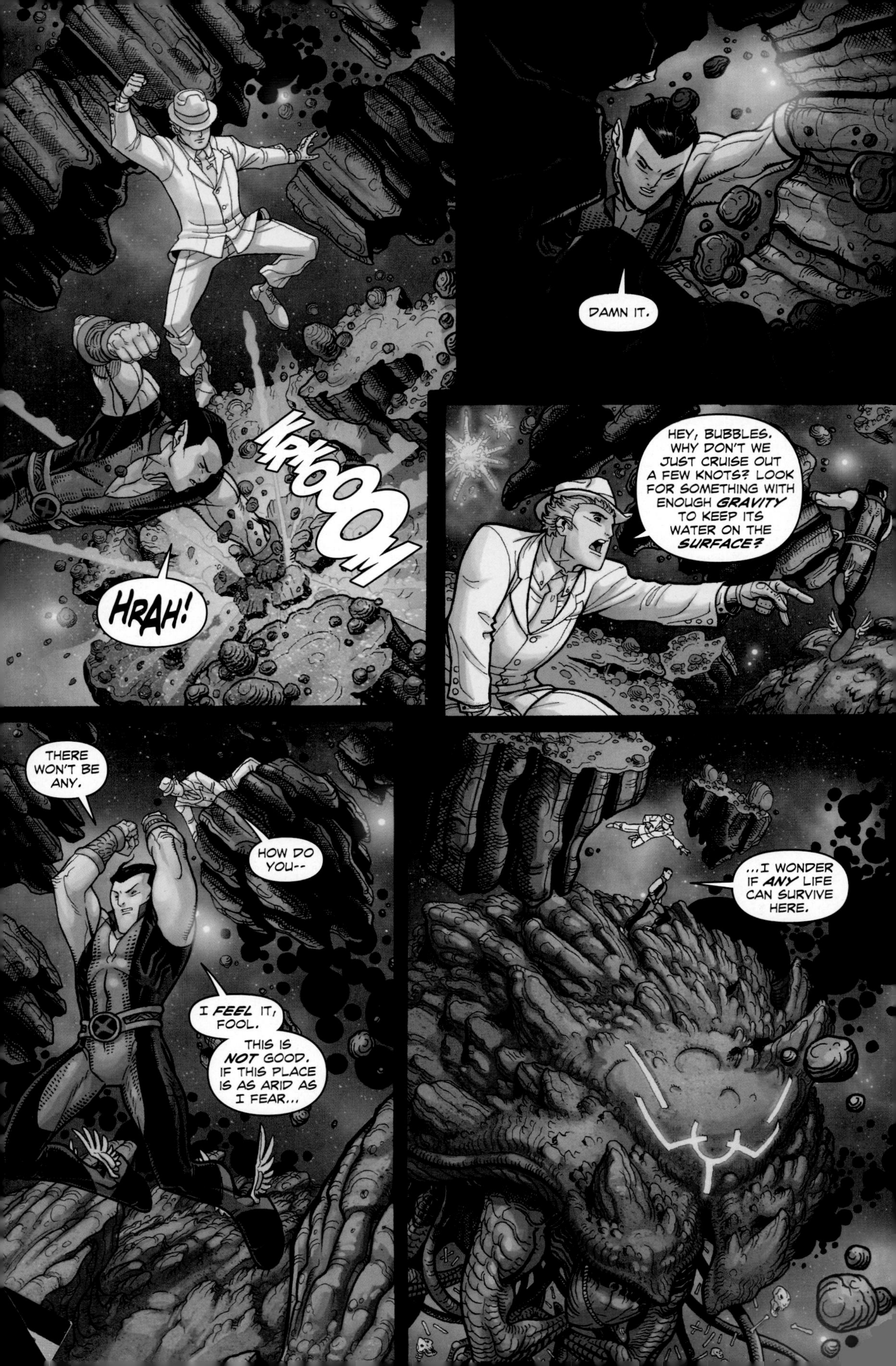
KRKOOOM
HRAH!
DAMN IT.
HEY, BUBBLES. WHY DON'T WE JUST CRUISE OUT A FEW KNOTS? LOOK FOR SOMETHING WITH ENOUGH GRAVITY TO KEEP ITS WATER ON THE SURFACE?
THERE WON'T BE ANY.
HOW DO YOU--
I FEEL IT, FOOL.
THIS IS NOT GOOD. IF THIS PLACE IS AS ARID AS I FEAR...
...I WONDER IF ANY LIFE CAN SURVIVE HERE.

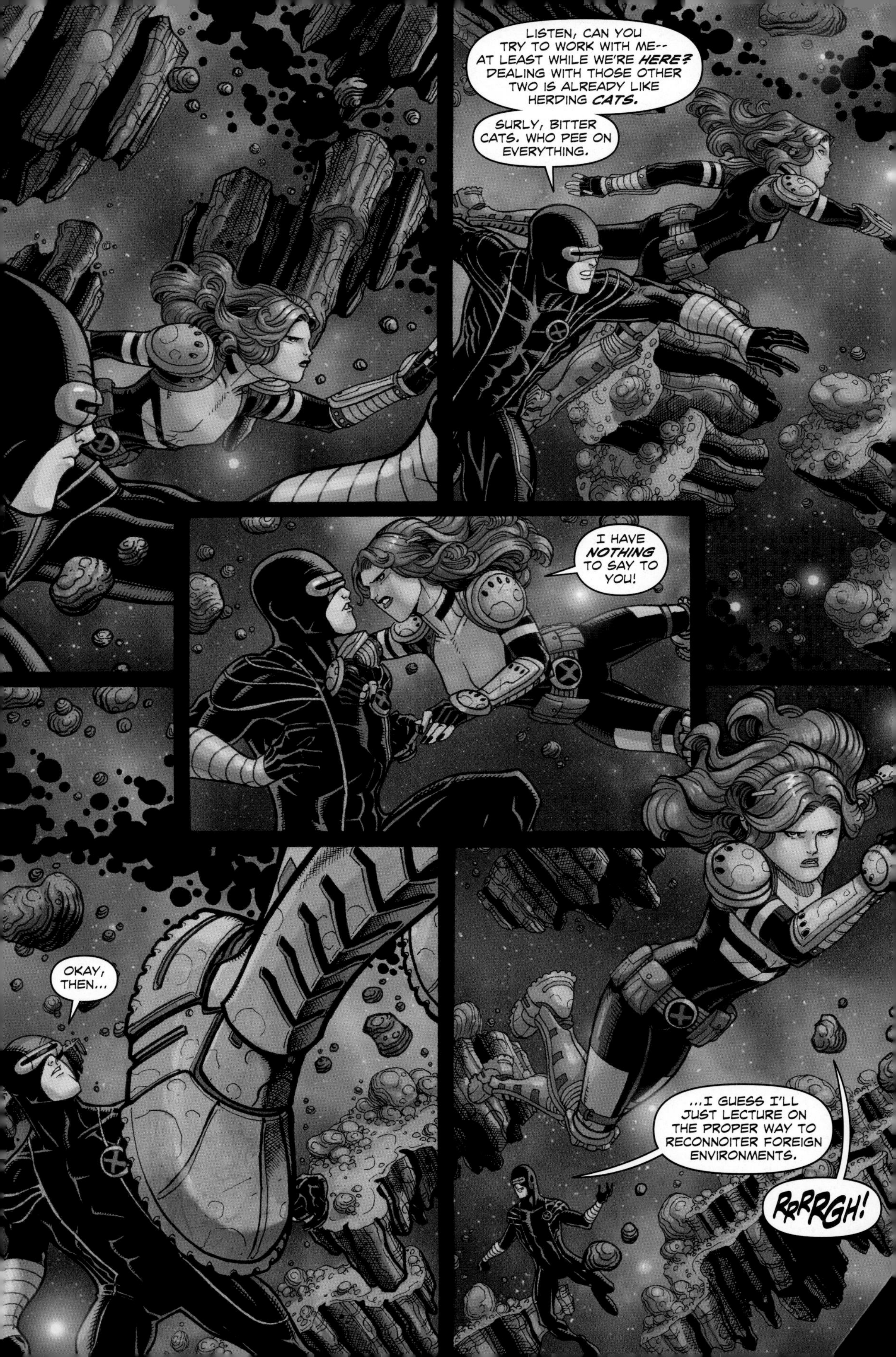
LISTEN, CAN YOU TRY TO WORK WITH ME-- AT LEAST WHILE WE'RE *HERE?* DEALING WITH THOSE OTHER TWO IS ALREADY LIKE HERDING *CATS.*
SURLY, BITTER CATS. WHO PEE ON EVERYTHING.
I HAVE *NOTHING* TO SAY TO YOU!
OKAY, THEN...
...I GUESS I'LL JUST LECTURE ON THE PROPER WAY TO RECONNOITER FOREIGN ENVIRONMENTS.
RRRRGH!

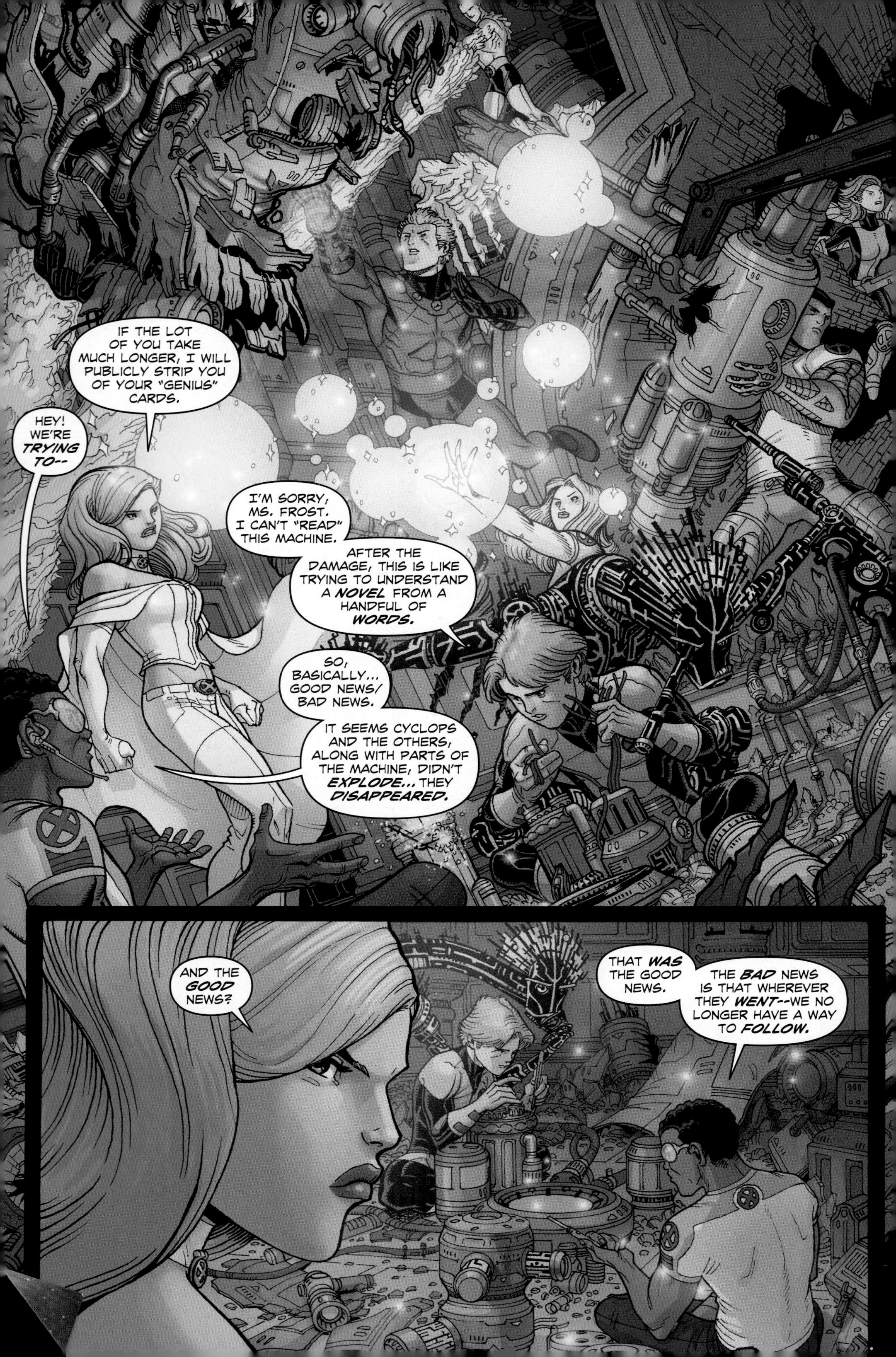
IF THE LOT OF YOU TAKE MUCH LONGER, I WILL PUBLICLY STRIP YOU OF YOUR "GENIUS" CARDS.
HEY! WE'RE *TRYING* TO--
I'M SORRY, MS. FROST. I CAN'T "READ" THIS MACHINE.
AFTER THE DAMAGE, THIS IS LIKE TRYING TO UNDERSTAND A *NOVEL* FROM A HANDFUL OF *WORDS.*
SO, BASICALLY... GOOD NEWS/ BAD NEWS.
IT SEEMS CYCLOPS AND THE OTHERS, ALONG WITH PARTS OF THE MACHINE, DIDN'T *EXPLODE...* THEY *DISAPPEARED.*
AND THE *GOOD* NEWS?
THAT *WAS* THE GOOD NEWS.
THE *BAD* NEWS IS THAT WHEREVER THEY *WENT*--WE NO LONGER HAVE A WAY TO *FOLLOW.*

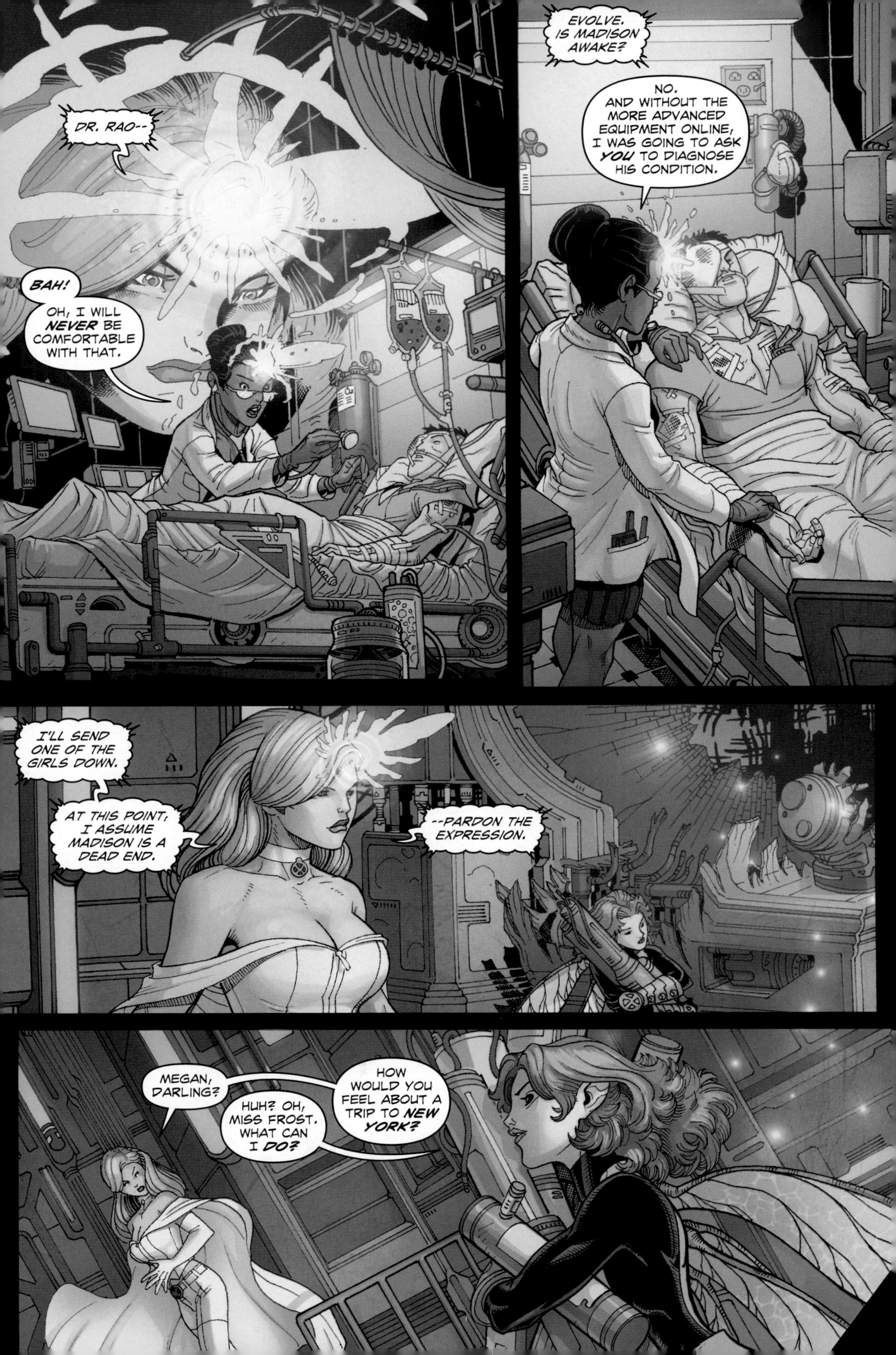
DR. RAO--
BAH!
OH, I WILL NEVER BE COMFORTABLE WITH THAT.
EVOLVE. IS MADISON AWAKE?
NO. AND WITHOUT THE MORE ADVANCED EQUIPMENT ONLINE, I WAS GOING TO ASK YOU TO DIAGNOSE HIS CONDITION.
I'LL SEND ONE OF THE GIRLS DOWN.
AT THIS POINT, I ASSUME MADISON IS A DEAD END.
--PARDON THE EXPRESSION.
MEGAN, DARLING?
HUH? OH, MISS FROST. WHAT CAN I DO?
HOW WOULD YOU FEEL ABOUT A TRIP TO NEW YORK?

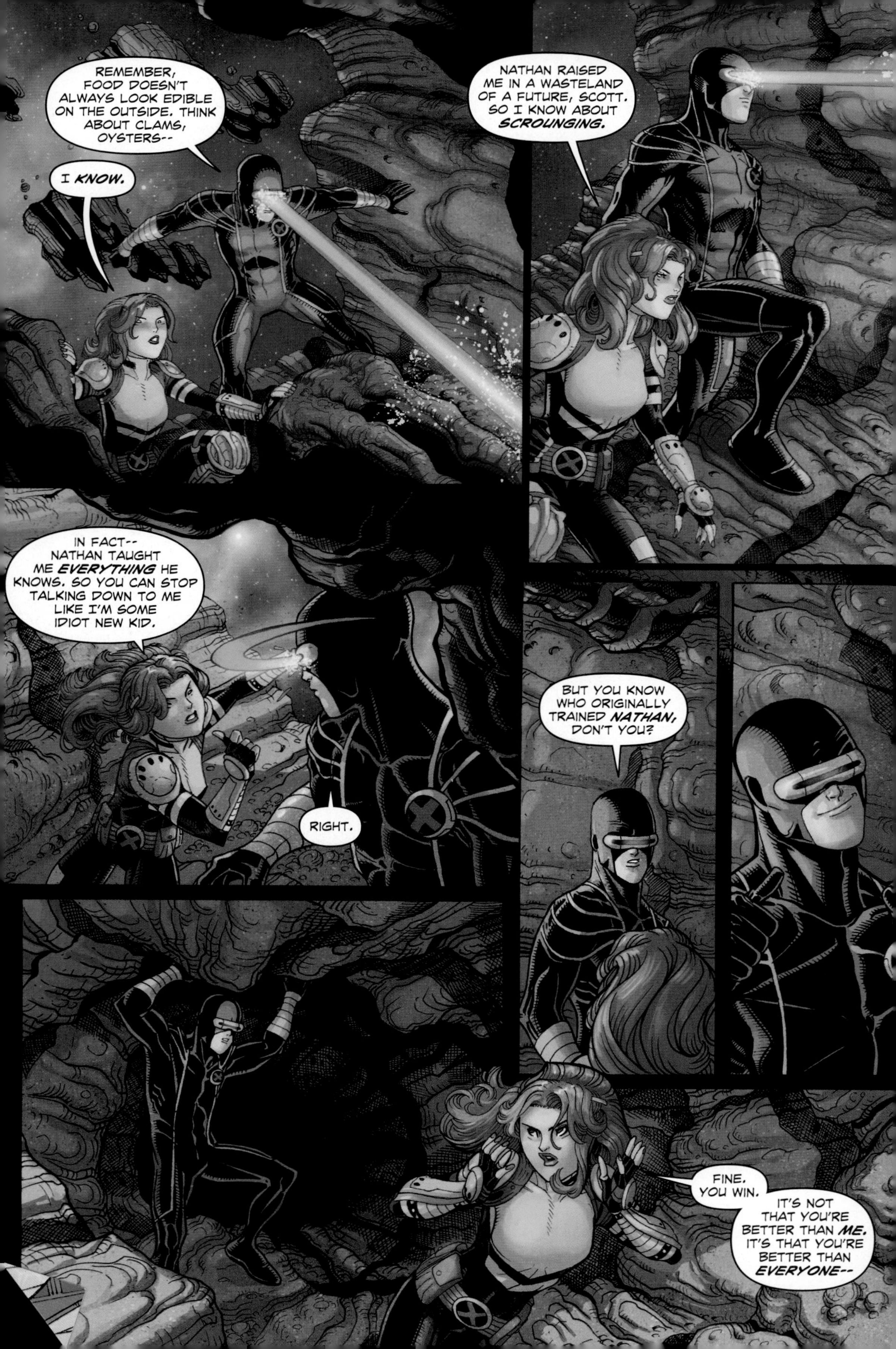
REMEMBER, FOOD DOESN'T ALWAYS LOOK EDIBLE ON THE OUTSIDE. THINK ABOUT CLAMS, OYSTERS--
I *KNOW.*
NATHAN RAISED ME IN A WASTELAND OF A FUTURE, SCOTT. SO I KNOW ABOUT *SCROUNGING.*
IN FACT-- NATHAN TAUGHT ME *EVERYTHING* HE KNOWS. SO YOU CAN STOP TALKING DOWN TO ME LIKE I'M SOME IDIOT NEW KID.
RIGHT.
BUT YOU KNOW WHO ORIGINALLY TRAINED *NATHAN,* DON'T YOU?
FINE. YOU WIN.
IT'S NOT THAT YOU'RE BETTER THAN *ME.* IT'S THAT YOU'RE BETTER THAN *EVERYONE--*

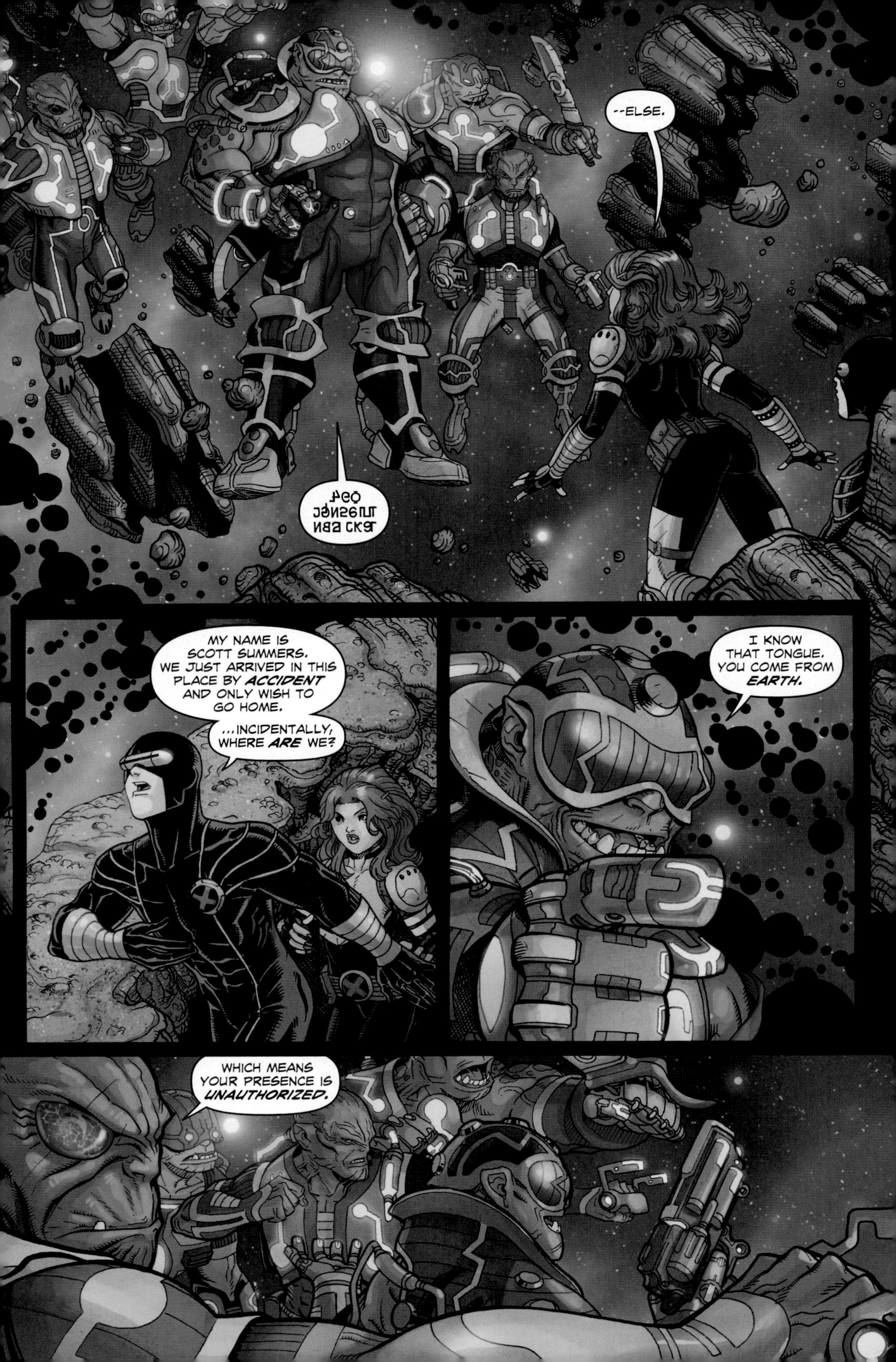
--ELSE.
MY NAME IS SCOTT SUMMERS. WE JUST ARRIVED IN THIS PLACE BY ACCIDENT AND ONLY WISH TO GO HOME.
...INCIDENTALLY, WHERE ARE WE?
I KNOW THAT TONGUE. YOU COME FROM EARTH.
WHICH MEANS YOUR PRESENCE IS UNAUTHORIZED.

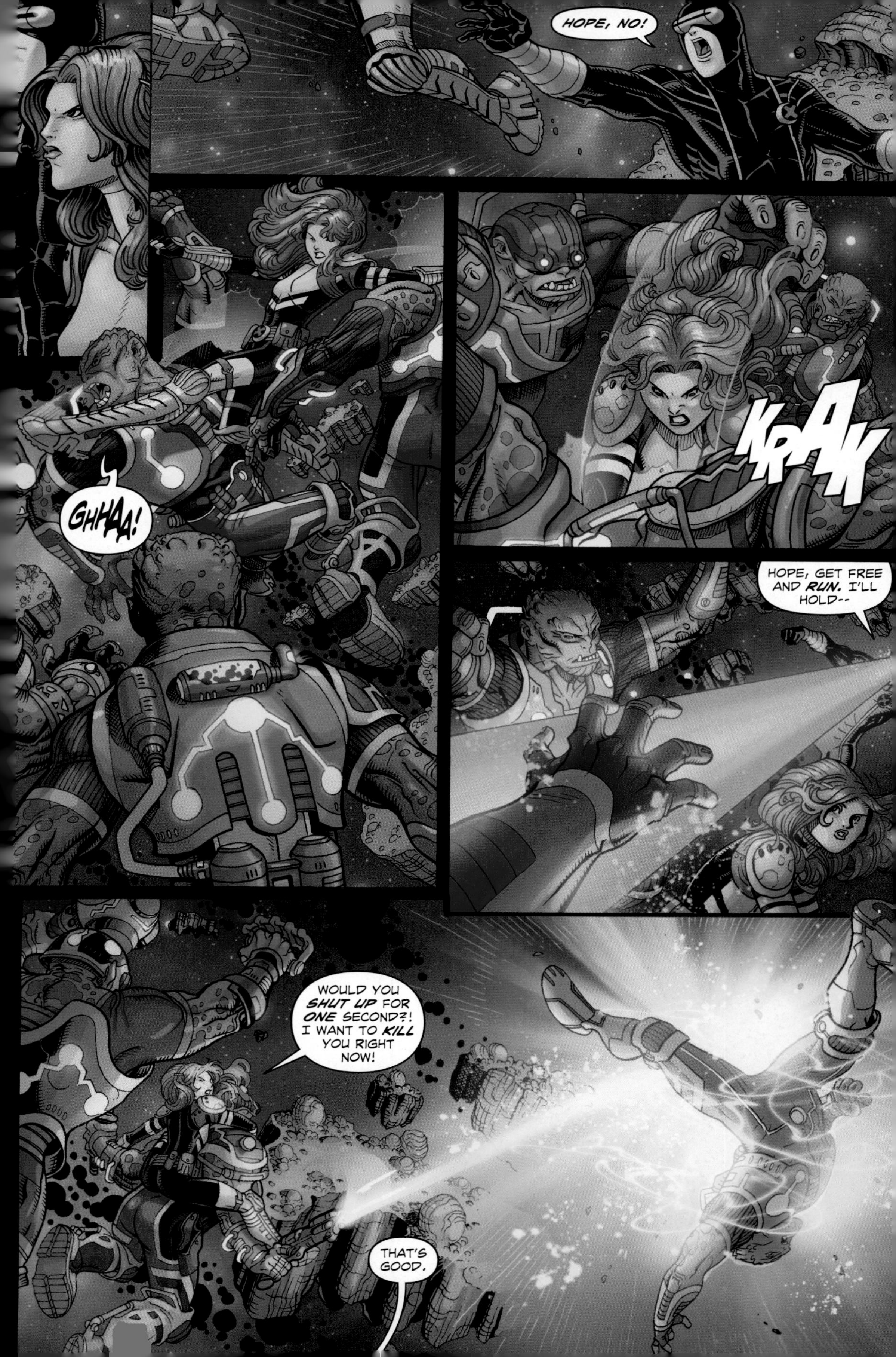
HOPE, NO!
KRAK
GHHAA!
HOPE, GET FREE AND RUN. I'LL HOLD--
WOULD YOU SHUT UP FOR ONE SECOND?! I WANT TO KILL YOU RIGHT NOW!
THAT'S GOOD.

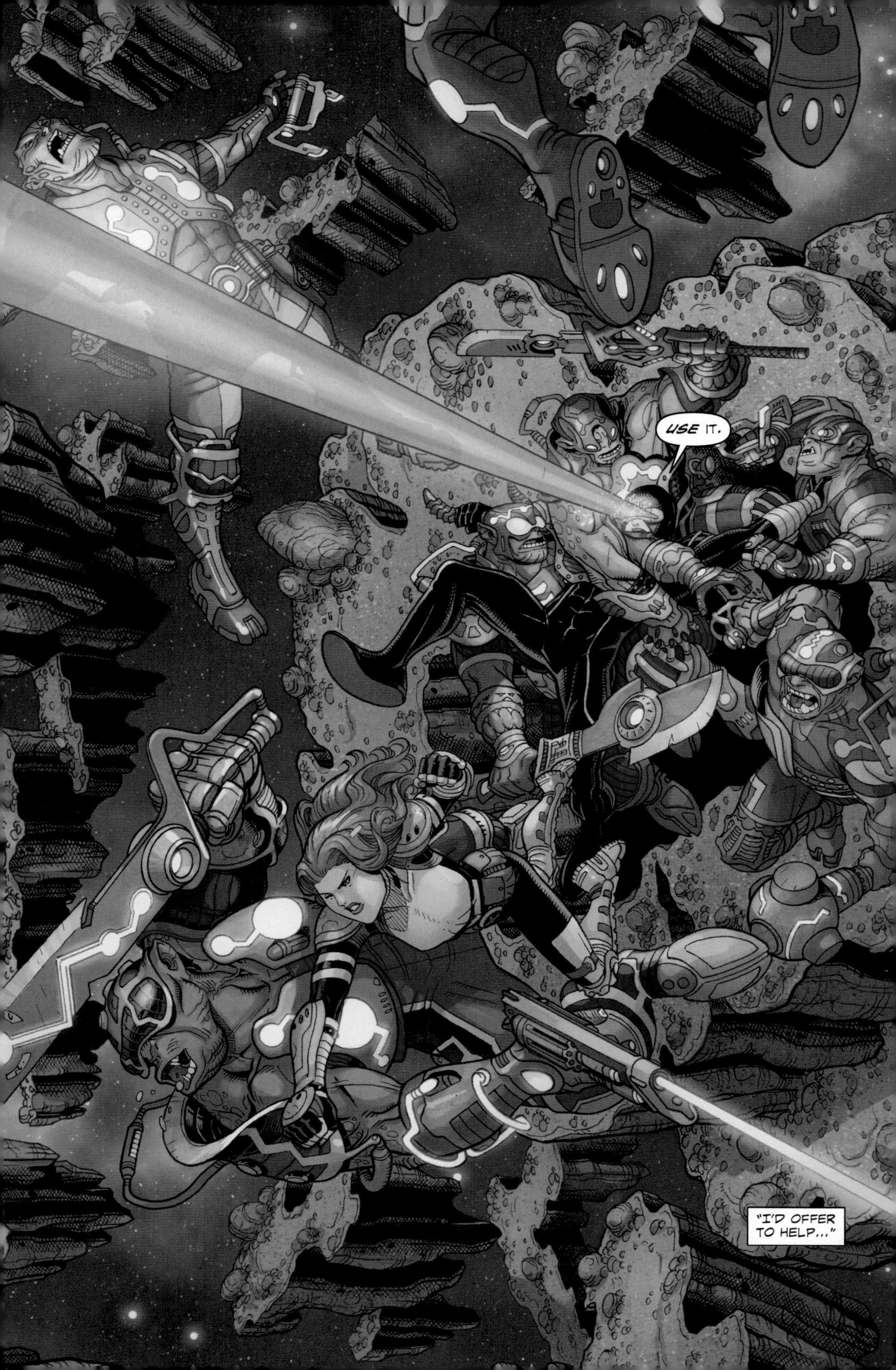
USE IT.
"I'D OFFER TO HELP..."

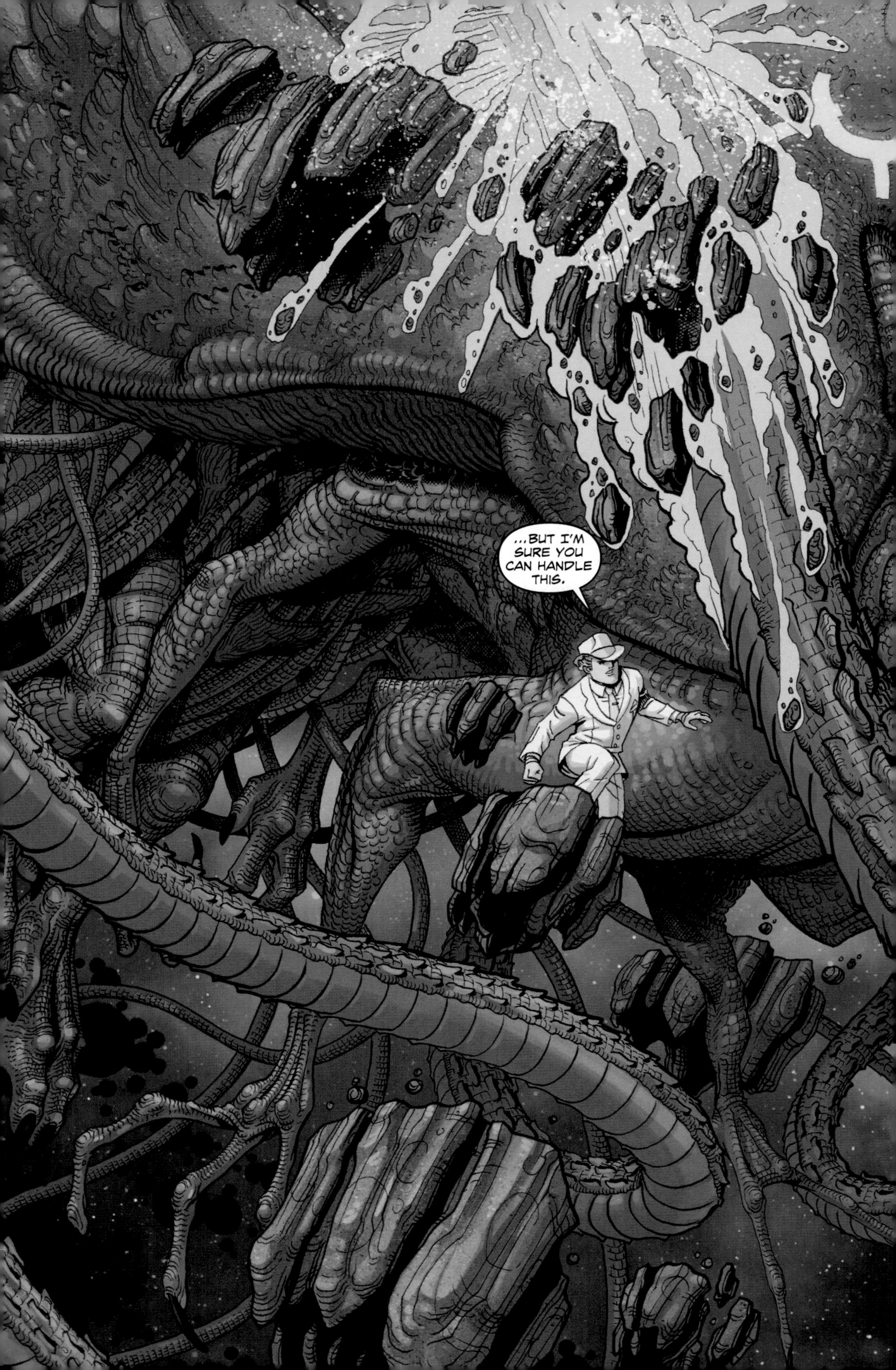
...BUT I'M SURE YOU CAN HANDLE THIS.

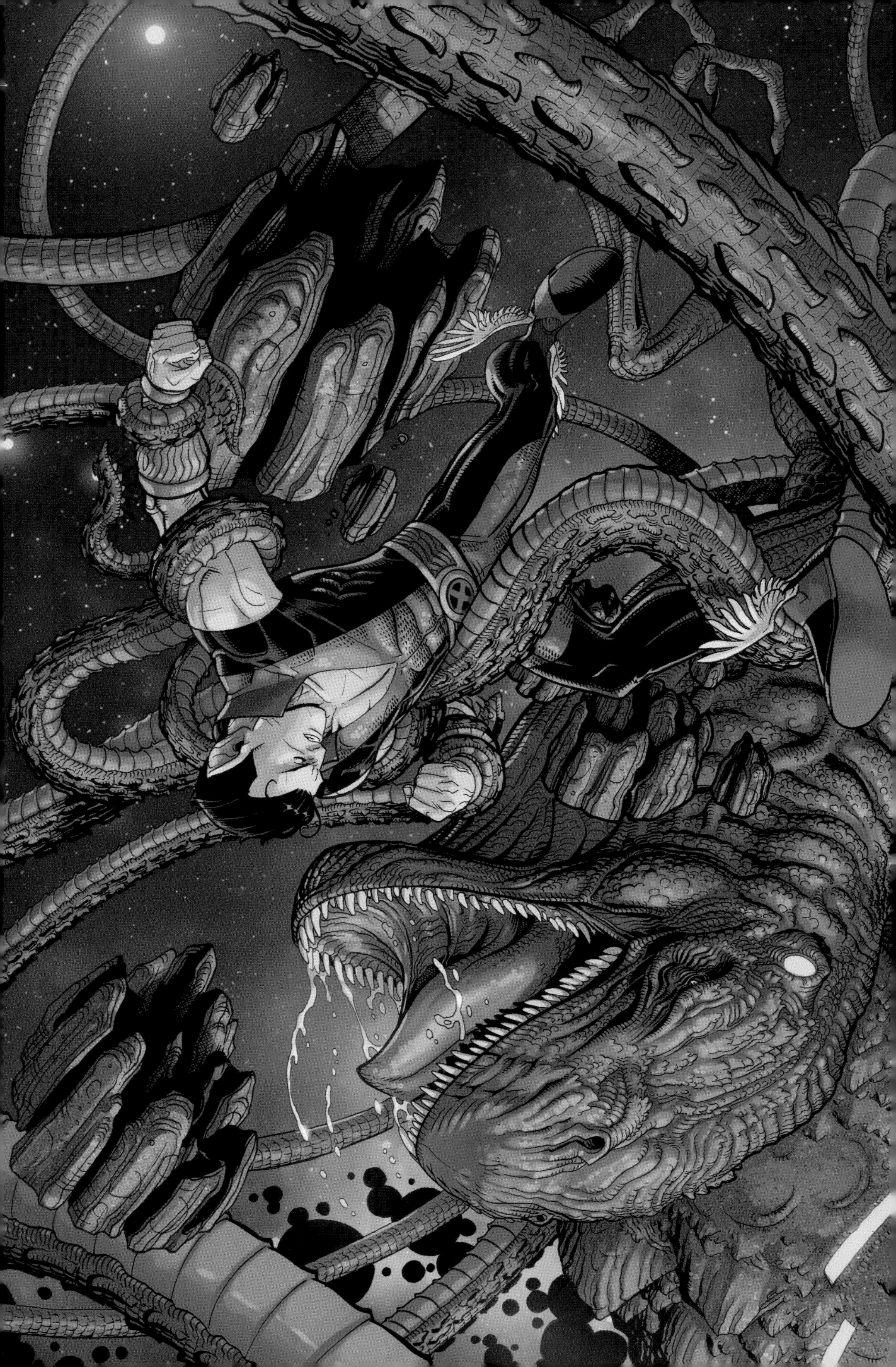

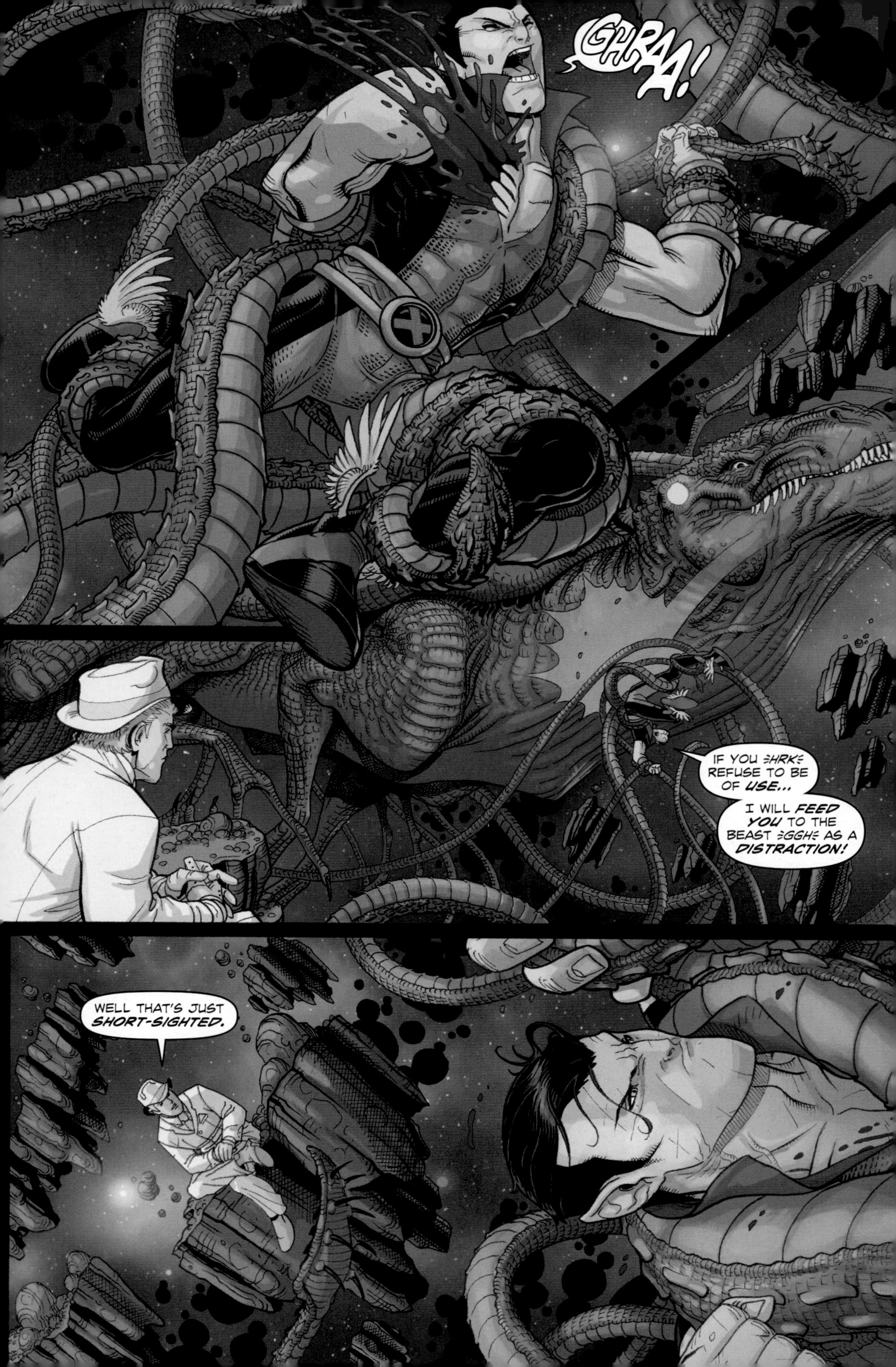
GHRAA!
IF YOU =HRK= REFUSE TO BE OF *USE*...
I WILL *FEED YOU* TO THE BEAST =GGH= AS A *DISTRACTION!*
WELL THAT'S JUST *SHORT-SIGHTED.*

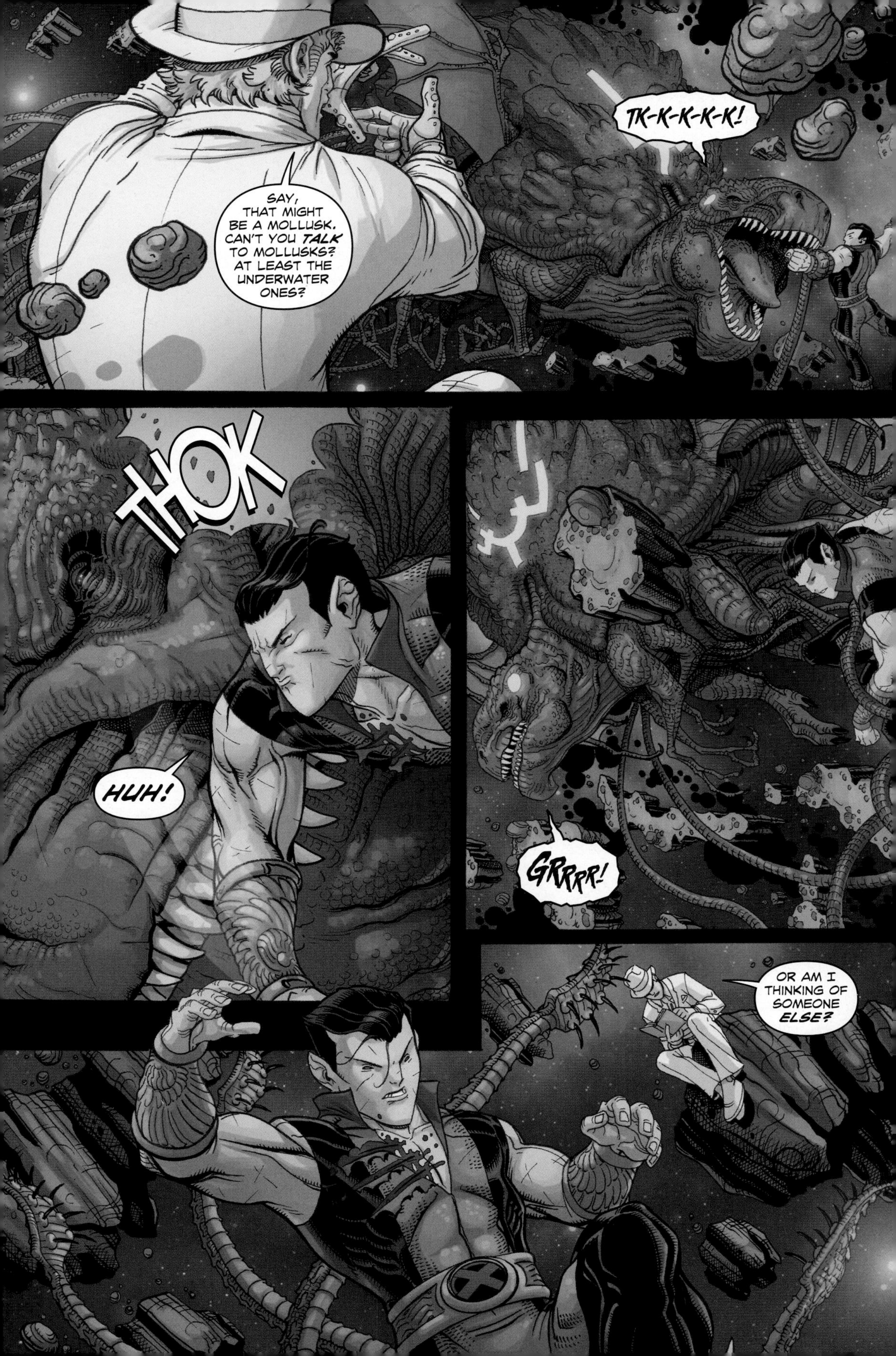
SAY, THAT MIGHT BE A MOLLUSK. CAN'T YOU *TALK* TO MOLLUSKS? AT LEAST THE UNDERWATER ONES?
TK-K-K-K-K!
THOK
HUH!
GRRRR!
OR AM I THINKING OF SOMEONE *ELSE?*

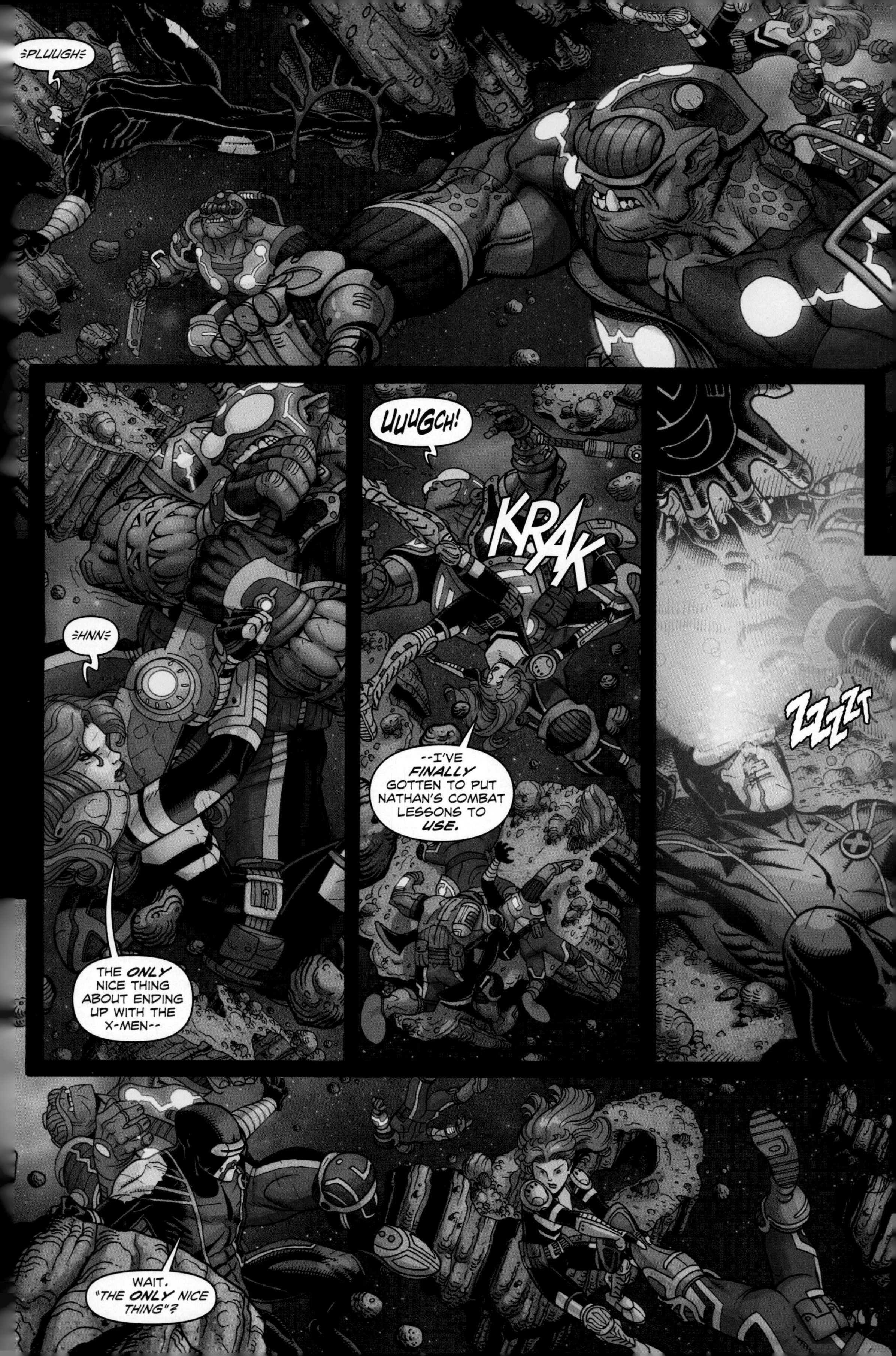

PLUUGH
HNN
THE ONLY NICE THING ABOUT ENDING UP WITH THE X-MEN--
UUUGCH!
KRAK
--I'VE FINALLY GOTTEN TO PUT NATHAN'S COMBAT LESSONS TO USE.
ZZZZZT
WAIT. "THE ONLY NICE THING"?

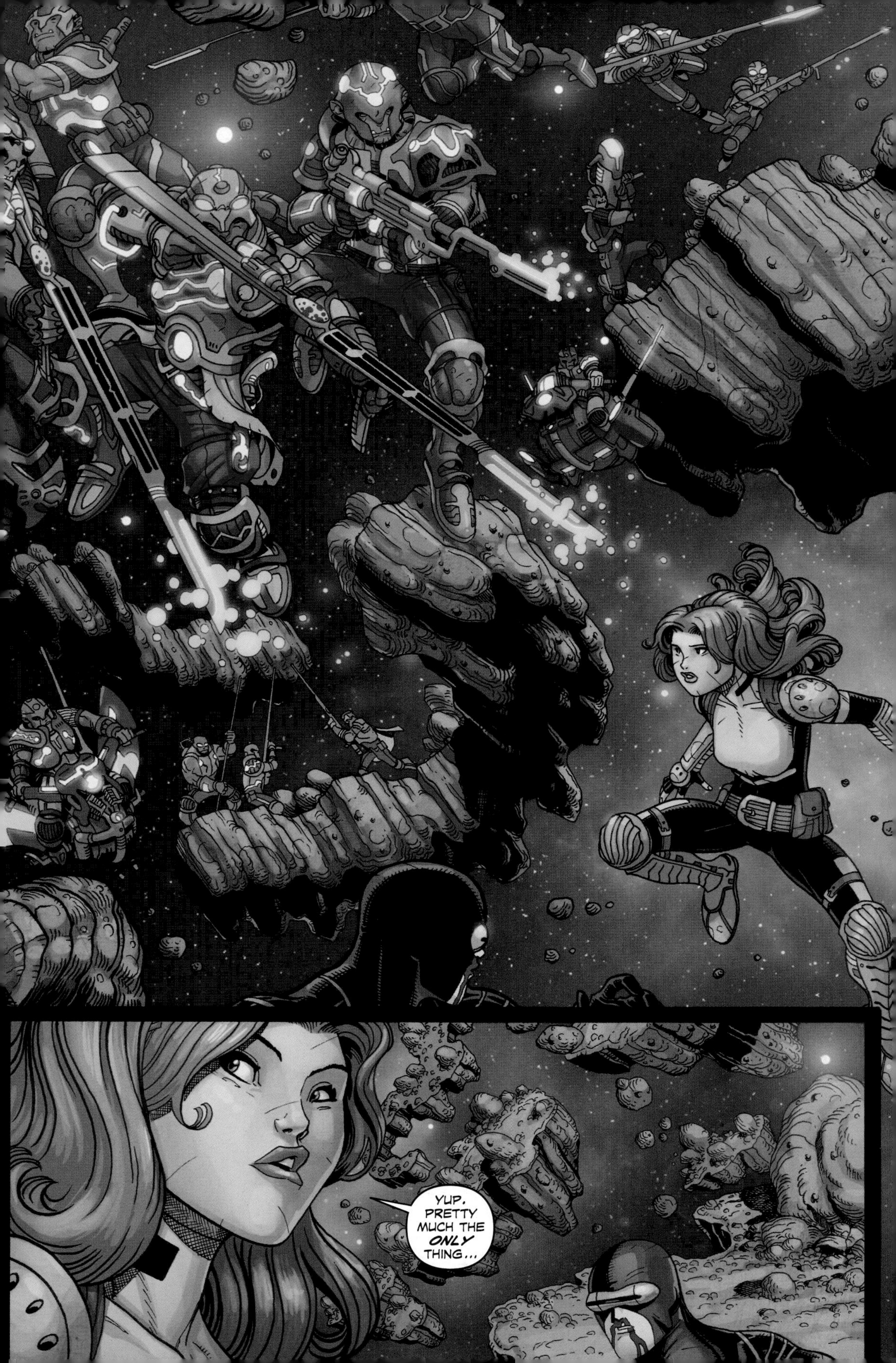
YUP. PRETTY MUCH THE *ONLY* THING...

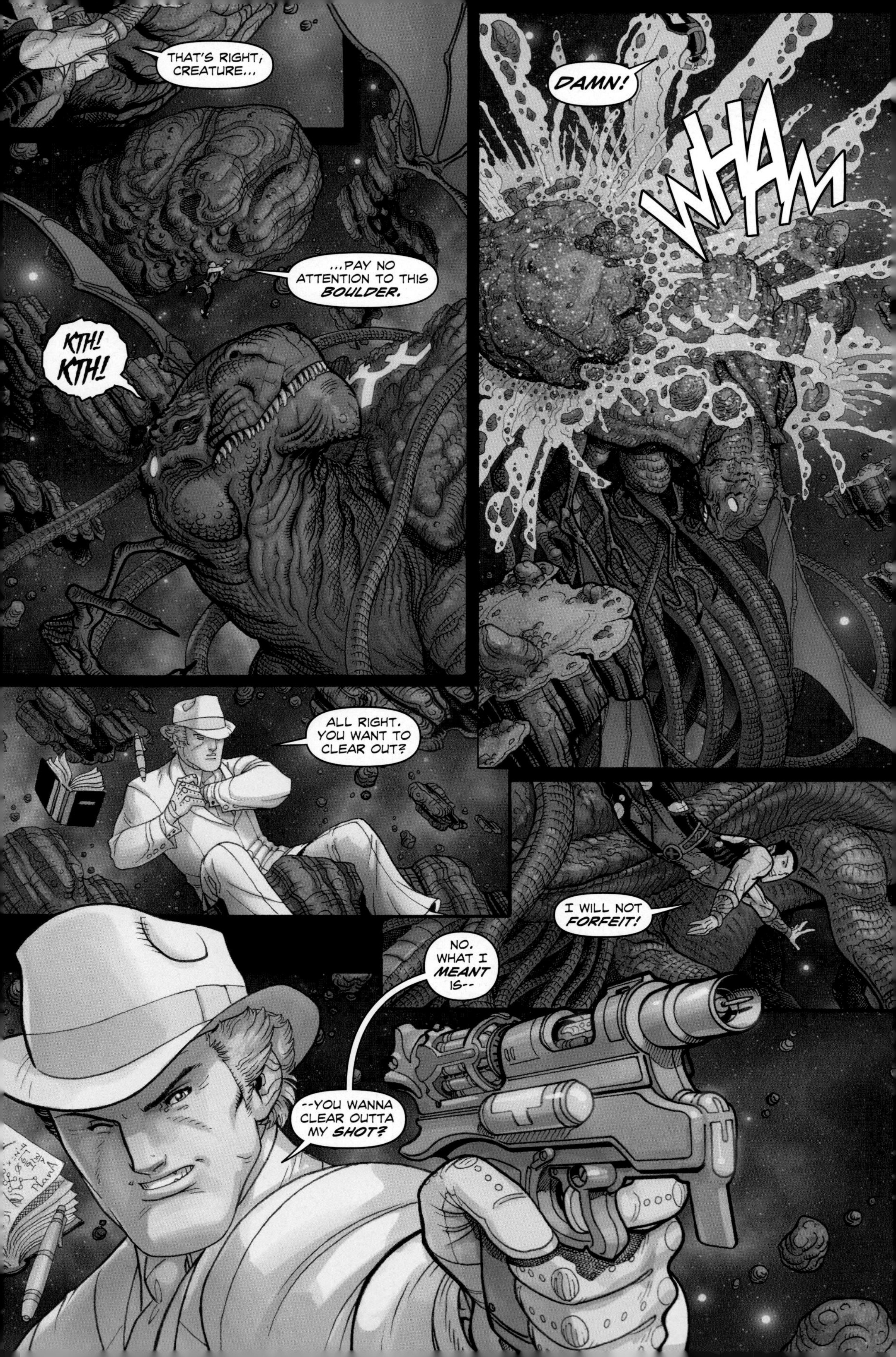
THAT'S RIGHT, CREATURE...
...PAY NO ATTENTION TO THIS *BOULDER.*
KTH! KTH!
DAMN!
WHAM
ALL RIGHT. YOU WANT TO CLEAR OUT?
I WILL NOT *FORFEIT!*
NO. WHAT I *MEANT* IS--
--YOU WANNA CLEAR OUTTA MY *SHOT?*

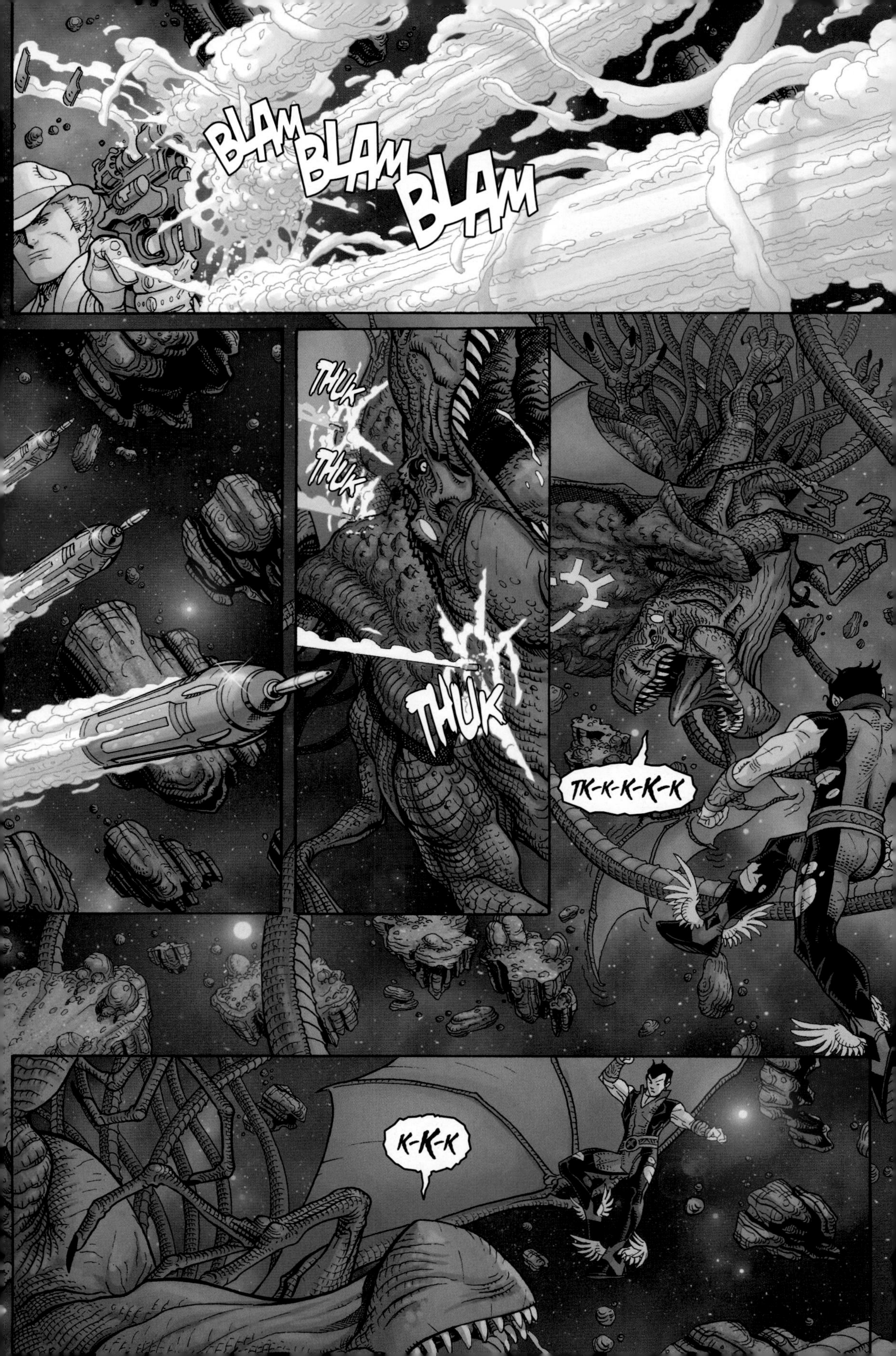
BLAM BLAM BLAM
THUK
THUK
THUK
TK-K-K-K-K
K-K-K

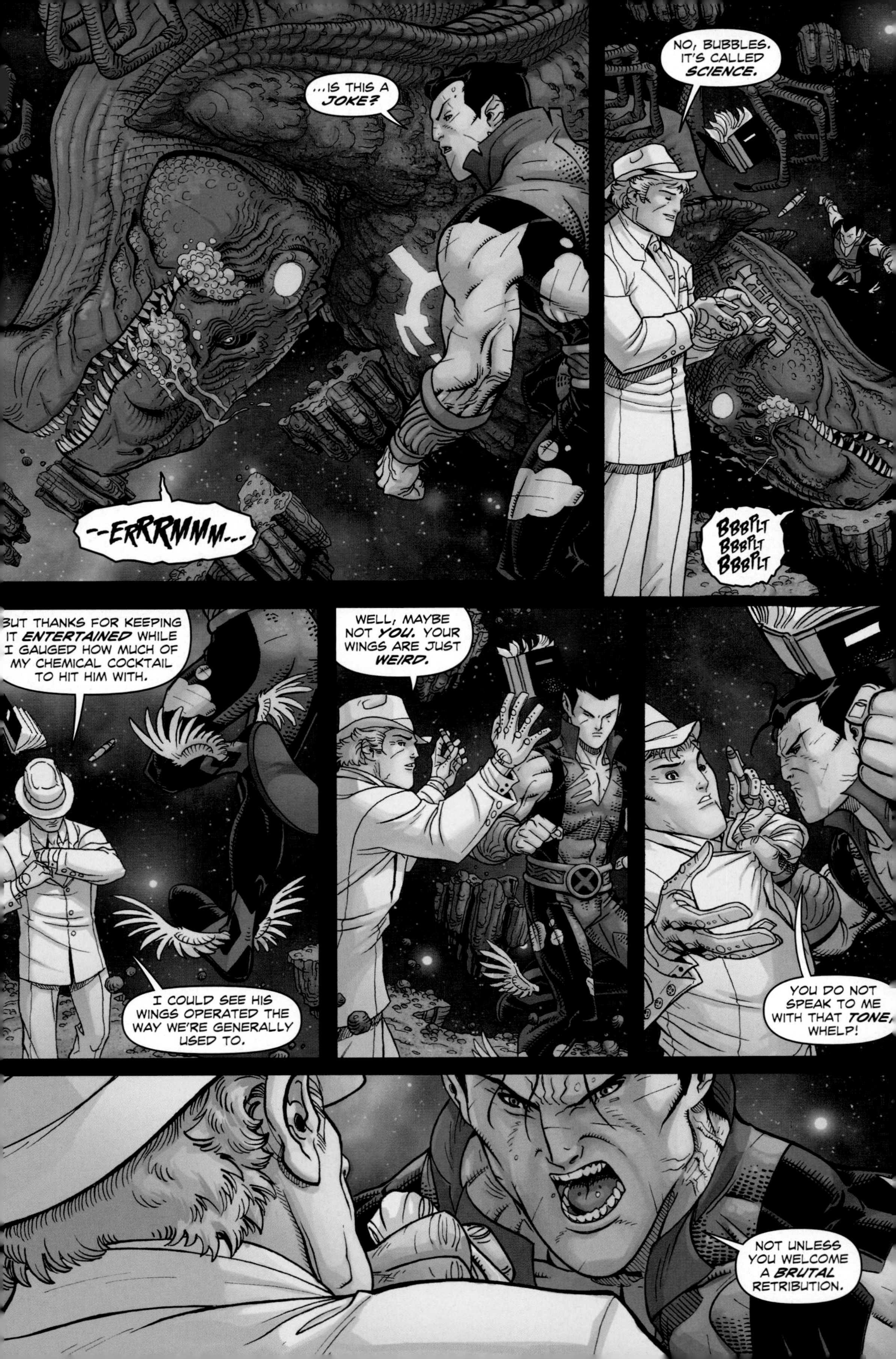
...IS THIS A JOKE?
--ERRRMMM...
NO, BUBBLES. IT'S CALLED SCIENCE.
BBBPLT BBBPLT BBBPLT
BUT THANKS FOR KEEPING IT ENTERTAINED WHILE I GAUGED HOW MUCH OF MY CHEMICAL COCKTAIL TO HIT HIM WITH.
I COULD SEE HIS WINGS OPERATED THE WAY WE'RE GENERALLY USED TO.
WELL, MAYBE NOT YOU. YOUR WINGS ARE JUST WEIRD.
YOU DO NOT SPEAK TO ME WITH THAT TONE, WHELP!
NOT UNLESS YOU WELCOME A BRUTAL RETRIBUTION.

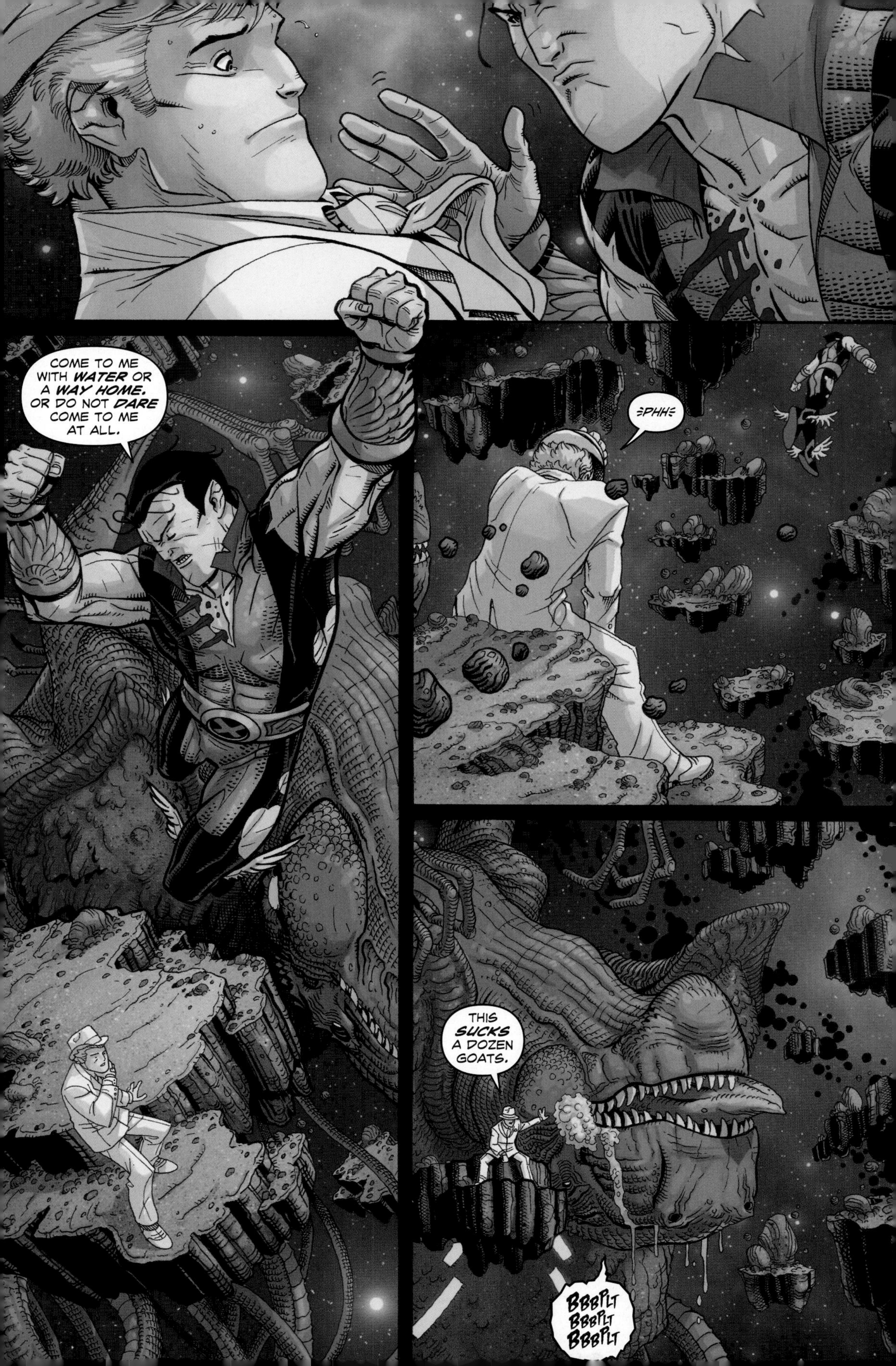
COME TO ME WITH WATER OR A WAY HOME. OR DO NOT DARE COME TO ME AT ALL.
PHH
THIS SUCKS A DOZEN GOATS.
BBBPLT
BBBPLT
BBBPLT

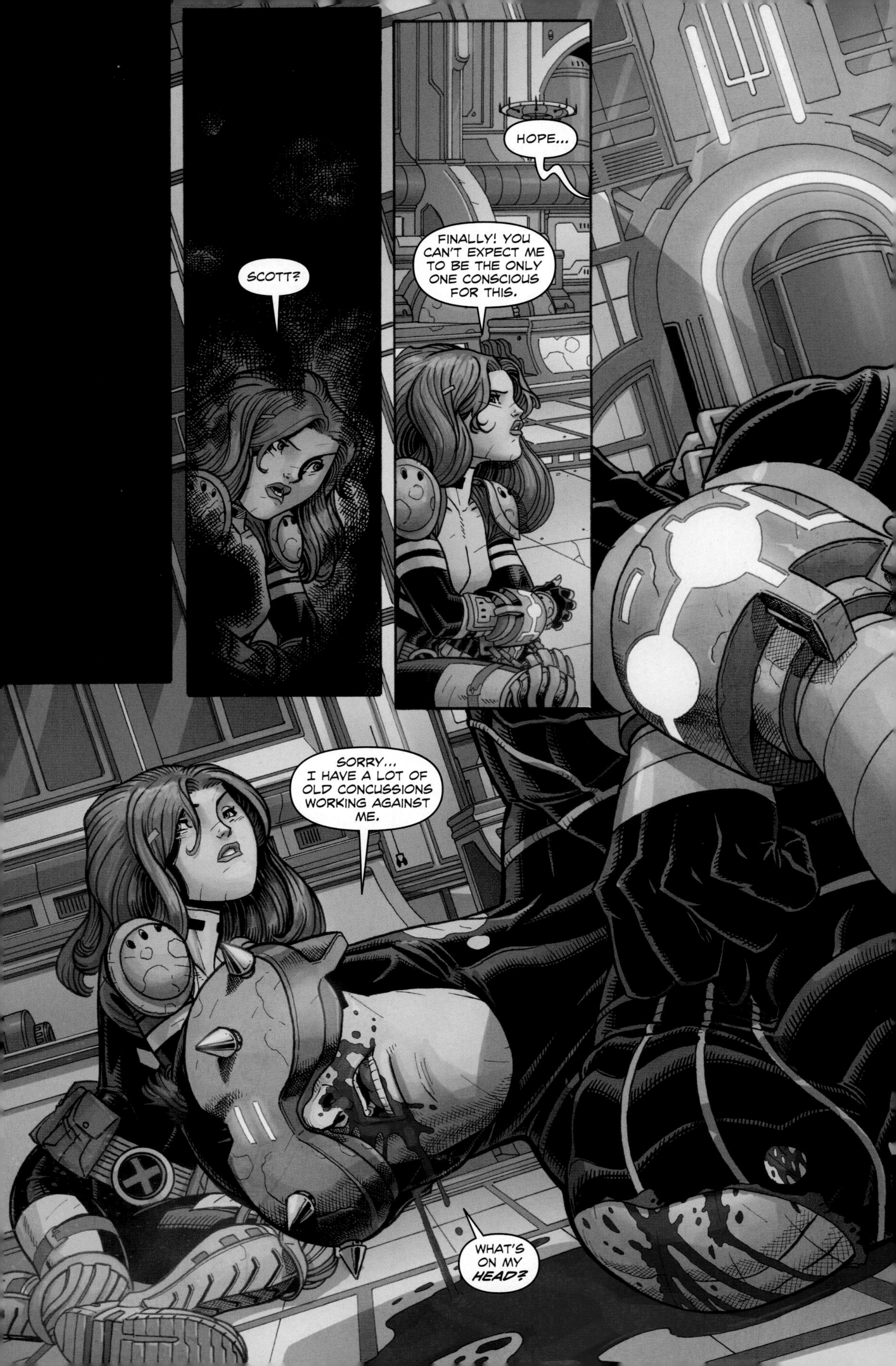
SCOTT?
HOPE...
FINALLY! YOU CAN'T EXPECT ME TO BE THE ONLY ONE CONSCIOUS FOR THIS.
SORRY... I HAVE A LOT OF OLD CONCUSSIONS WORKING AGAINST ME.
WHAT'S ON MY *HEAD?*

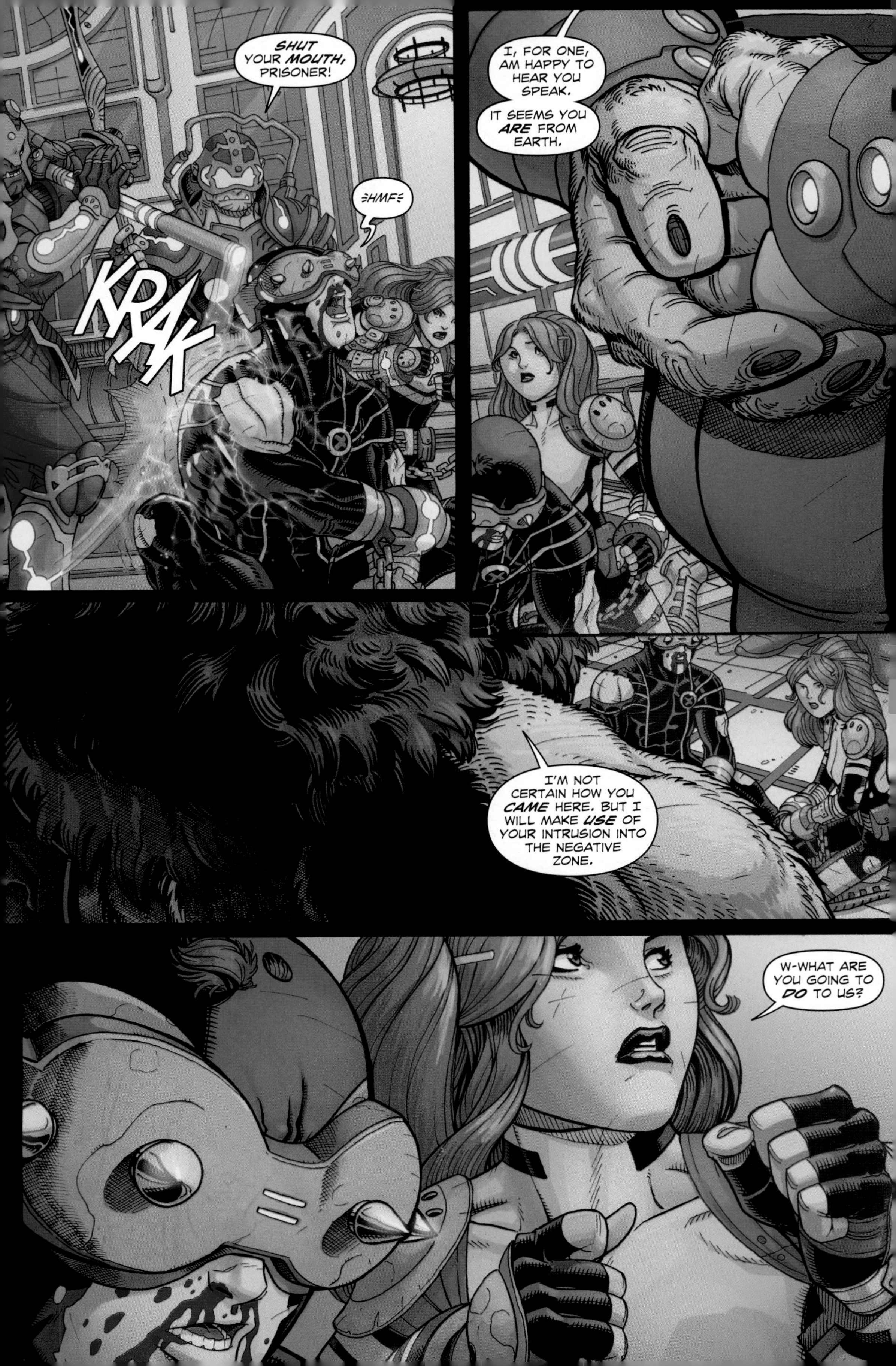
SHUT YOUR MOUTH, PRISONER!
=HMF=
KRAK
I, FOR ONE, AM HAPPY TO HEAR YOU SPEAK.
IT SEEMS YOU ARE FROM EARTH.
I'M NOT CERTAIN HOW YOU CAME HERE, BUT I WILL MAKE USE OF YOUR INTRUSION INTO THE NEGATIVE ZONE.
W-WHAT ARE YOU GOING TO DO TO US?

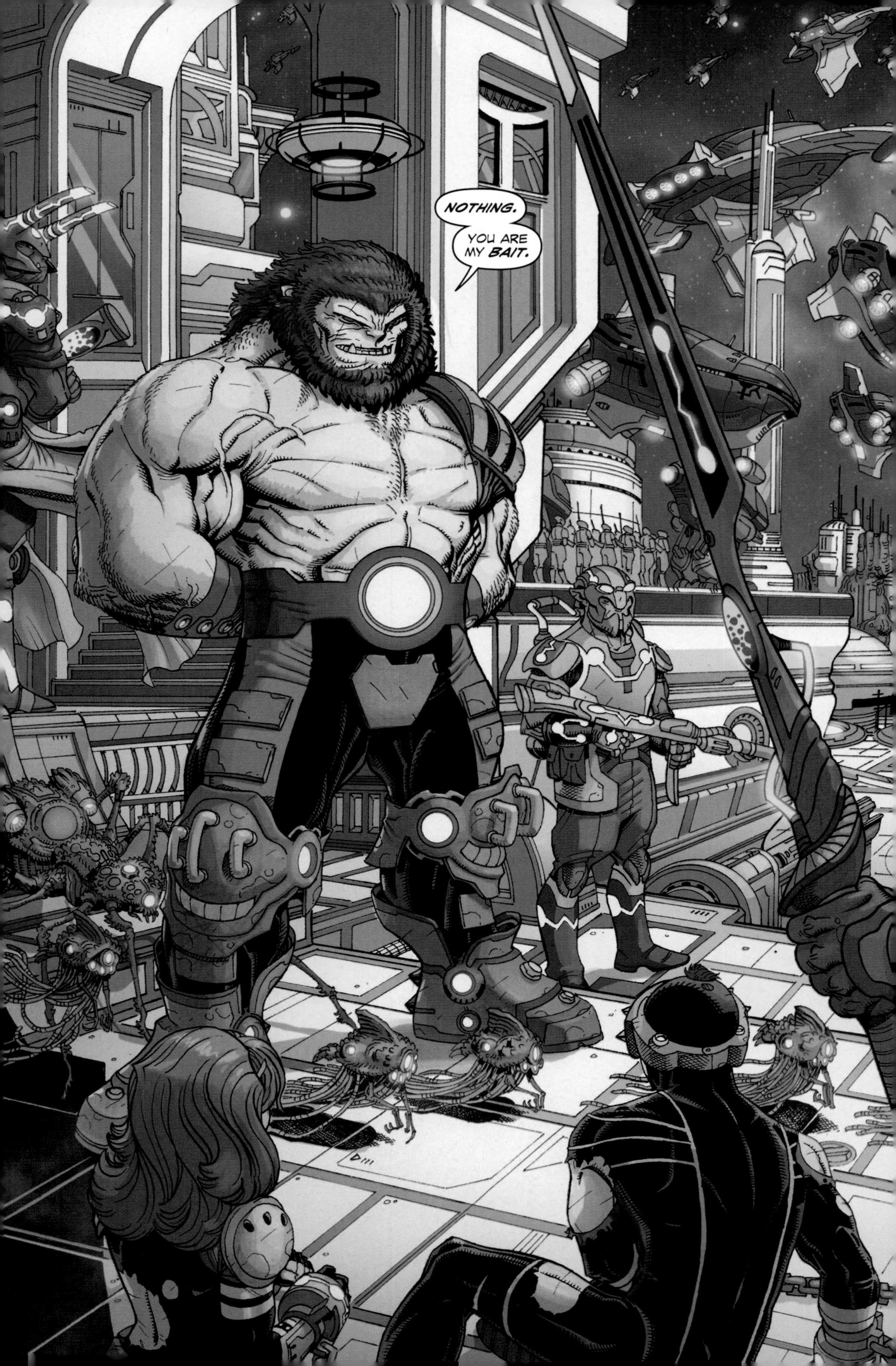
NOTHING.
YOU ARE MY BAIT.

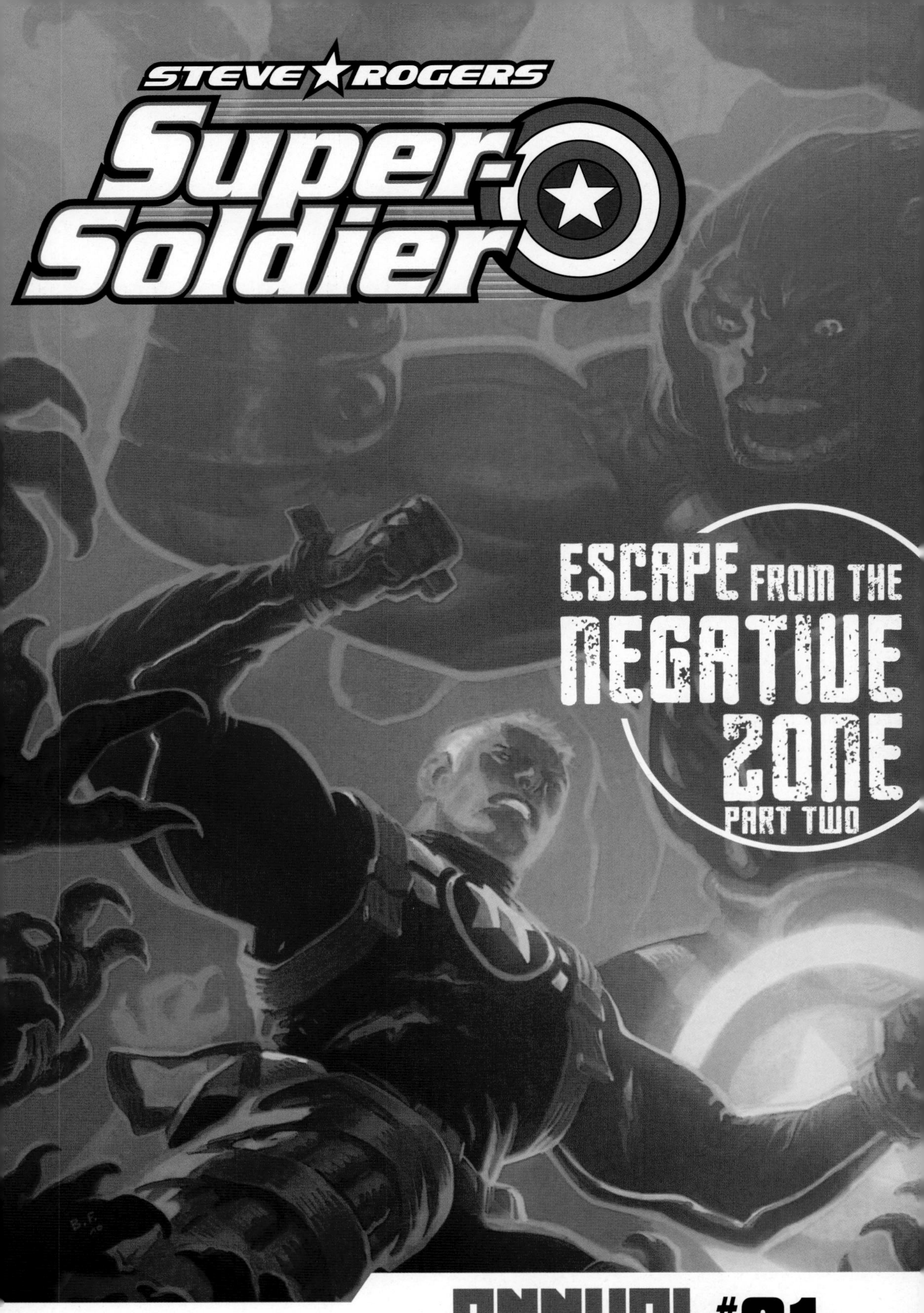
STEVE ROGERS
Super-Soldier
ESCAPE FROM THE
NEGATIVE
ZONE
PART TWO
B.F. '10

ANNUAL #01 2011

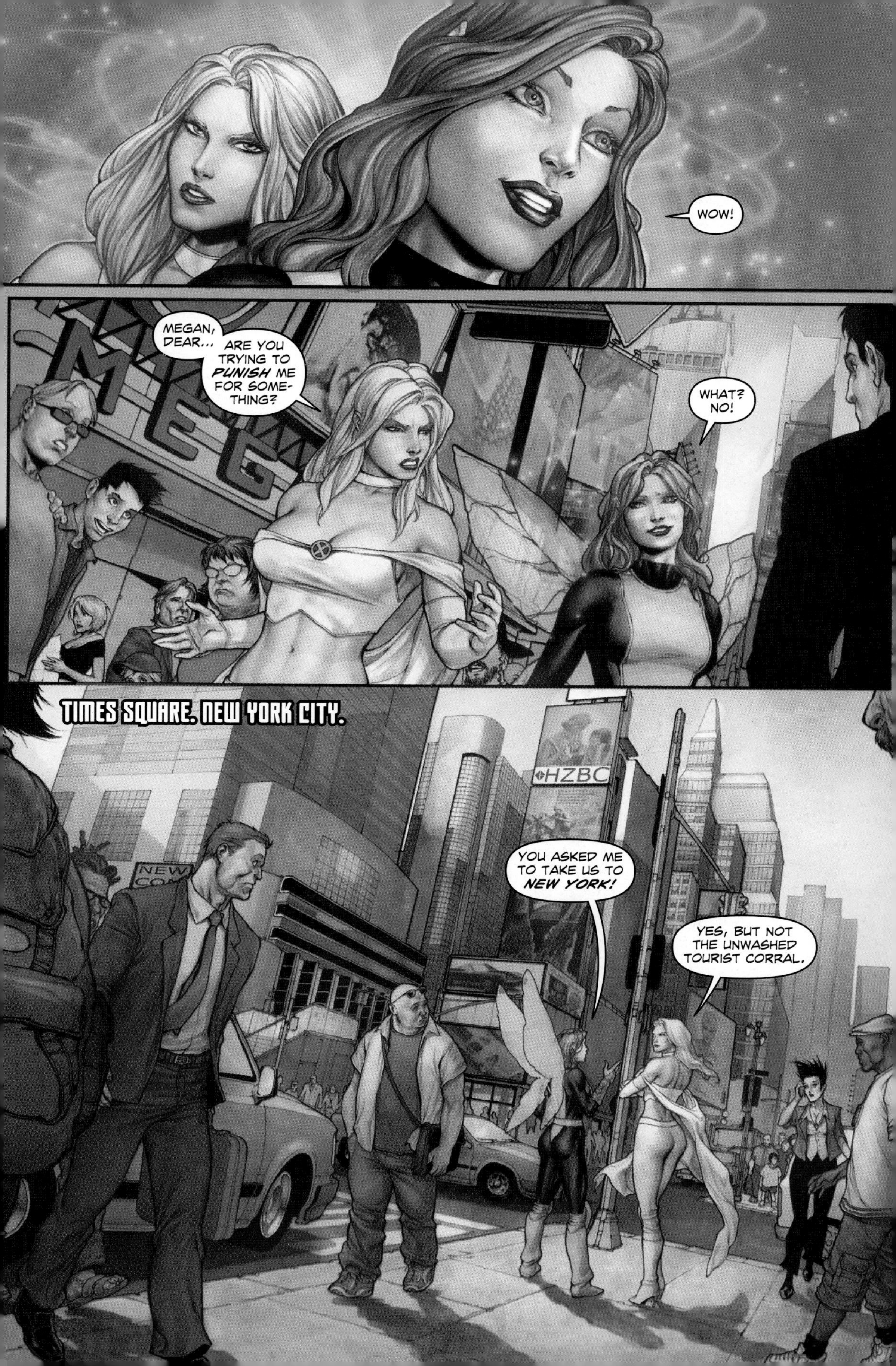
WOW!
MEGAN, DEAR...
ARE YOU TRYING TO *PUNISH* ME FOR SOME-THING?
WHAT? NO!
TIMES SQUARE. NEW YORK CITY.
HZBC
YOU ASKED ME TO TAKE US TO *NEW YORK!*
YES, BUT NOT THE UNWASHED TOURIST CORRAL.

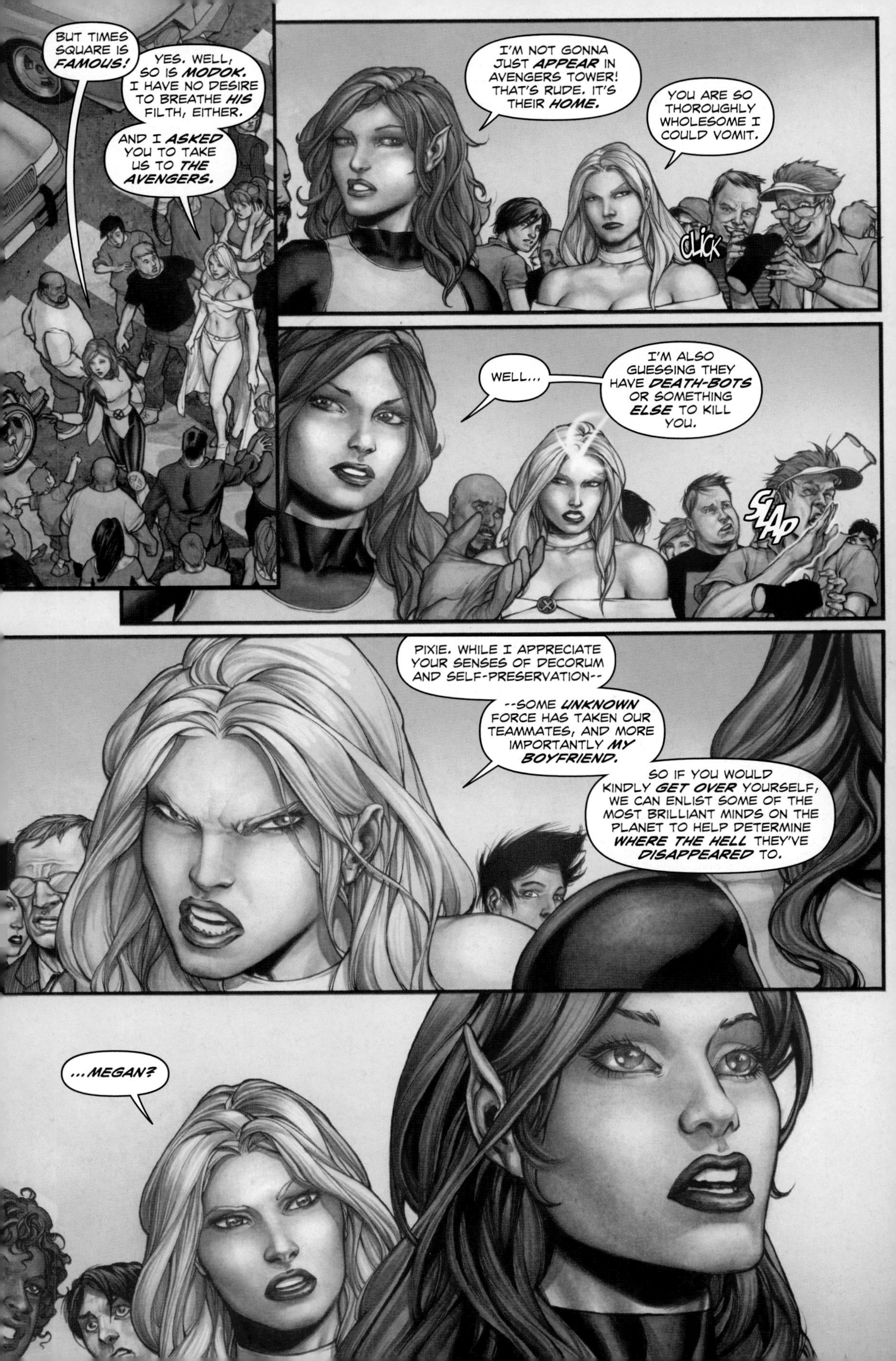
BUT TIMES SQUARE IS **FAMOUS!**
YES. WELL, SO IS **MODOK.** I HAVE NO DESIRE TO BREATHE **HIS** FILTH, EITHER.
AND I **ASKED** YOU TO TAKE US TO **THE AVENGERS.**
I'M NOT GONNA JUST **APPEAR** IN AVENGERS TOWER! THAT'S RUDE. IT'S THEIR **HOME.**
YOU ARE SO THOROUGHLY WHOLESOME I COULD VOMIT.
CLICK
WELL...
I'M ALSO GUESSING THEY HAVE **DEATH-BOTS** OR SOMETHING **ELSE** TO KILL YOU.
SLAP
PIXIE. WHILE I APPRECIATE YOUR SENSES OF DECORUM AND SELF-PRESERVATION--
--SOME **UNKNOWN** FORCE HAS TAKEN OUR TEAMMATES, AND MORE IMPORTANTLY **MY BOYFRIEND.**
SO IF YOU WOULD KINDLY **GET OVER** YOURSELF, WE CAN ENLIST SOME OF THE MOST BRILLIANT MINDS ON THE PLANET TO HELP DETERMINE **WHERE THE HELL** THEY'VE **DISAPPEARED** TO.
...MEGAN?

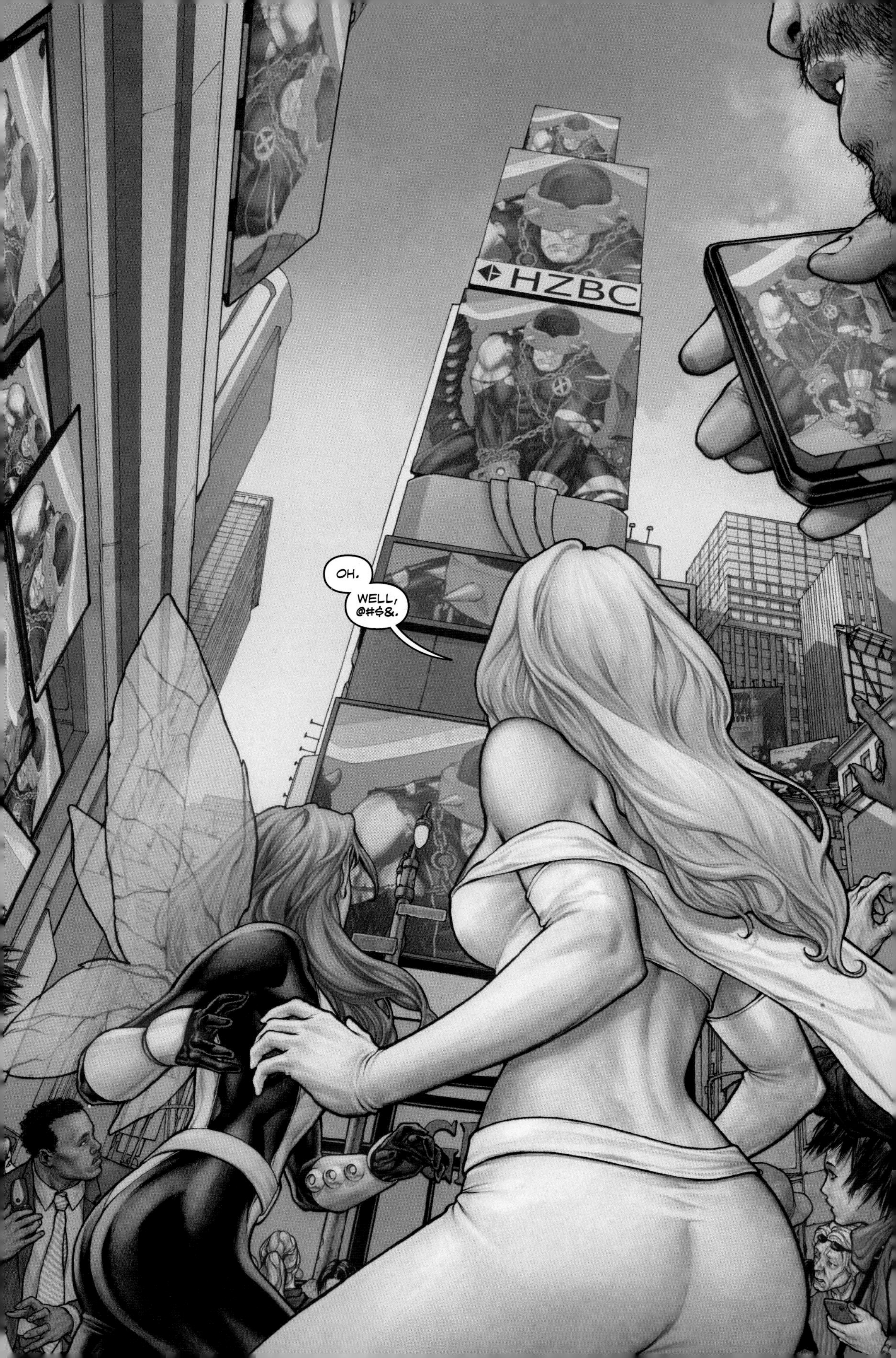
HZBC
OH.
WELL, @#$&.

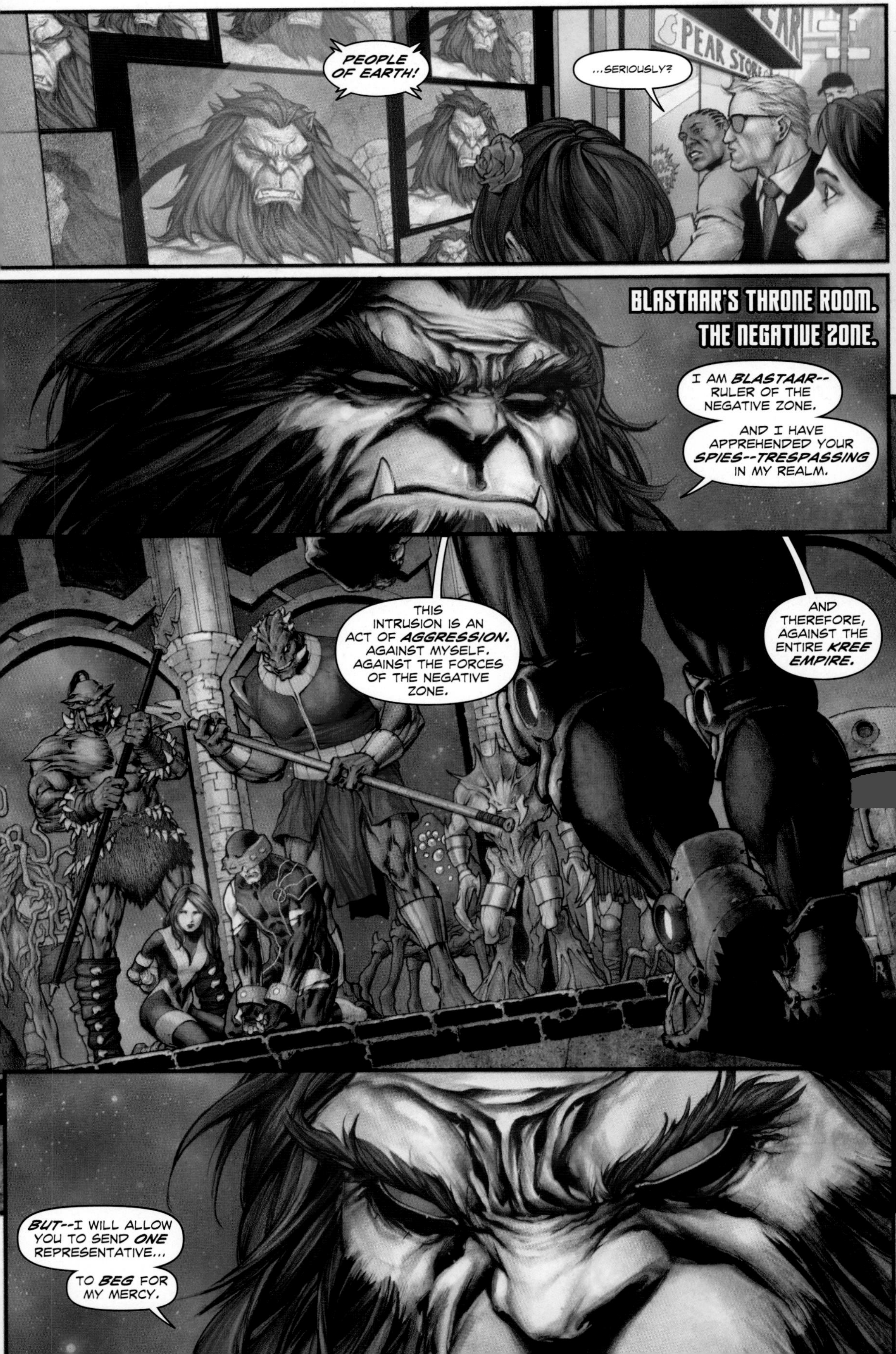
PEAR STORE
PEOPLE OF EARTH!
...SERIOUSLY?
BLASTAAR'S THRONE ROOM. THE NEGATIVE ZONE.
I AM BLASTAAR-- RULER OF THE NEGATIVE ZONE.
AND I HAVE APPREHENDED YOUR SPIES--TRESPASSING IN MY REALM.
THIS INTRUSION IS AN ACT OF AGGRESSION. AGAINST MYSELF. AGAINST THE FORCES OF THE NEGATIVE ZONE.
AND THEREFORE, AGAINST THE ENTIRE KREE EMPIRE.
BUT--I WILL ALLOW YOU TO SEND ONE REPRESENTATIVE...
TO BEG FOR MY MERCY.

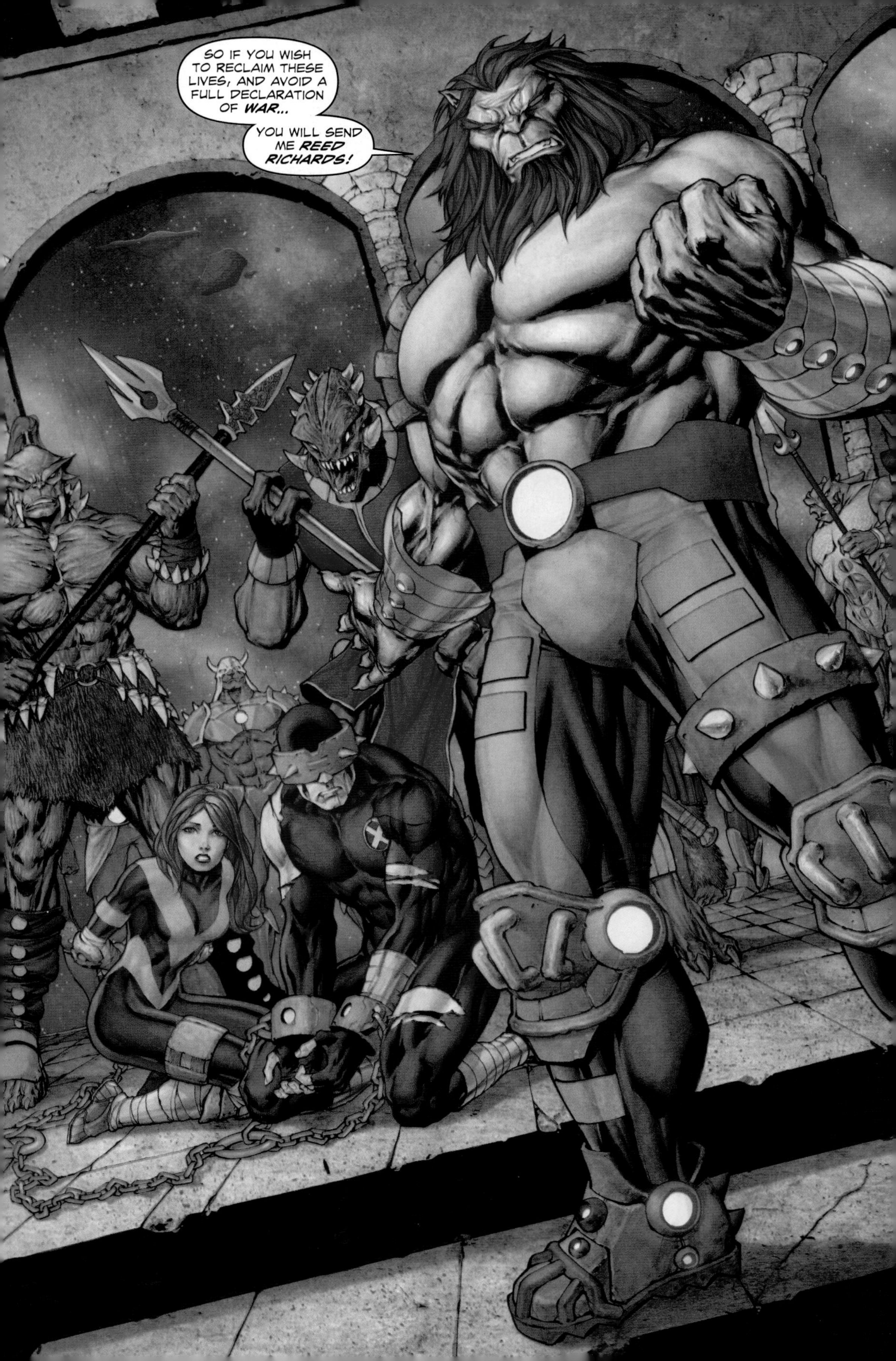
SO IF YOU WISH TO RECLAIM THESE LIVES, AND AVOID A FULL DECLARATION OF **WAR...**
YOU WILL SEND ME **REED RICHARDS!**

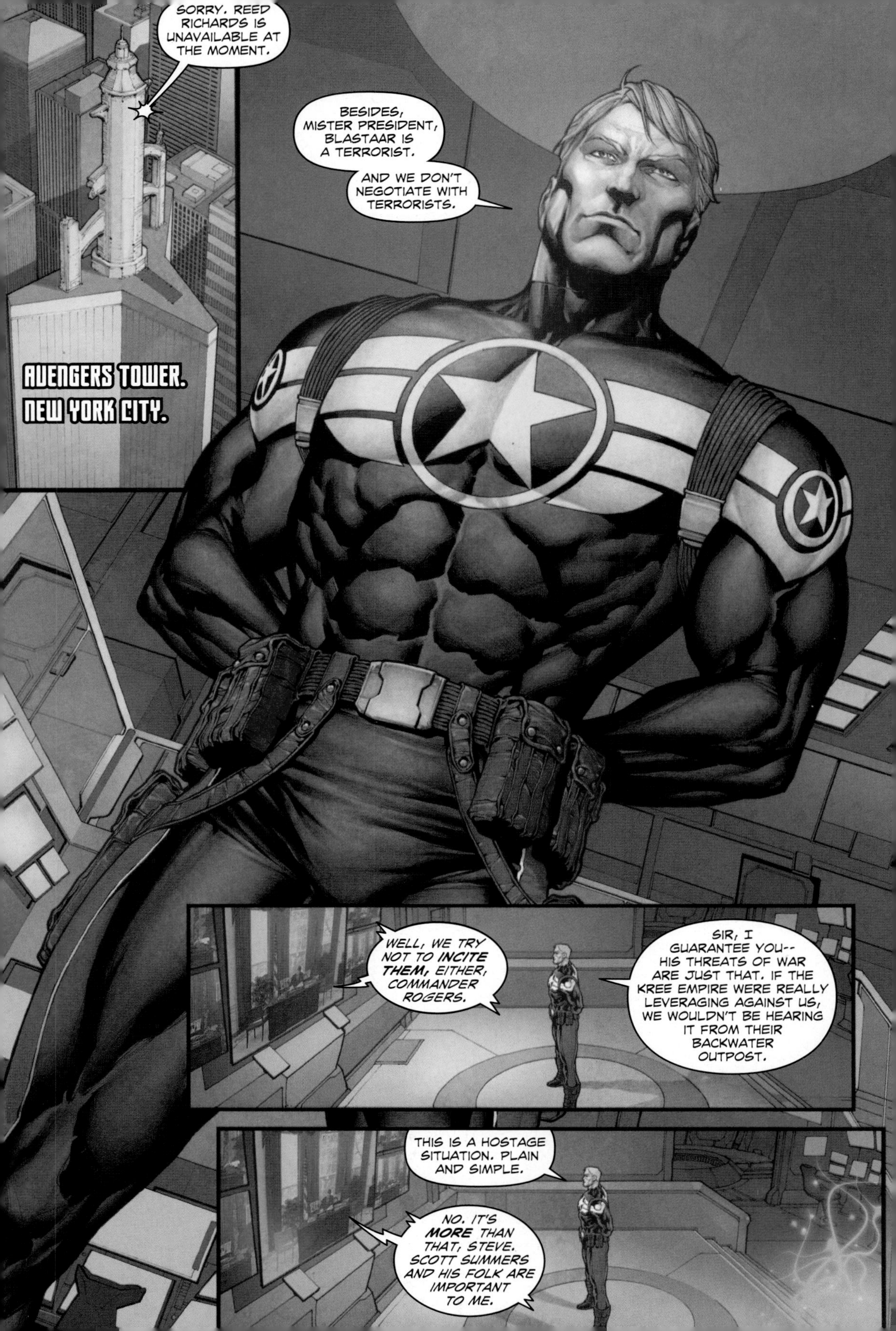
SORRY. REED RICHARDS IS UNAVAILABLE AT THE MOMENT.
AVENGERS TOWER. NEW YORK CITY.
BESIDES, MISTER PRESIDENT, BLASTAAR IS A TERRORIST.
AND WE DON'T NEGOTIATE WITH TERRORISTS.
WELL, WE TRY NOT TO **INCITE THEM,** EITHER, COMMANDER ROGERS.
SIR, I GUARANTEE YOU-- HIS THREATS OF WAR ARE JUST THAT. IF THE KREE EMPIRE WERE REALLY LEVERAGING AGAINST US, WE WOULDN'T BE HEARING IT FROM THEIR BACKWATER OUTPOST.
THIS IS A HOSTAGE SITUATION. PLAIN AND SIMPLE.
NO. IT'S **MORE** THAN THAT, STEVE. SCOTT SUMMERS AND HIS FOLK ARE IMPORTANT TO ME.

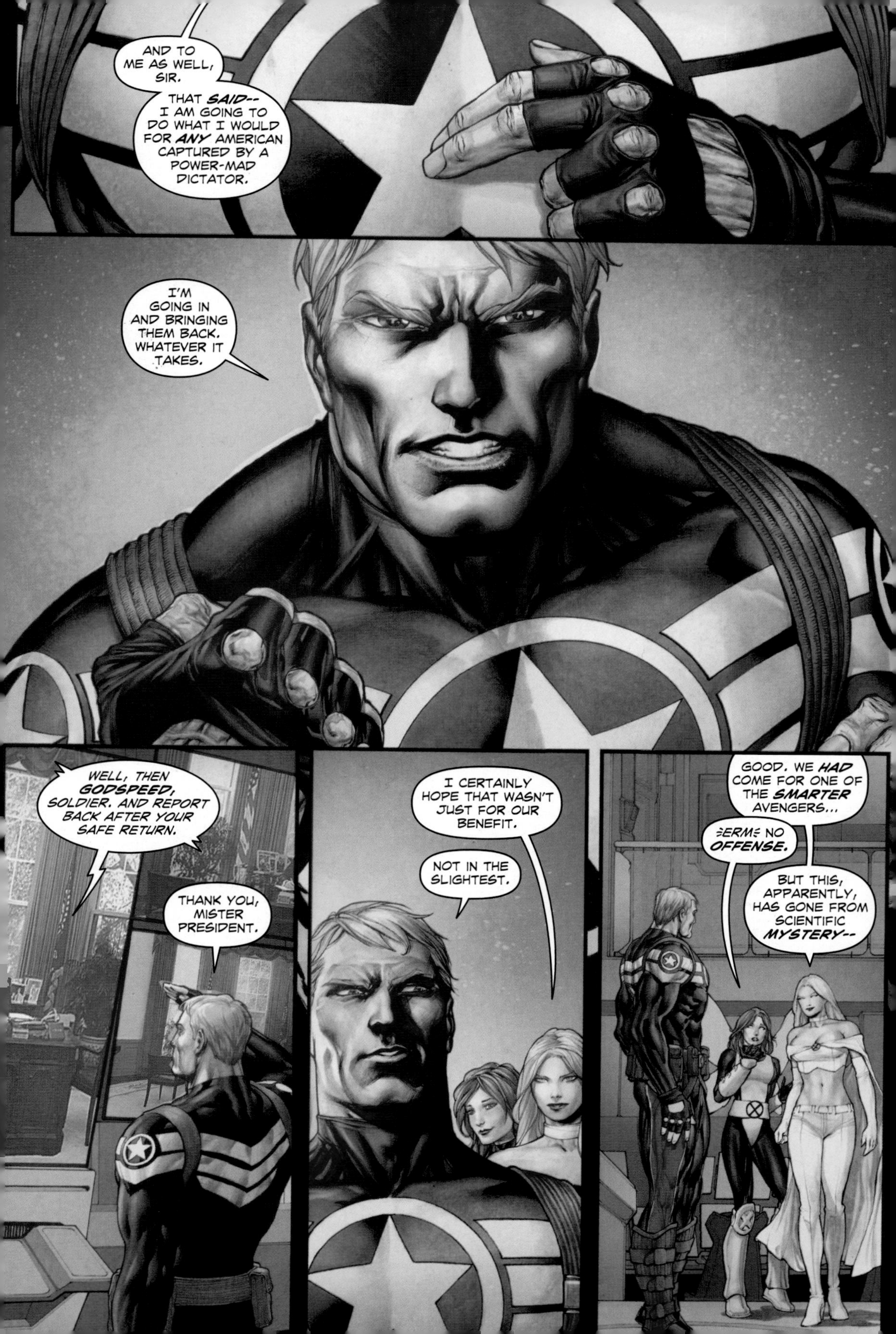
AND TO ME AS WELL, SIR.
THAT SAID-- I AM GOING TO DO WHAT I WOULD FOR ANY AMERICAN CAPTURED BY A POWER-MAD DICTATOR.
I'M GOING IN AND BRINGING THEM BACK. WHATEVER IT TAKES.
WELL, THEN GODSPEED, SOLDIER. AND REPORT BACK AFTER YOUR SAFE RETURN.
THANK YOU, MISTER PRESIDENT.
I CERTAINLY HOPE THAT WASN'T JUST FOR OUR BENEFIT.
NOT IN THE SLIGHTEST.
GOOD. WE HAD COME FOR ONE OF THE SMARTER AVENGERS...
ERM NO OFFENSE.
BUT THIS, APPARENTLY, HAS GONE FROM SCIENTIFIC MYSTERY--

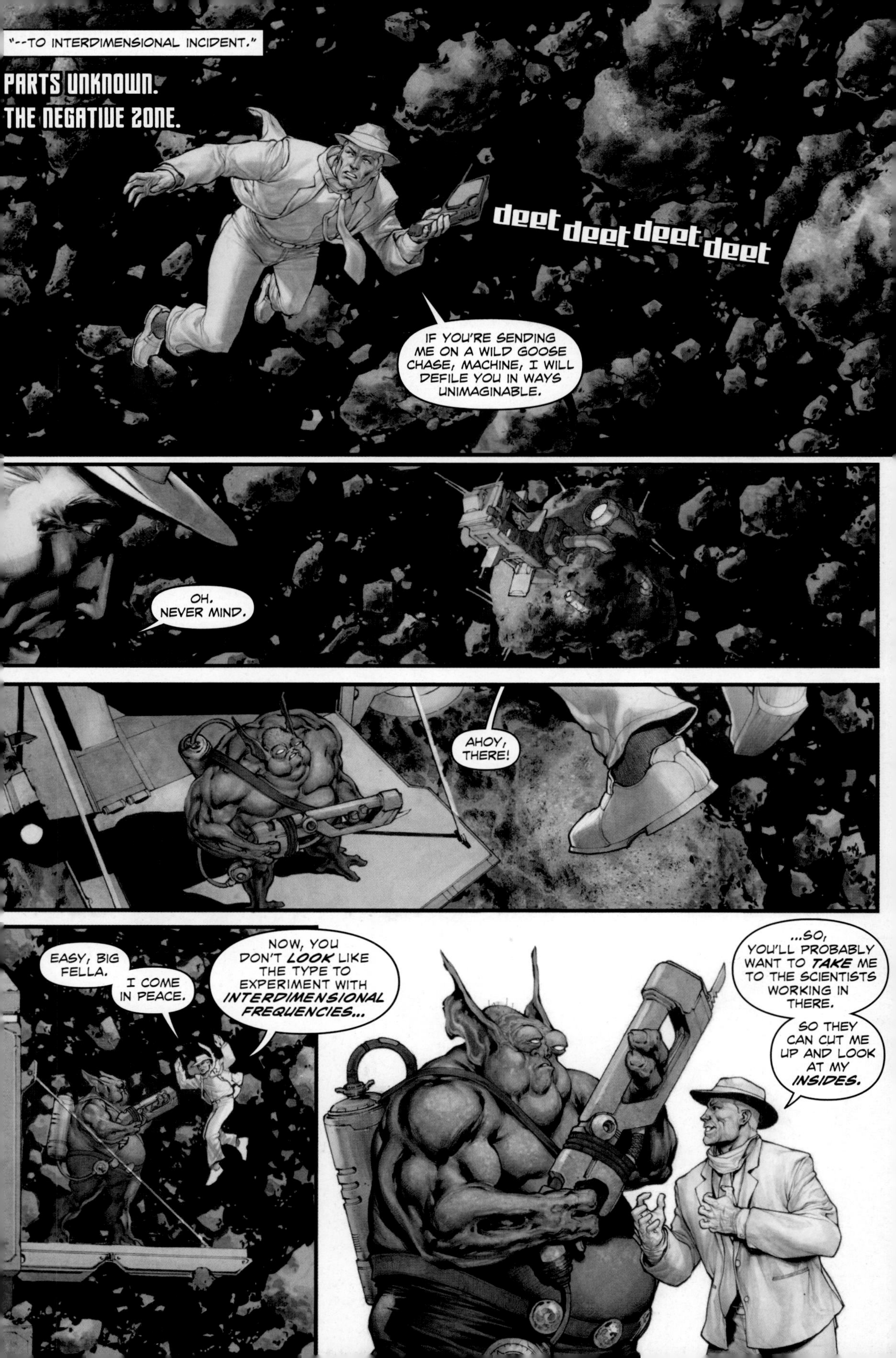
"--TO INTERDIMENSIONAL INCIDENT."
PARTS UNKNOWN.
THE NEGATIVE ZONE.
deet deet deet deet
IF YOU'RE SENDING ME ON A WILD GOOSE CHASE, MACHINE, I WILL DEFILE YOU IN WAYS UNIMAGINABLE.
OH. NEVER MIND.
AHOY, THERE!
EASY, BIG FELLA.
I COME IN PEACE.
NOW, YOU DON'T LOOK LIKE THE TYPE TO EXPERIMENT WITH INTERDIMENSIONAL FREQUENCIES...
...SO, YOU'LL PROBABLY WANT TO TAKE ME TO THE SCIENTISTS WORKING IN THERE.
SO THEY CAN CUT ME UP AND LOOK AT MY INSIDES.

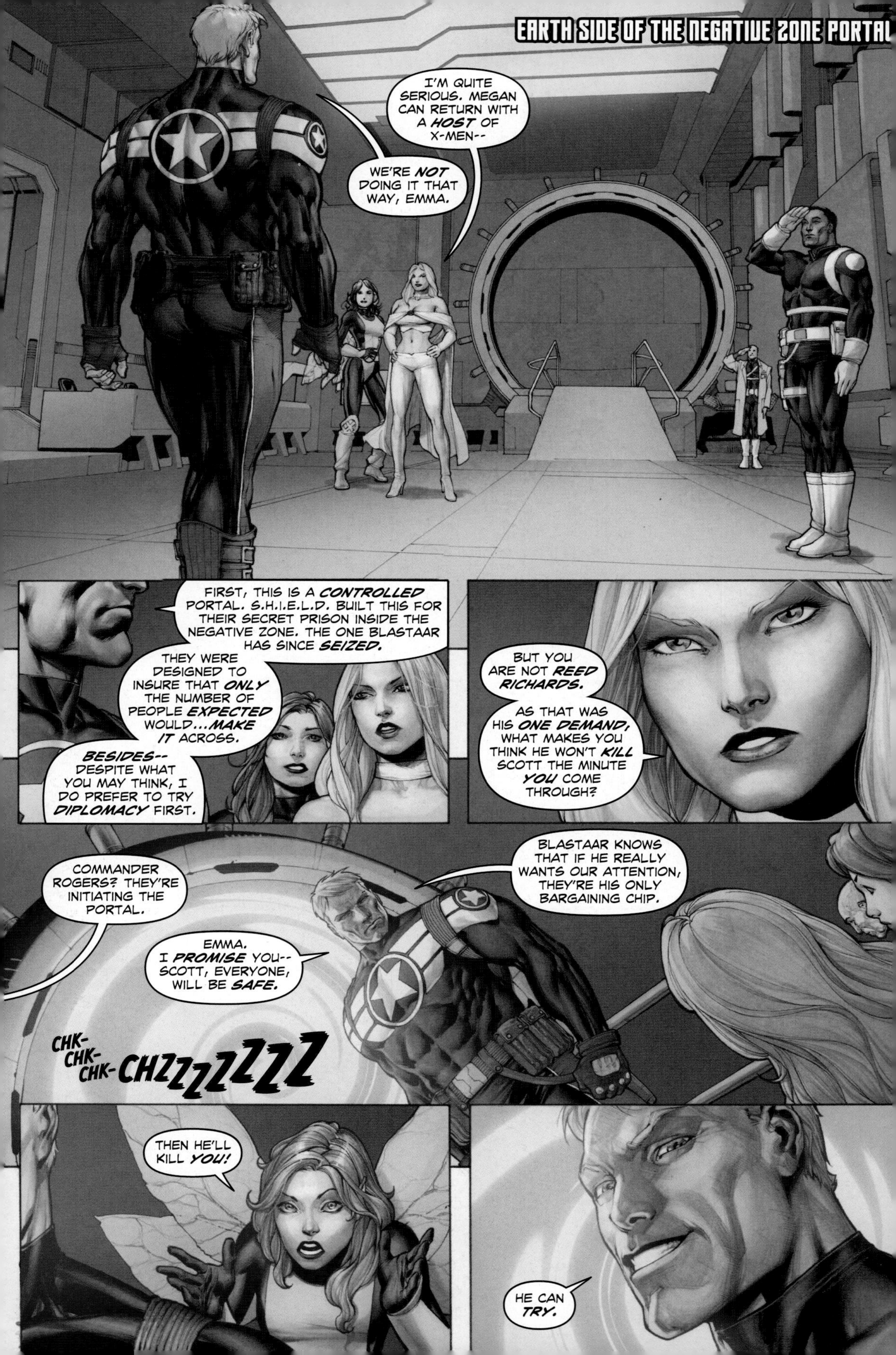
EARTH SIDE OF THE NEGATIVE ZONE PORTAL
I'M QUITE SERIOUS. MEGAN CAN RETURN WITH A HOST OF X-MEN--
WE'RE NOT DOING IT THAT WAY, EMMA.
FIRST, THIS IS A CONTROLLED PORTAL. S.H.I.E.L.D. BUILT THIS FOR THEIR SECRET PRISON INSIDE THE NEGATIVE ZONE. THE ONE BLASTAAR HAS SINCE SEIZED.
THEY WERE DESIGNED TO INSURE THAT ONLY THE NUMBER OF PEOPLE EXPECTED WOULD...MAKE IT ACROSS.
BESIDES-- DESPITE WHAT YOU MAY THINK, I DO PREFER TO TRY DIPLOMACY FIRST.
BUT YOU ARE NOT REED RICHARDS.
AS THAT WAS HIS ONE DEMAND, WHAT MAKES YOU THINK HE WON'T KILL SCOTT THE MINUTE YOU COME THROUGH?
COMMANDER ROGERS? THEY'RE INITIATING THE PORTAL.
BLASTAAR KNOWS THAT IF HE REALLY WANTS OUR ATTENTION, THEY'RE HIS ONLY BARGAINING CHIP.
EMMA. I PROMISE YOU-- SCOTT, EVERYONE, WILL BE SAFE.
CHK- CHK- CHK-CHZZZZZZZZ
THEN HE'LL KILL YOU!
HE CAN TRY.

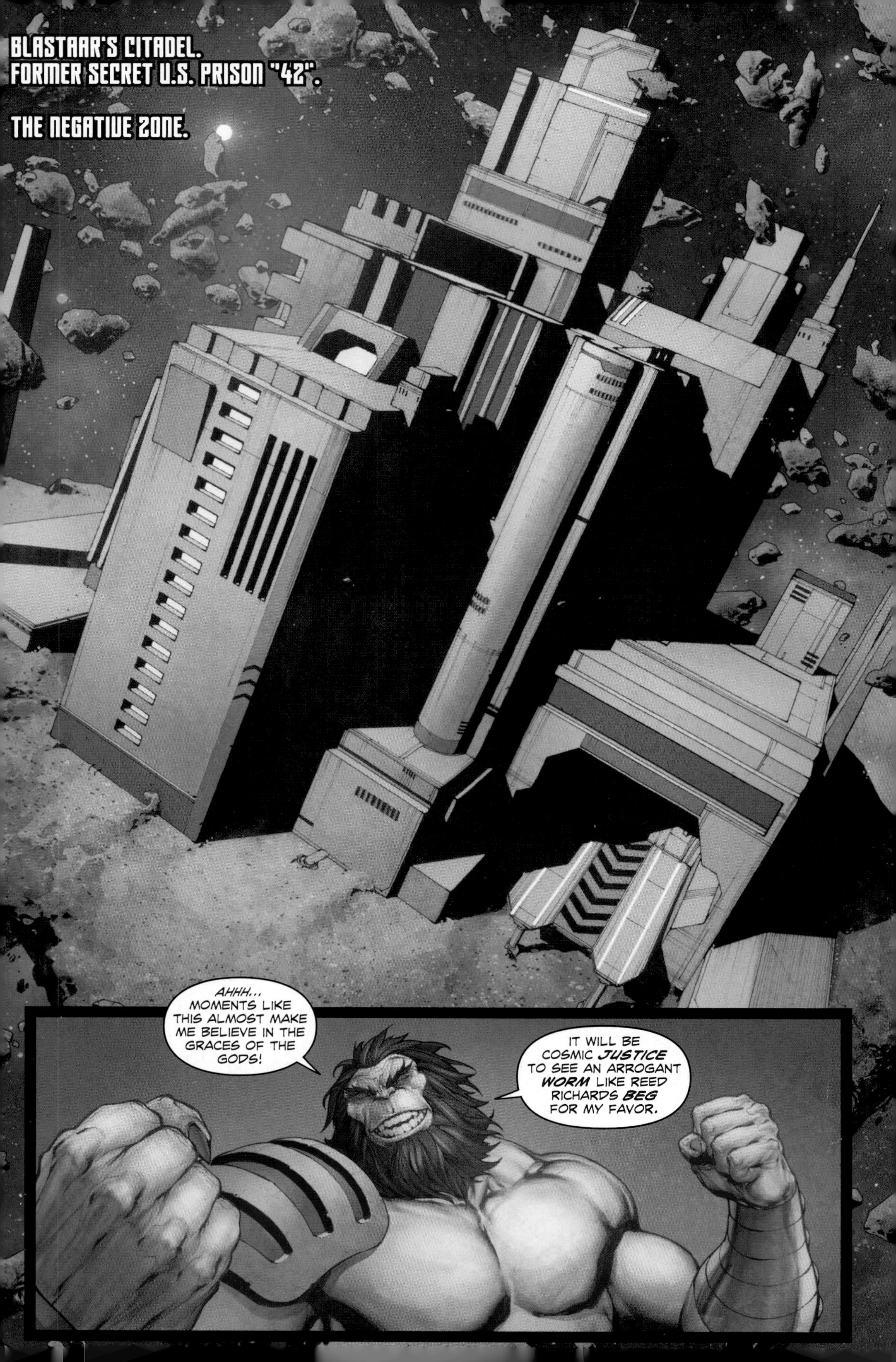
BLASTAAR'S CITADEL.
FORMER SECRET U.S. PRISON "42".
THE NEGATIVE ZONE.
AHHH... MOMENTS LIKE THIS ALMOST MAKE ME BELIEVE IN THE GRACES OF THE GODS!
IT WILL BE COSMIC JUSTICE TO SEE AN ARROGANT WORM LIKE REED RICHARDS BEG FOR MY FAVOR.

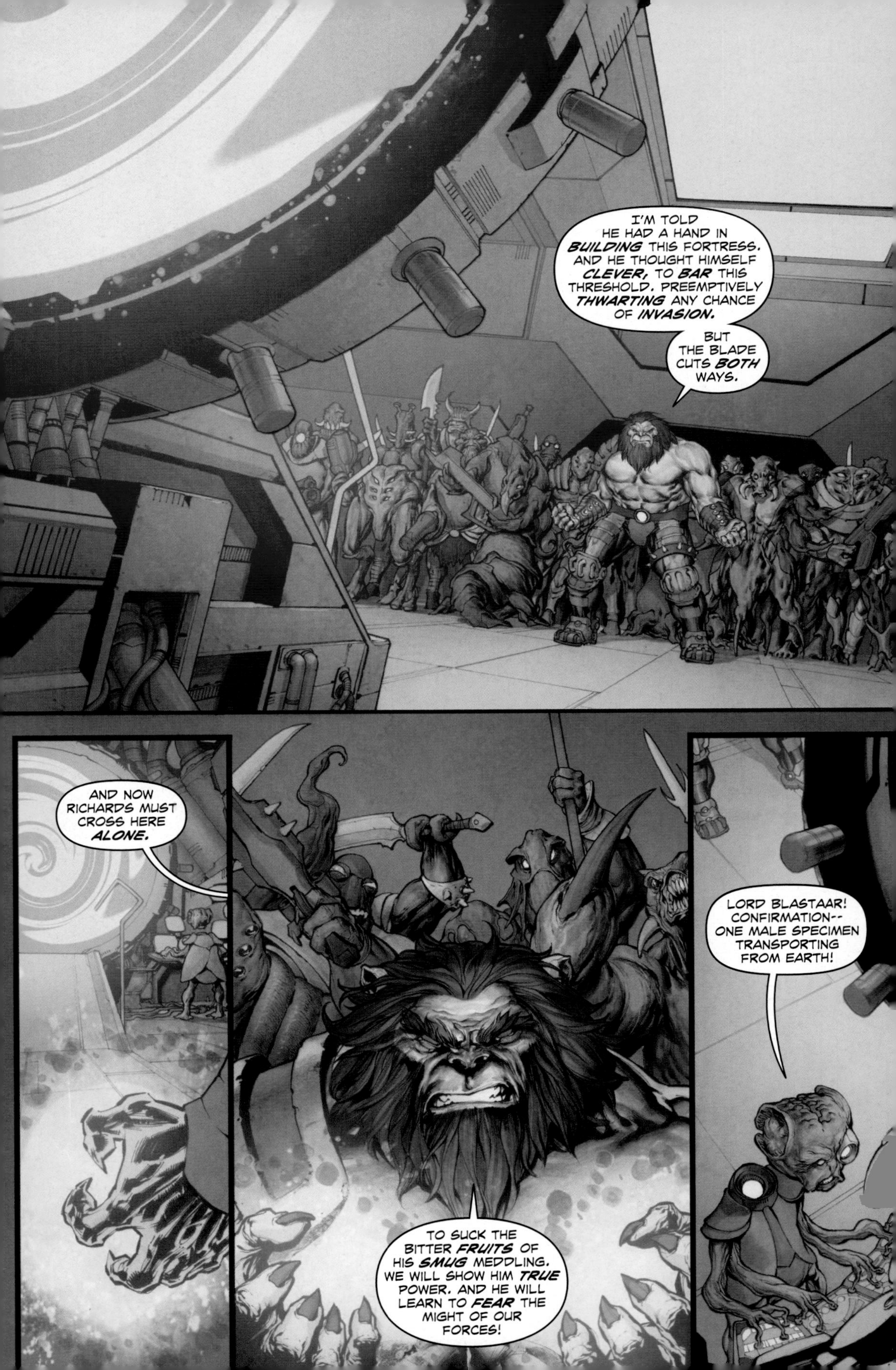
I'M TOLD HE HAD A HAND IN BUILDING THIS FORTRESS. AND HE THOUGHT HIMSELF CLEVER, TO BAR THIS THRESHOLD. PREEMPTIVELY THWARTING ANY CHANCE OF INVASION.
BUT THE BLADE CUTS BOTH WAYS.
AND NOW RICHARDS MUST CROSS HERE ALONE.
TO SUCK THE BITTER FRUITS OF HIS SMUG MEDDLING. WE WILL SHOW HIM TRUE POWER. AND HE WILL LEARN TO FEAR THE MIGHT OF OUR FORCES!
LORD BLASTAAR! CONFIRMATION-- ONE MALE SPECIMEN TRANSPORTING FROM EARTH!

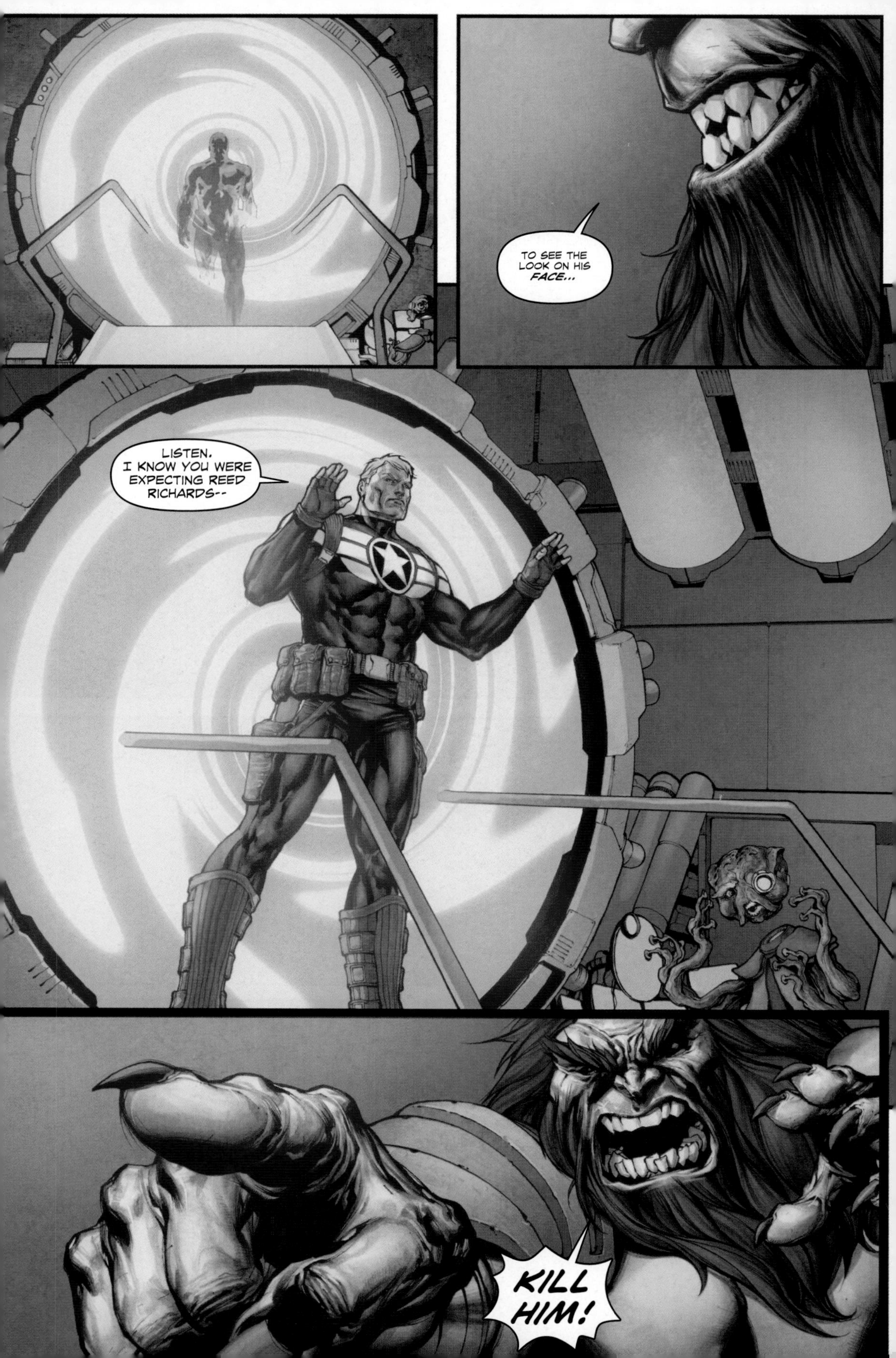
TO SEE THE LOOK ON HIS *FACE...*
LISTEN. I KNOW YOU WERE EXPECTING REED RICHARDS--
KILL HIM!

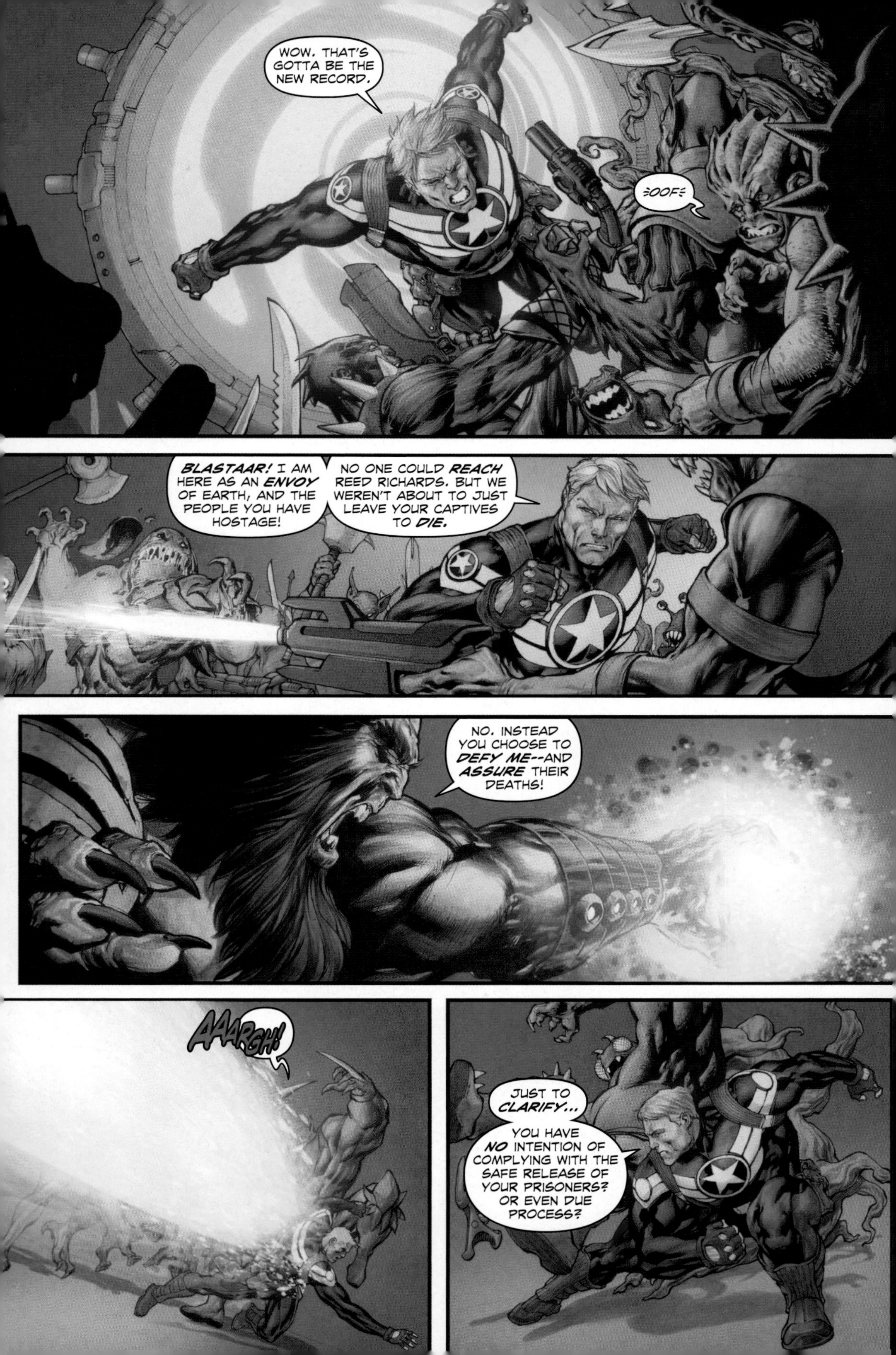
WOW. THAT'S GOTTA BE THE NEW RECORD.
=OOF=
BLASTAAR! I AM HERE AS AN ENVOY OF EARTH, AND THE PEOPLE YOU HAVE HOSTAGE!
NO ONE COULD REACH REED RICHARDS. BUT WE WEREN'T ABOUT TO JUST LEAVE YOUR CAPTIVES TO DIE.
NO. INSTEAD YOU CHOOSE TO DEFY ME--AND ASSURE THEIR DEATHS!
AAARGH!
JUST TO CLARIFY...
YOU HAVE NO INTENTION OF COMPLYING WITH THE SAFE RELEASE OF YOUR PRISONERS? OR EVEN DUE PROCESS?

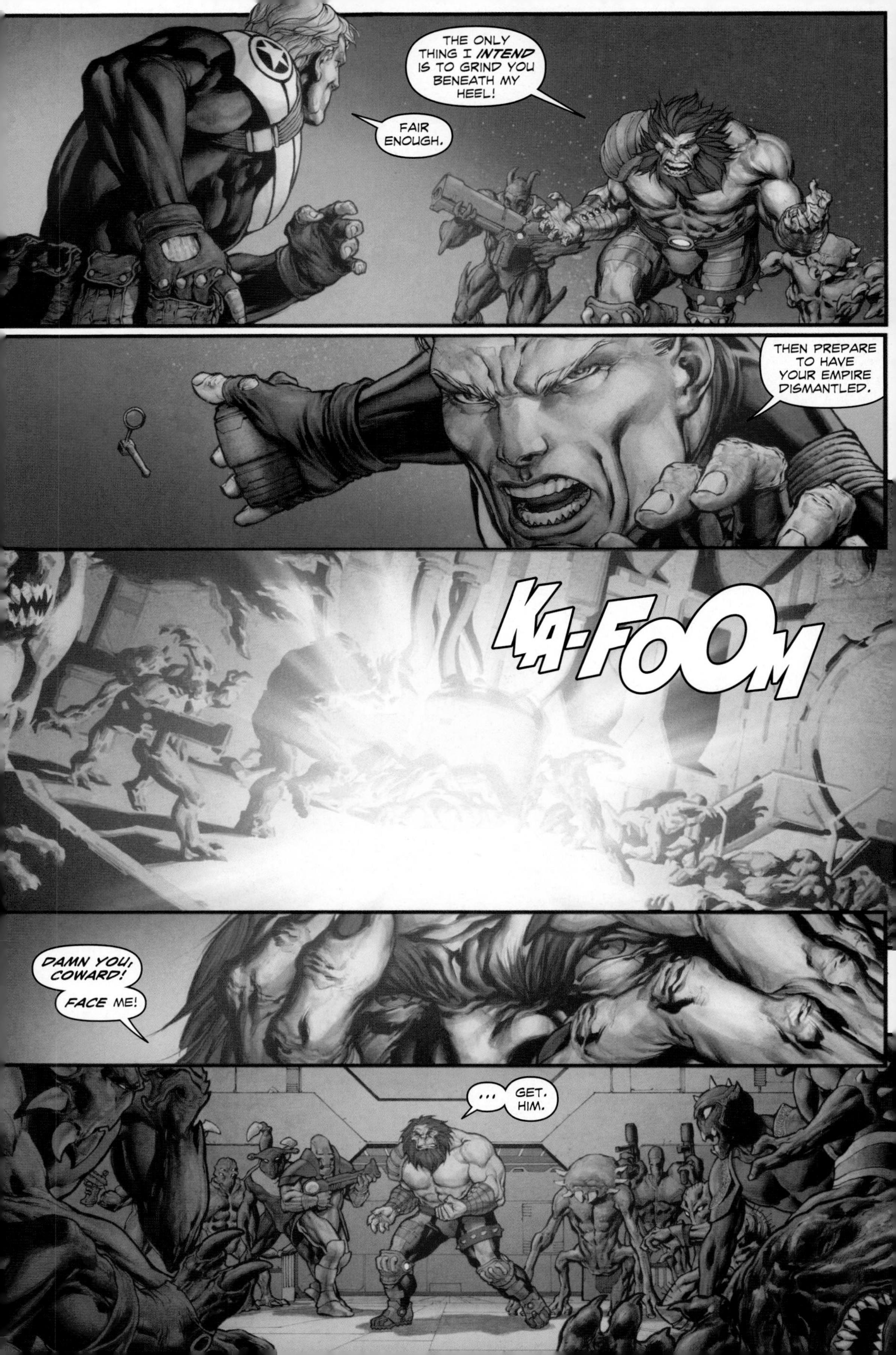
THE ONLY THING I *INTEND* IS TO GRIND YOU BENEATH MY HEEL!
FAIR ENOUGH.
THEN PREPARE TO HAVE YOUR EMPIRE DISMANTLED.
KA-FOOM
DAMN YOU, COWARD!
FACE ME!
... GET. HIM.

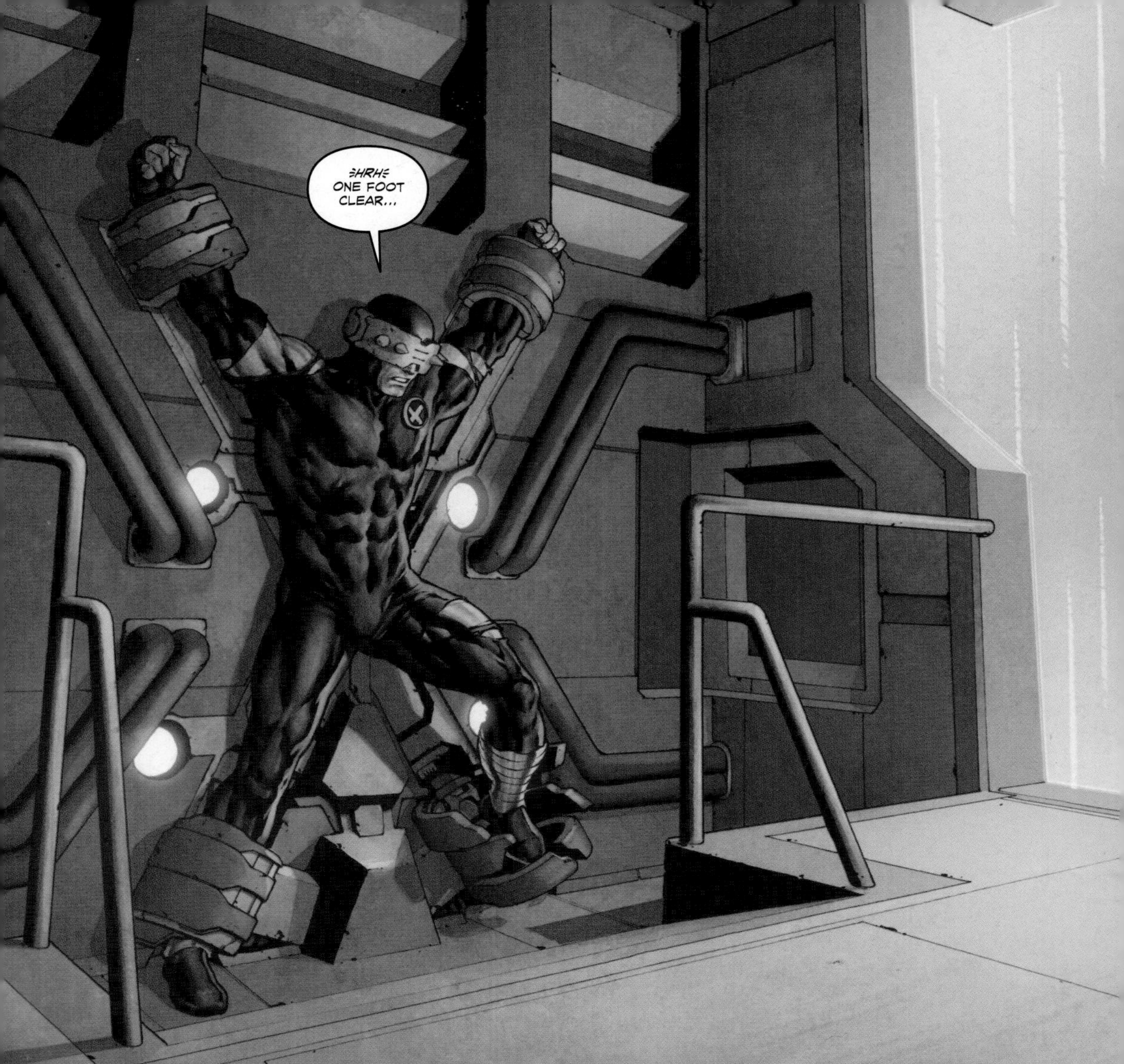

HRH
ONE FOOT CLEAR...

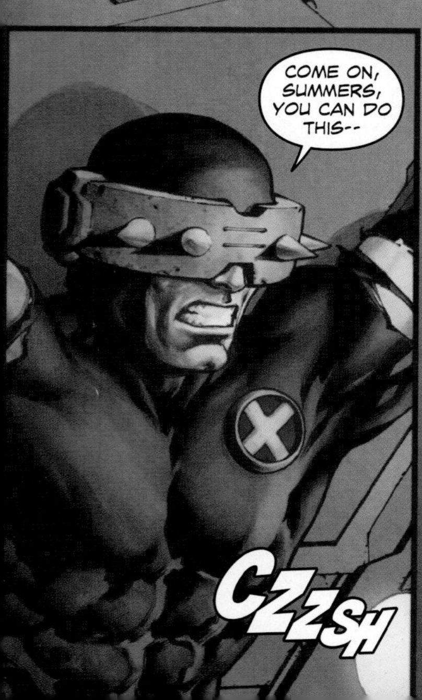

COME ON, SUMMERS, YOU CAN DO THIS--
CZZSH

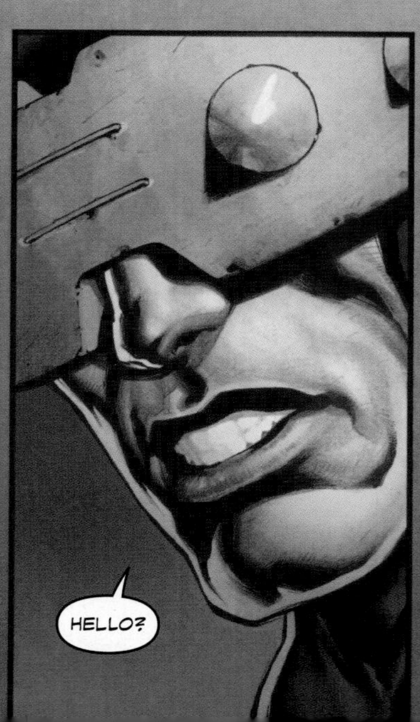

HELLO?

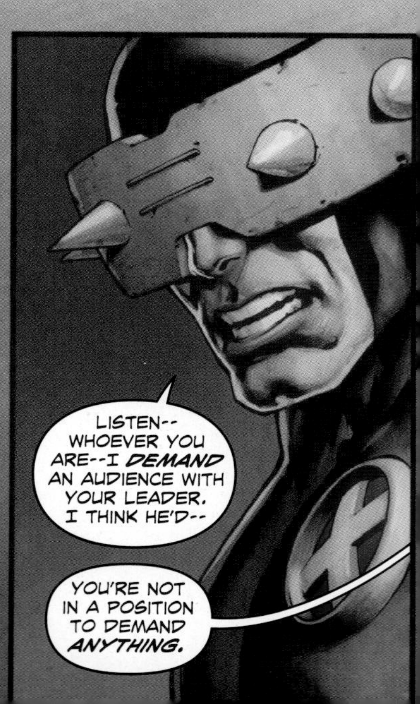

LISTEN-- WHOEVER YOU ARE--I *DEMAND* AN AUDIENCE WITH YOUR LEADER. I THINK HE'D--
YOU'RE NOT IN A POSITION TO DEMAND ***ANYTHING.***

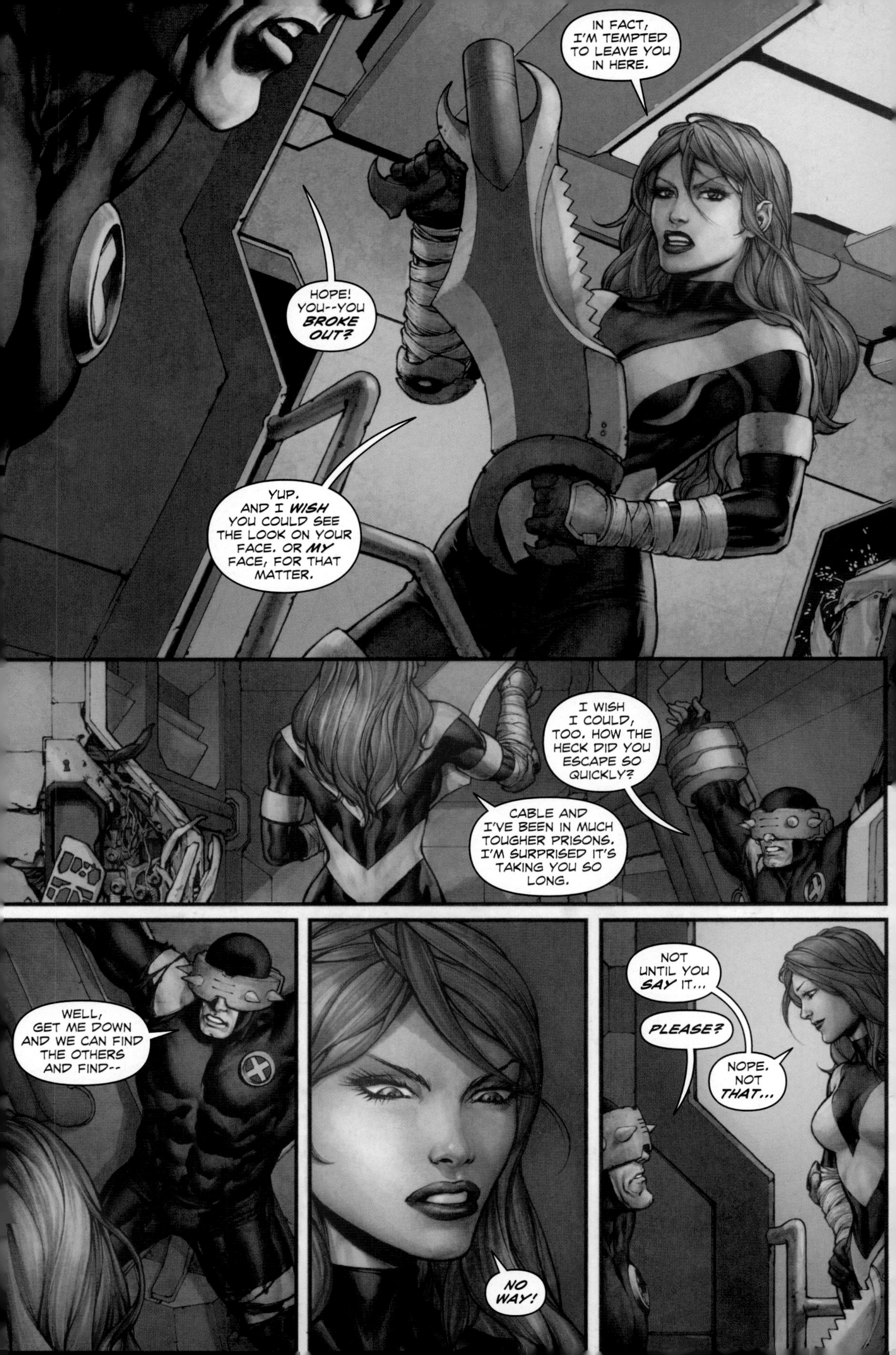
HOPE! YOU--YOU BROKE OUT?
IN FACT, I'M TEMPTED TO LEAVE YOU IN HERE.
YUP. AND I WISH YOU COULD SEE THE LOOK ON YOUR FACE. OR MY FACE, FOR THAT MATTER.
I WISH I COULD, TOO. HOW THE HECK DID YOU ESCAPE SO QUICKLY?
CABLE AND I'VE BEEN IN MUCH TOUGHER PRISONS. I'M SURPRISED IT'S TAKING YOU SO LONG.
WELL, GET ME DOWN AND WE CAN FIND THE OTHERS AND FIND--
NO WAY!
NOT UNTIL YOU SAY IT...
PLEASE?
NOPE. NOT THAT...

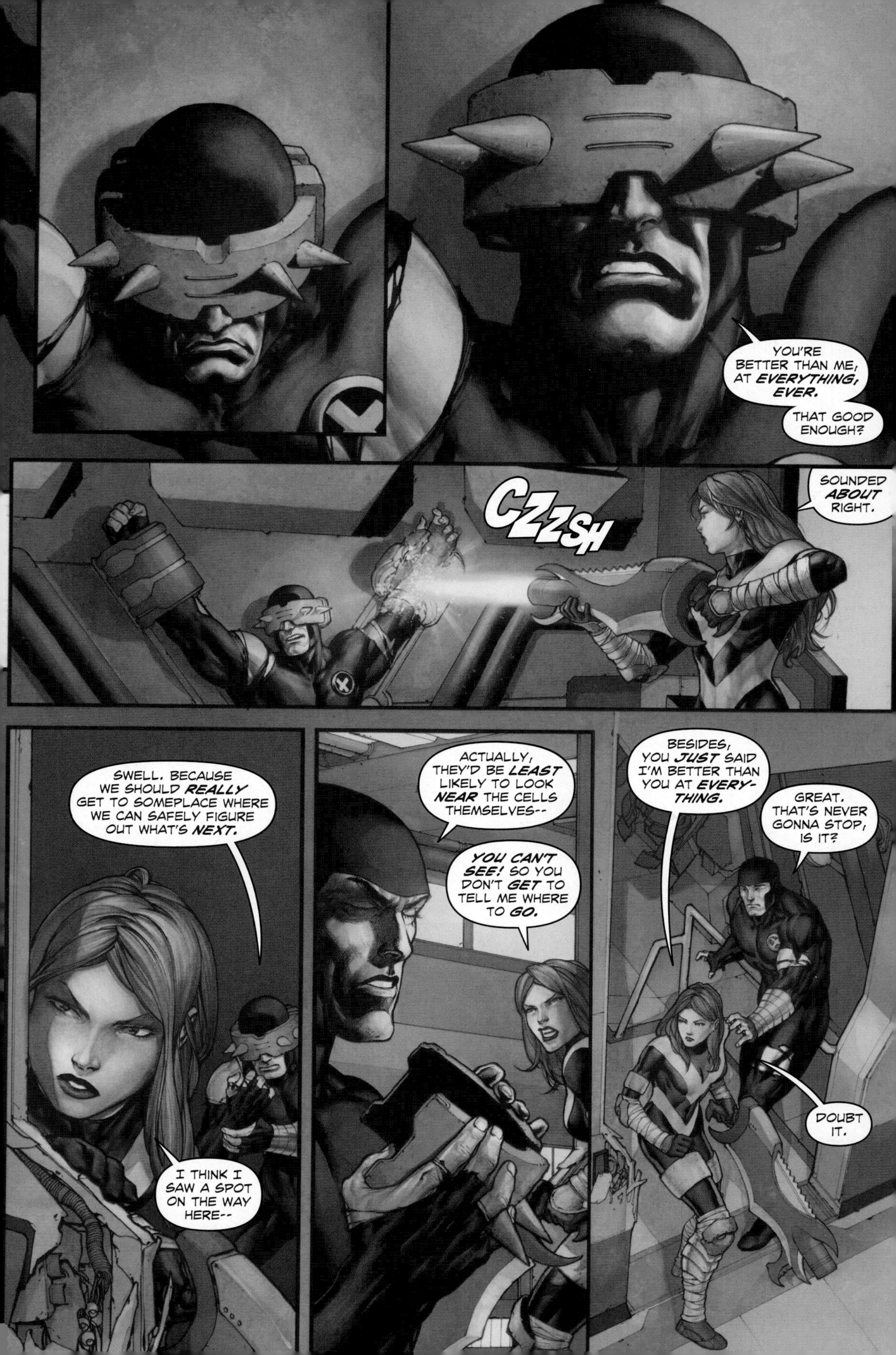
YOU'RE BETTER THAN ME, AT EVERYTHING, EVER.
THAT GOOD ENOUGH?
SOUNDED ABOUT RIGHT.
CZZSH
SWELL. BECAUSE WE SHOULD REALLY GET TO SOMEPLACE WHERE WE CAN SAFELY FIGURE OUT WHAT'S NEXT.
I THINK I SAW A SPOT ON THE WAY HERE--
ACTUALLY, THEY'D BE LEAST LIKELY TO LOOK NEAR THE CELLS THEMSELVES--
YOU CAN'T SEE! SO YOU DON'T GET TO TELL ME WHERE TO GO.
BESIDES, YOU JUST SAID I'M BETTER THAN YOU AT EVERY-THING.
GREAT. THAT'S NEVER GONNA STOP, IS IT?
DOUBT IT.

"...WHAT THE--?

--WHO INSISTS ON THE SAME DISH FOR EVERY SINGLE MEAL?!

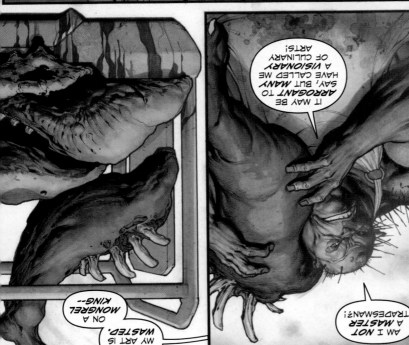

ON A MONGREL KING--

BUT HERE MY ART IS WASTED,

AM I NOT A MASTER TRADESMAN?!

IT MAY BE ARROGANT TO SAY, BUT MANY HAVE CALLED ME A VISIONARY OF CULINARY ARTS!

OF ALL THE INDIGNITIES!

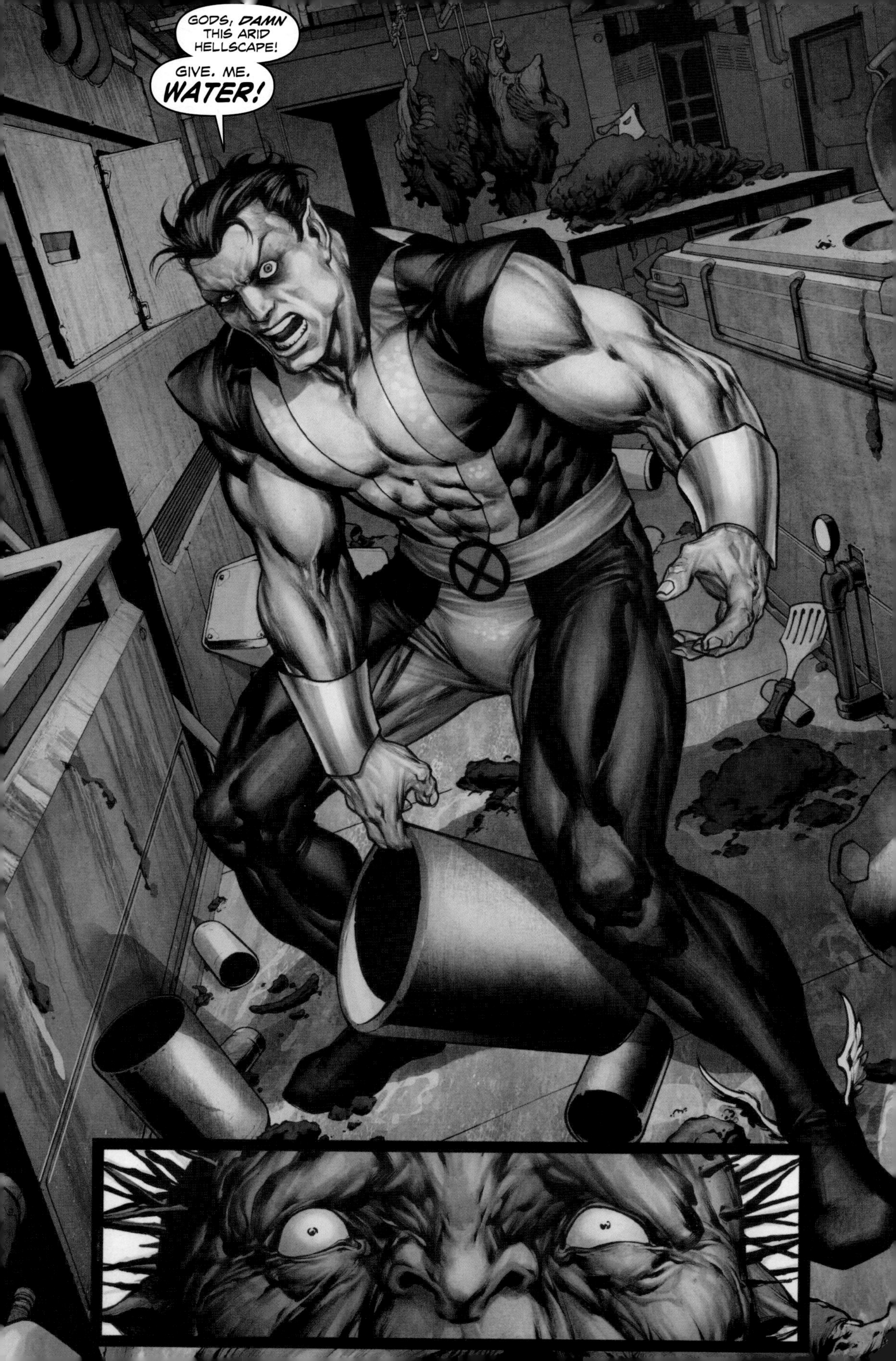
GODS, *DAMN* THIS ARID HELLSCAPE!
GIVE. ME. ***WATER!***

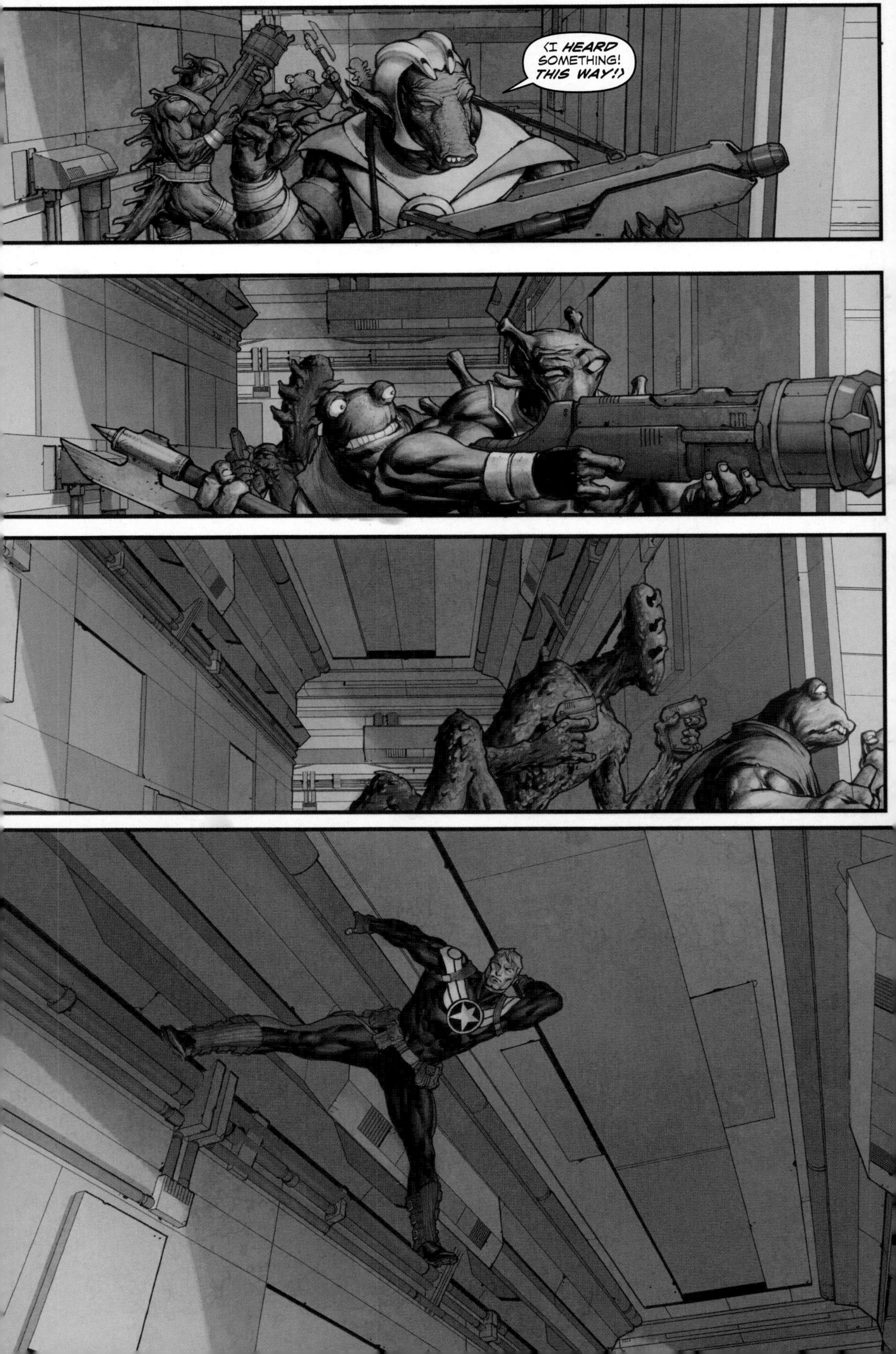

‹I HEARD SOMETHING! THIS WAY!›

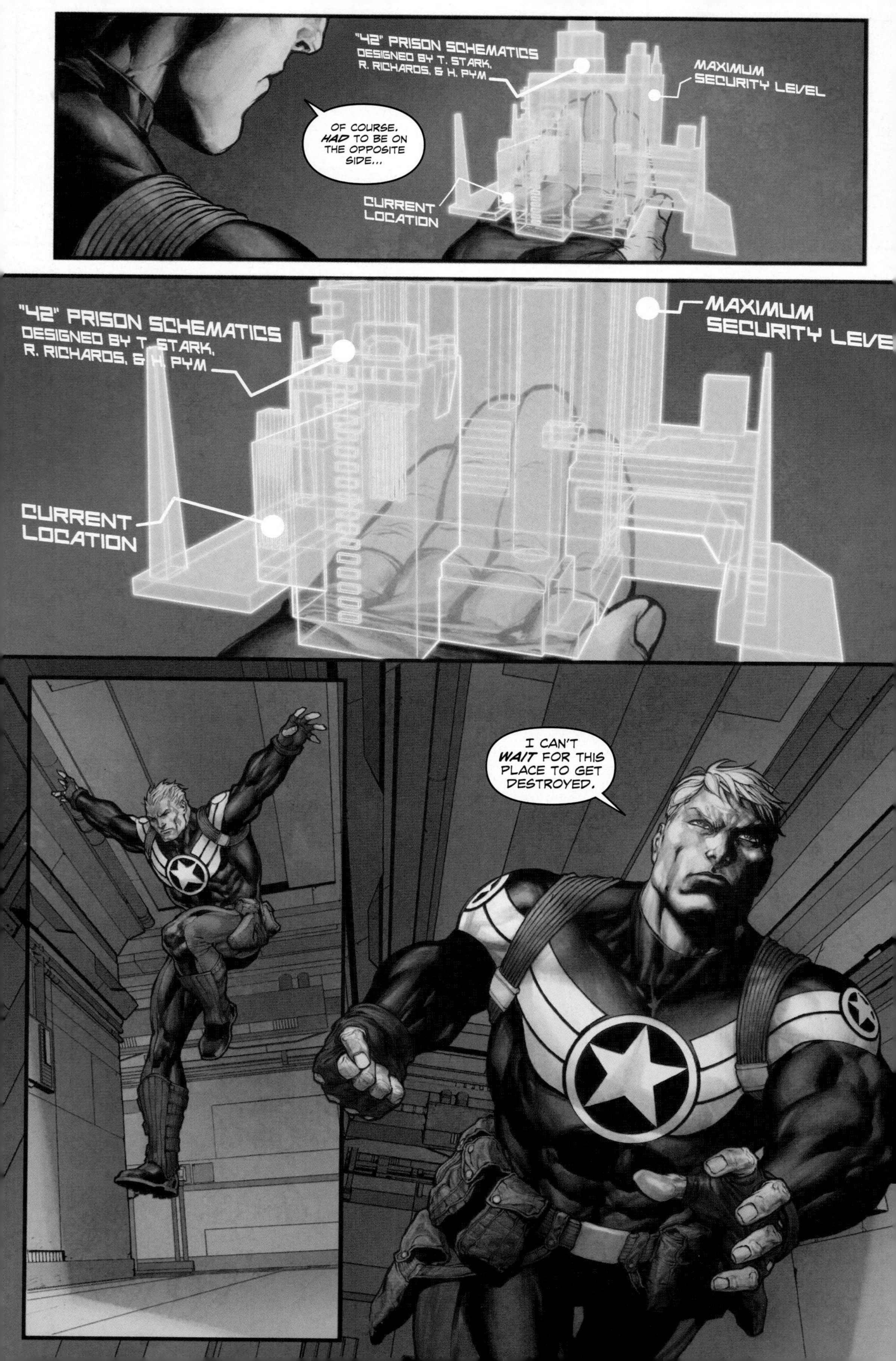
"42" PRISON SCHEMATICS
DESIGNED BY T. STARK, R. RICHARDS, & H. PYM
MAXIMUM SECURITY LEVEL
OF COURSE. HAD TO BE ON THE OPPOSITE SIDE...
CURRENT LOCATION
"42" PRISON SCHEMATICS
DESIGNED BY T. STARK, R. RICHARDS, & H. PYM
MAXIMUM SECURITY LEVE
CURRENT LOCATION
I CAN'T WAIT FOR THIS PLACE TO GET DESTROYED.

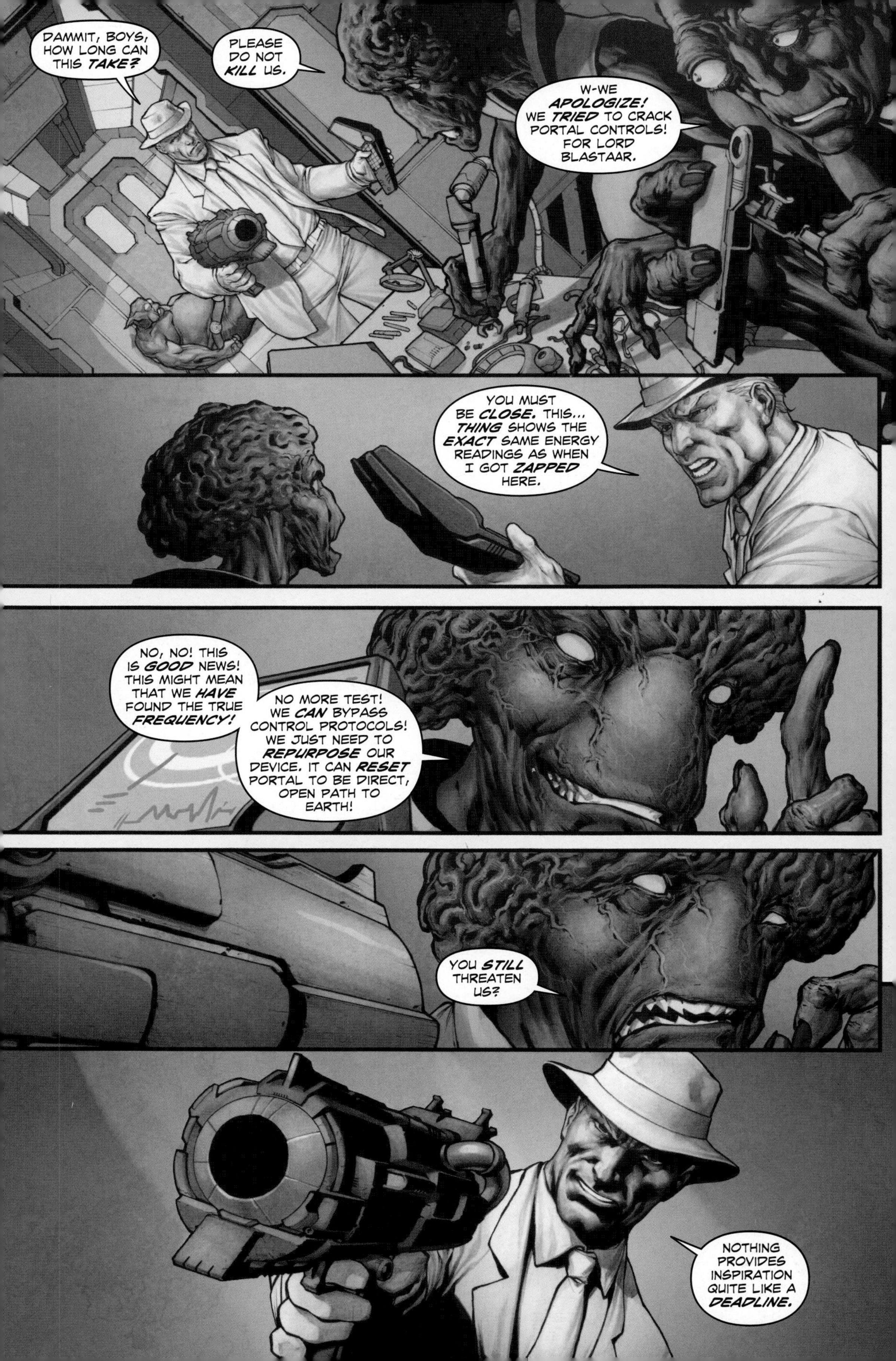
DAMMIT, BOYS, HOW LONG CAN THIS *TAKE?*
PLEASE DO NOT *KILL* US.
W-WE *APOLOGIZE!* WE *TRIED* TO CRACK PORTAL CONTROLS! FOR LORD BLASTAAR.
YOU MUST BE *CLOSE.* THIS... *THING* SHOWS THE *EXACT* SAME ENERGY READINGS AS WHEN I GOT *ZAPPED* HERE.
NO, NO! THIS IS *GOOD* NEWS! THIS MIGHT MEAN THAT WE *HAVE* FOUND THE TRUE *FREQUENCY!*
NO MORE TEST! WE *CAN* BYPASS CONTROL PROTOCOLS! WE JUST NEED TO *REPURPOSE* OUR DEVICE. IT CAN *RESET* PORTAL TO BE DIRECT, OPEN PATH TO EARTH!
YOU *STILL* THREATEN US?
NOTHING PROVIDES INSPIRATION QUITE LIKE A *DEADLINE.*

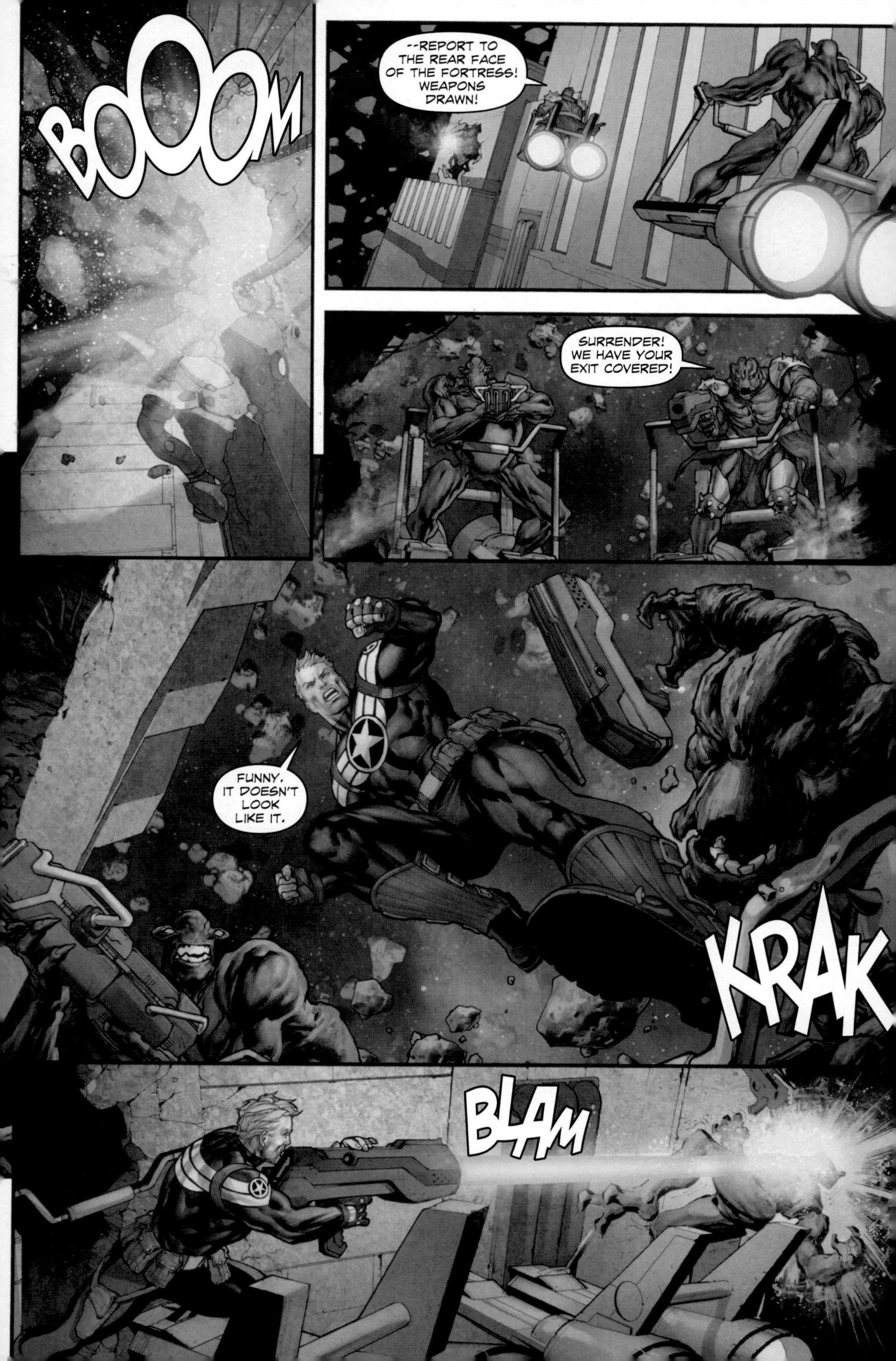
BOOOM
--REPORT TO THE REAR FACE OF THE FORTRESS! WEAPONS DRAWN!
SURRENDER! WE HAVE YOUR EXIT COVERED!
FUNNY. IT DOESN'T LOOK LIKE IT.
KRAK
BLAM

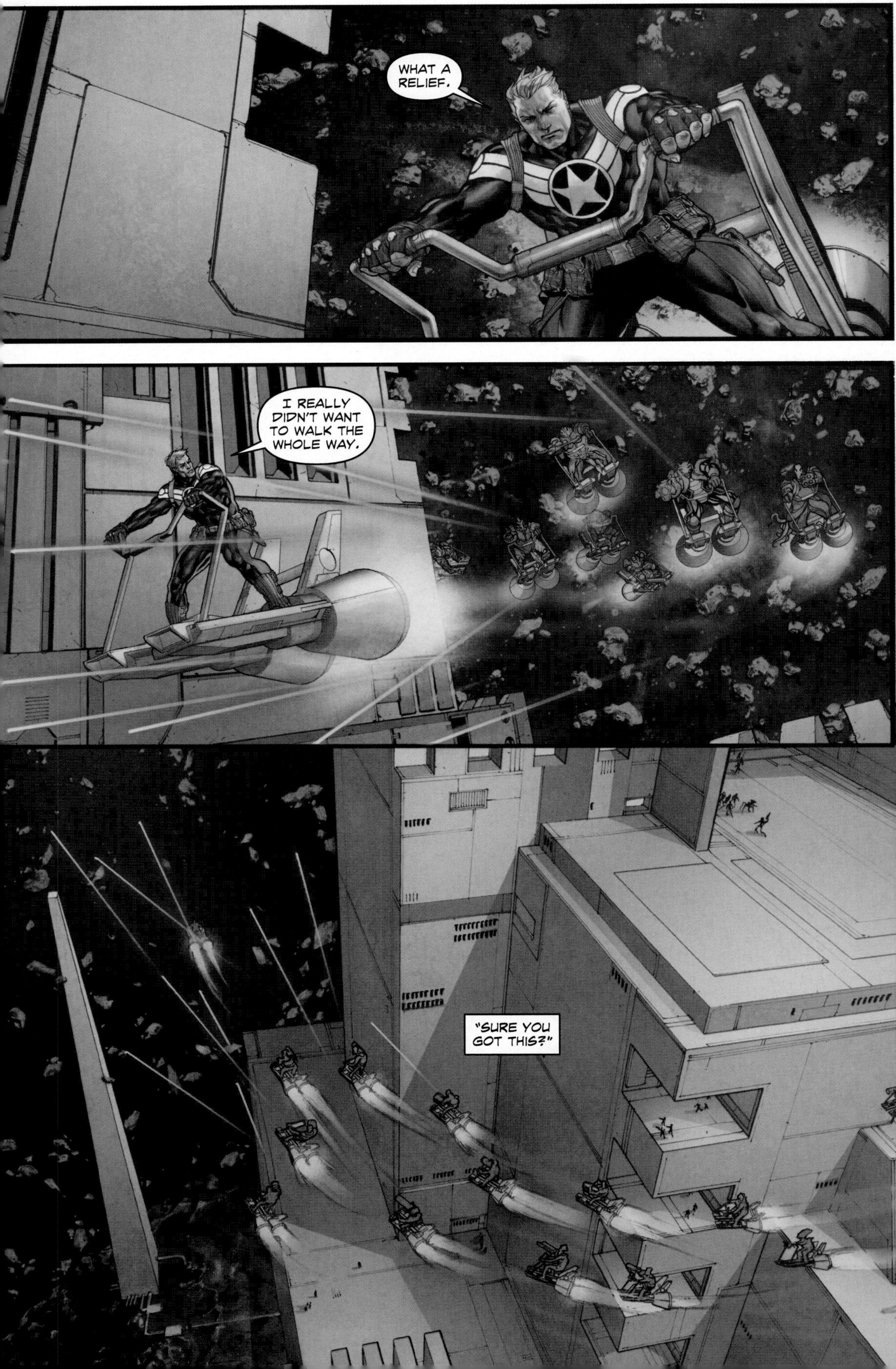
WHAT A RELIEF.
I REALLY DIDN'T WANT TO WALK THE WHOLE WAY.
"SURE YOU GOT THIS?"

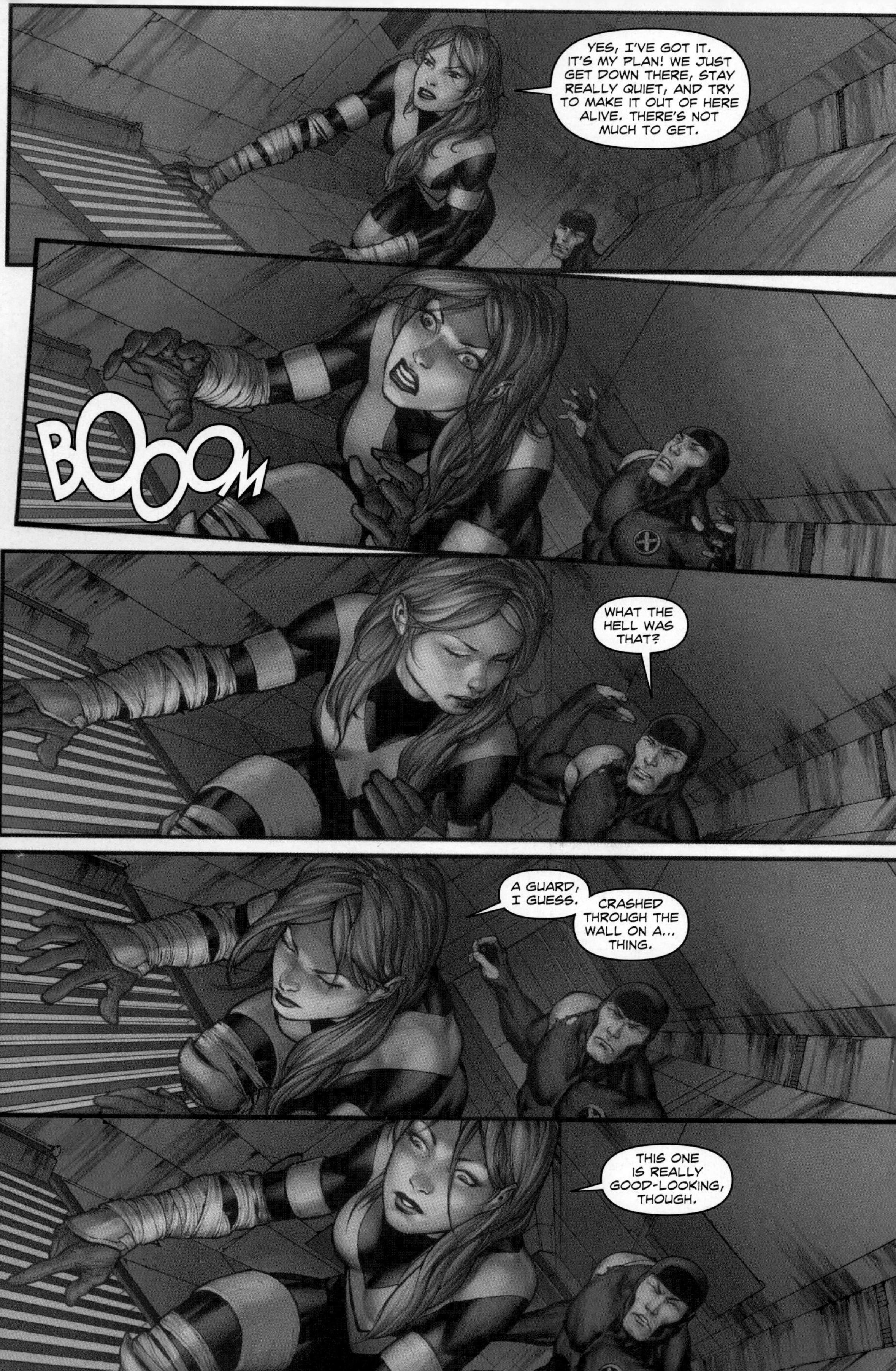
YES, I'VE GOT IT. IT'S MY PLAN! WE JUST GET DOWN THERE, STAY REALLY QUIET, AND TRY TO MAKE IT OUT OF HERE ALIVE. THERE'S NOT MUCH TO GET.
BOOOOM
WHAT THE HELL WAS THAT?
A GUARD, I GUESS.
CRASHED THROUGH THE WALL ON A... THING.
THIS ONE IS REALLY GOOD-LOOKING, THOUGH.

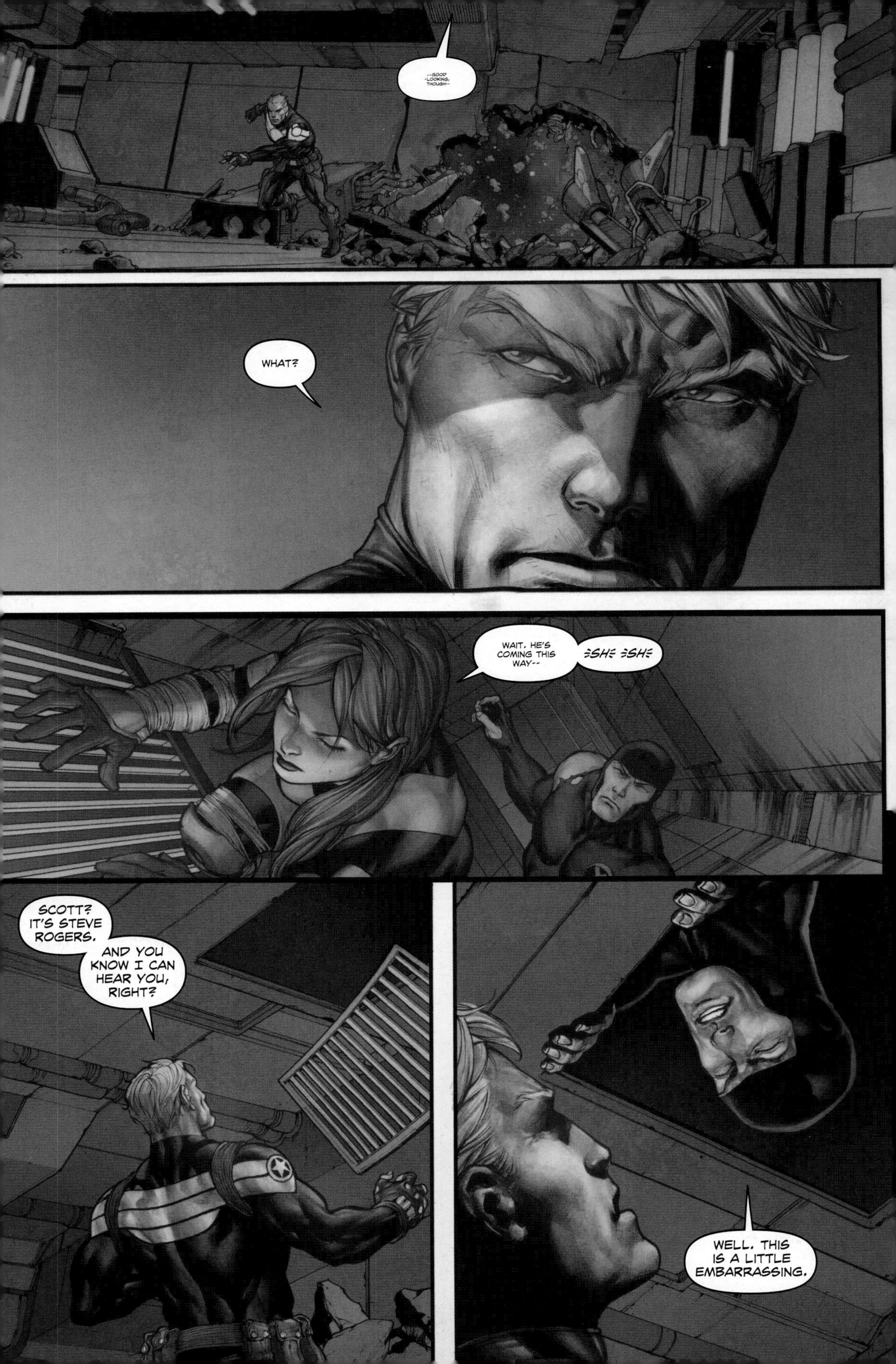
--GOOD-LOOKING, THOUGH--
WHAT?
WAIT. HE'S COMING THIS WAY--
SH SH
SCOTT? IT'S STEVE ROGERS.
AND YOU KNOW I CAN HEAR YOU, RIGHT?
WELL. THIS IS A LITTLE EMBARRASSING.

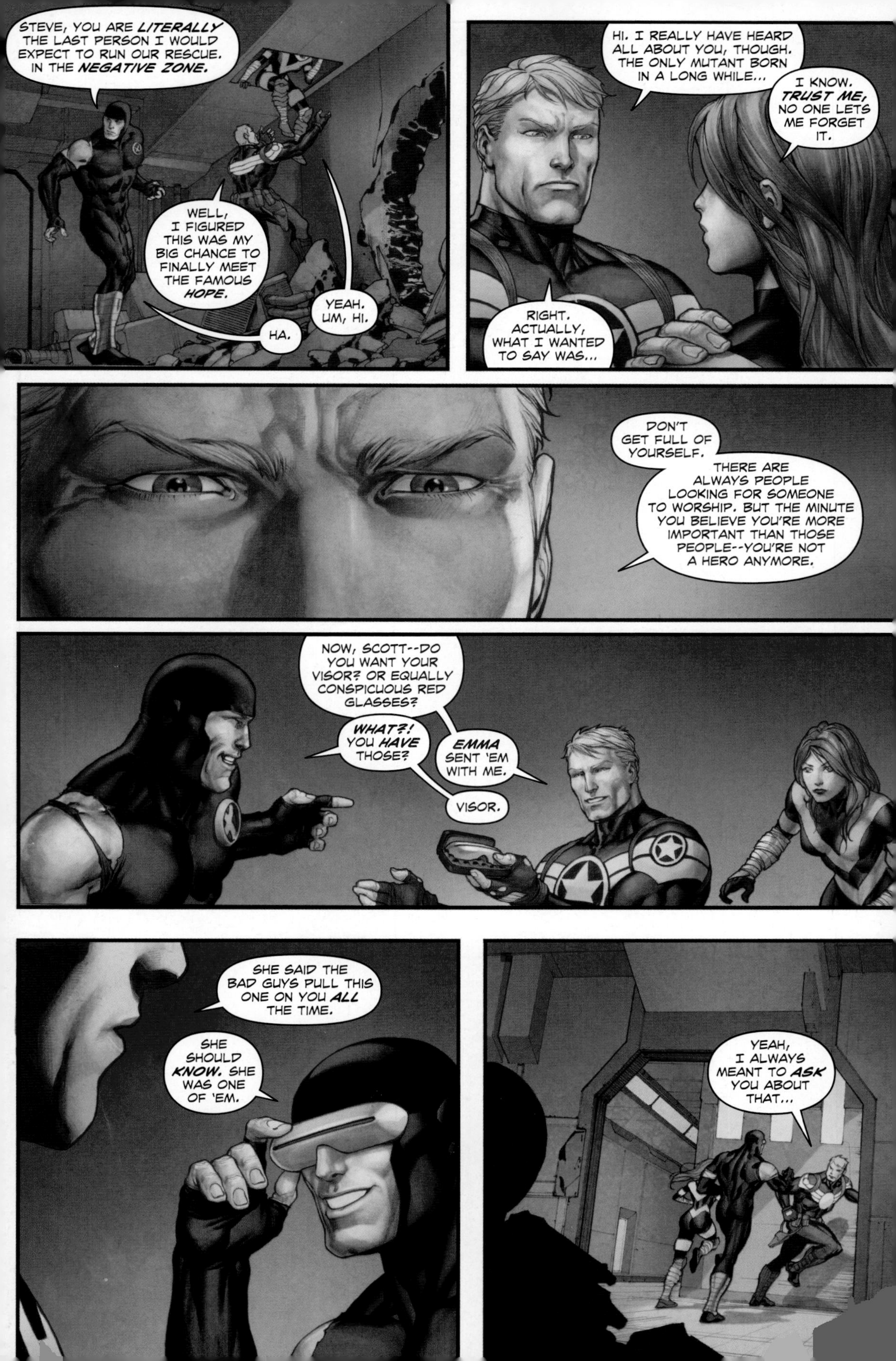
STEVE, YOU ARE *LITERALLY* THE LAST PERSON I WOULD EXPECT TO RUN OUR RESCUE. IN THE *NEGATIVE ZONE.*
WELL, I FIGURED THIS WAS MY BIG CHANCE TO FINALLY MEET THE FAMOUS *HOPE.*
YEAH. UM, HI.
HA.
HI. I REALLY HAVE HEARD ALL ABOUT YOU, THOUGH. THE ONLY MUTANT BORN IN A LONG WHILE...
I KNOW. *TRUST ME,* NO ONE LETS ME FORGET IT.
RIGHT. ACTUALLY, WHAT I WANTED TO SAY WAS...
DON'T GET FULL OF YOURSELF.
THERE ARE ALWAYS PEOPLE LOOKING FOR SOMEONE TO WORSHIP. BUT THE MINUTE YOU BELIEVE YOU'RE MORE IMPORTANT THAN THOSE PEOPLE--YOU'RE NOT A HERO ANYMORE.
NOW, SCOTT--DO YOU WANT YOUR VISOR? OR EQUALLY CONSPICUOUS RED GLASSES?
WHAT?! YOU *HAVE* THOSE?
EMMA SENT 'EM WITH ME.
VISOR.
SHE SAID THE BAD GUYS PULL THIS ONE ON YOU *ALL* THE TIME.
SHE SHOULD *KNOW.* SHE WAS ONE OF 'EM.
YEAH, I ALWAYS MEANT TO *ASK* YOU ABOUT THAT...

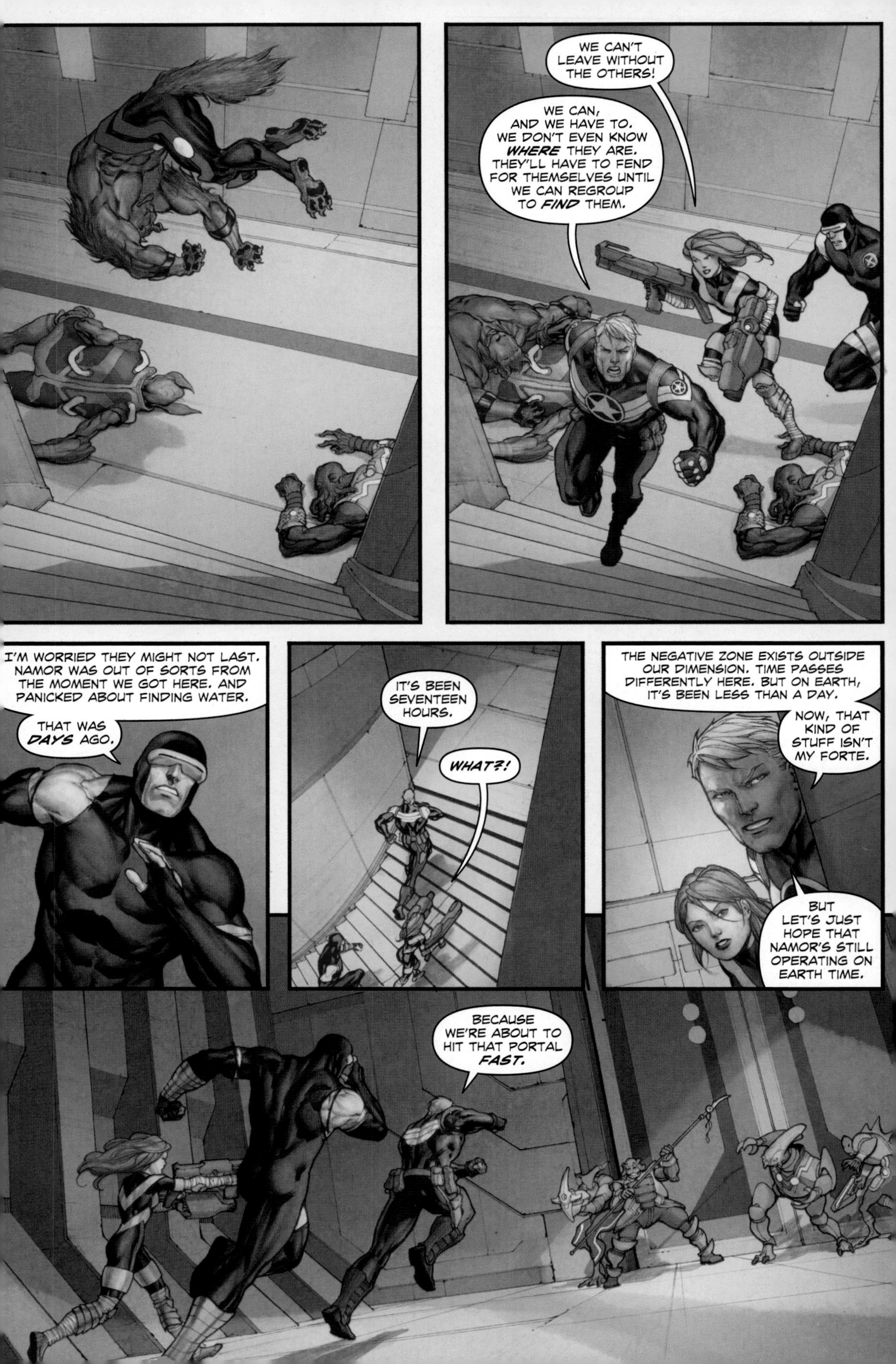
WE CAN'T LEAVE WITHOUT THE OTHERS!
WE CAN, AND WE HAVE TO. WE DON'T EVEN KNOW *WHERE* THEY ARE. THEY'LL HAVE TO FEND FOR THEMSELVES UNTIL WE CAN REGROUP TO *FIND* THEM.
I'M WORRIED THEY MIGHT NOT LAST. NAMOR WAS OUT OF SORTS FROM THE MOMENT WE GOT HERE. AND PANICKED ABOUT FINDING WATER.
THAT WAS *DAYS* AGO.
IT'S BEEN SEVENTEEN HOURS.
WHAT?!
THE NEGATIVE ZONE EXISTS OUTSIDE OUR DIMENSION. TIME PASSES DIFFERENTLY HERE. BUT ON EARTH, IT'S BEEN LESS THAN A DAY.
NOW, THAT KIND OF STUFF ISN'T MY FORTE.
BUT LET'S JUST HOPE THAT NAMOR'S STILL OPERATING ON EARTH TIME.
BECAUSE WE'RE ABOUT TO HIT THAT PORTAL *FAST*.

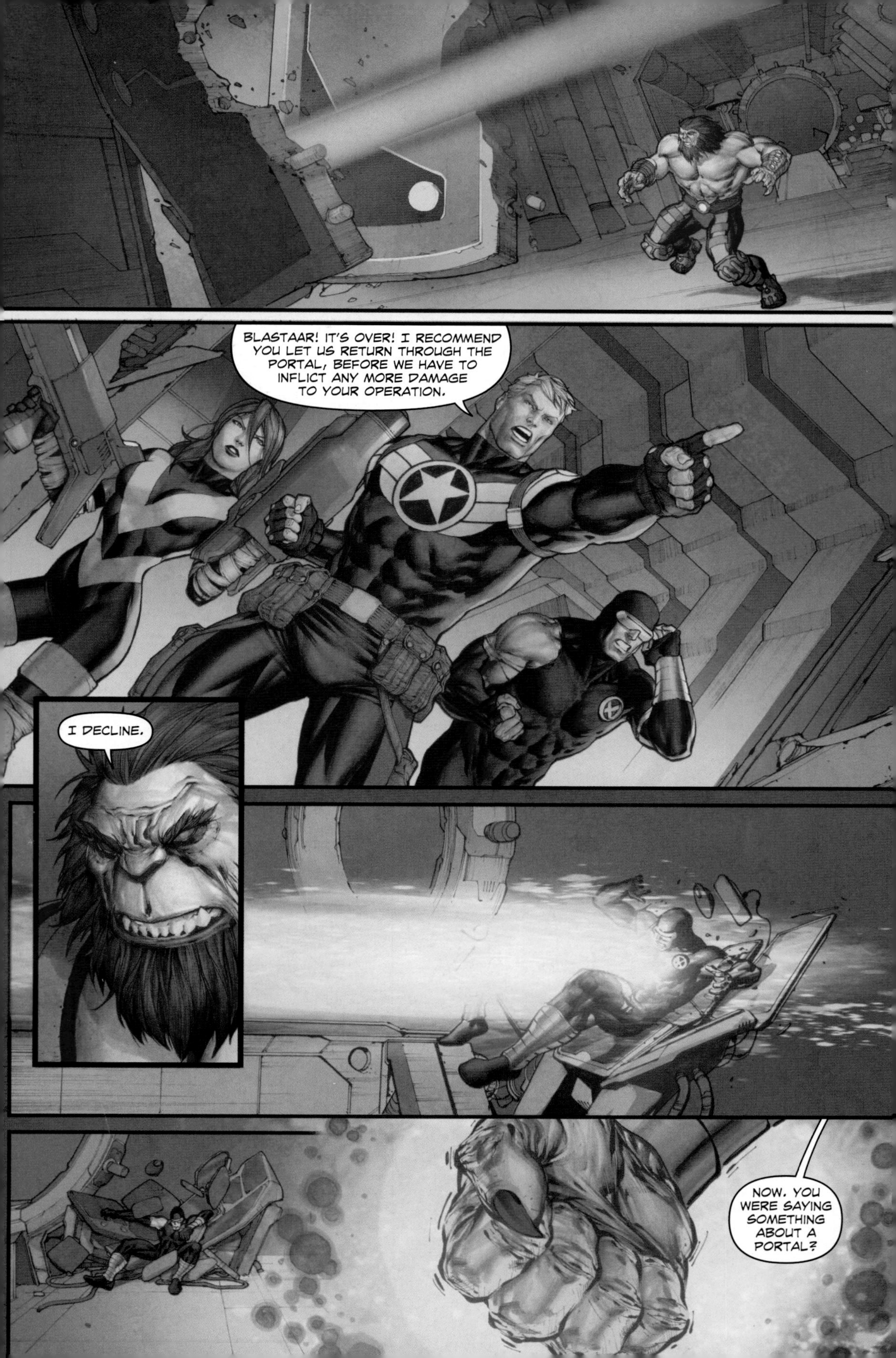
BLASTAAR! IT'S OVER! I RECOMMEND YOU LET US RETURN THROUGH THE PORTAL, BEFORE WE HAVE TO INFLICT ANY MORE DAMAGE TO YOUR OPERATION.
I DECLINE.
NOW, YOU WERE SAYING SOMETHING ABOUT A PORTAL?

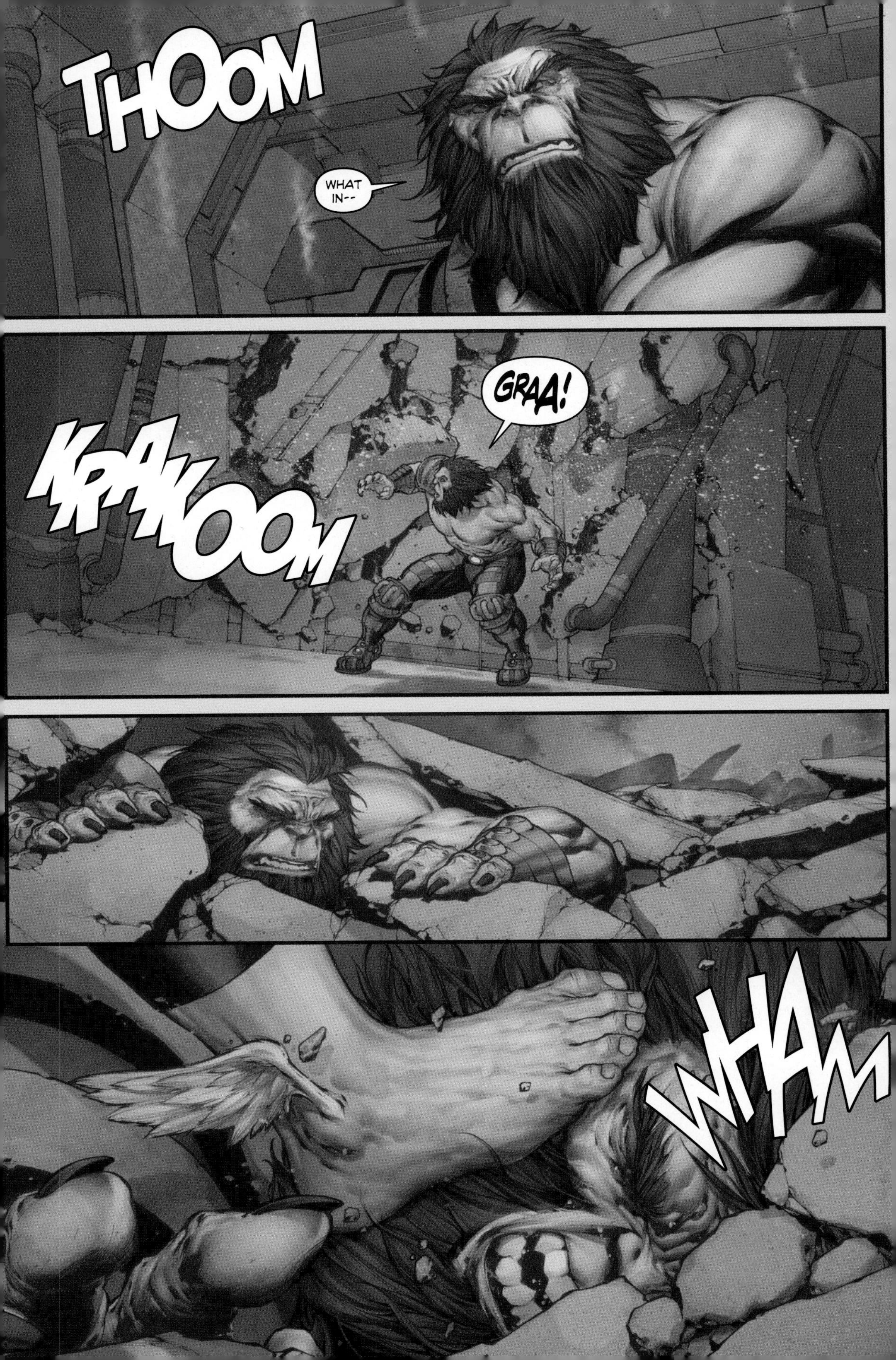
THOOM
WHAT IN--
KRAKOOM
GRAA!
WHAM

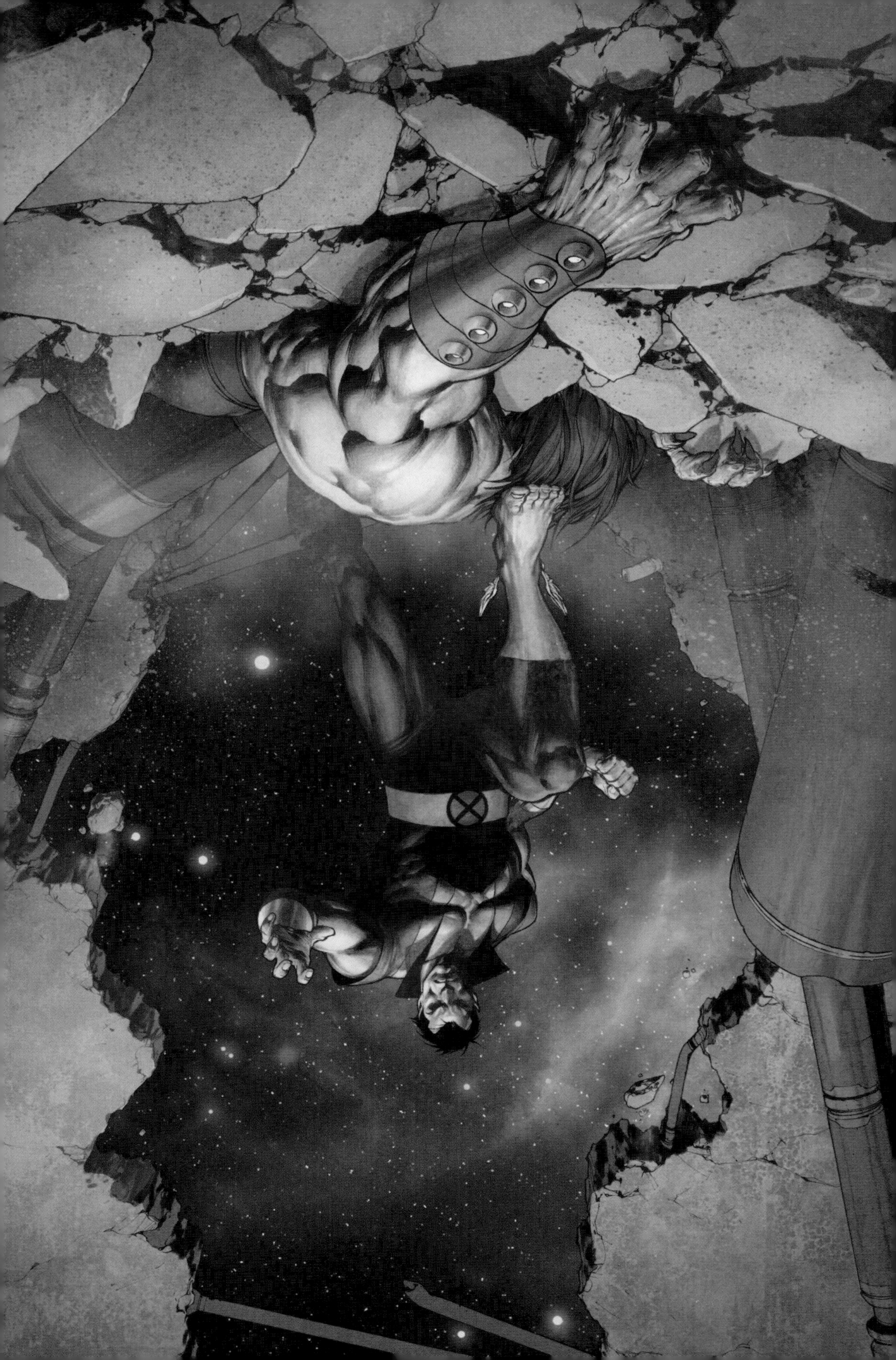

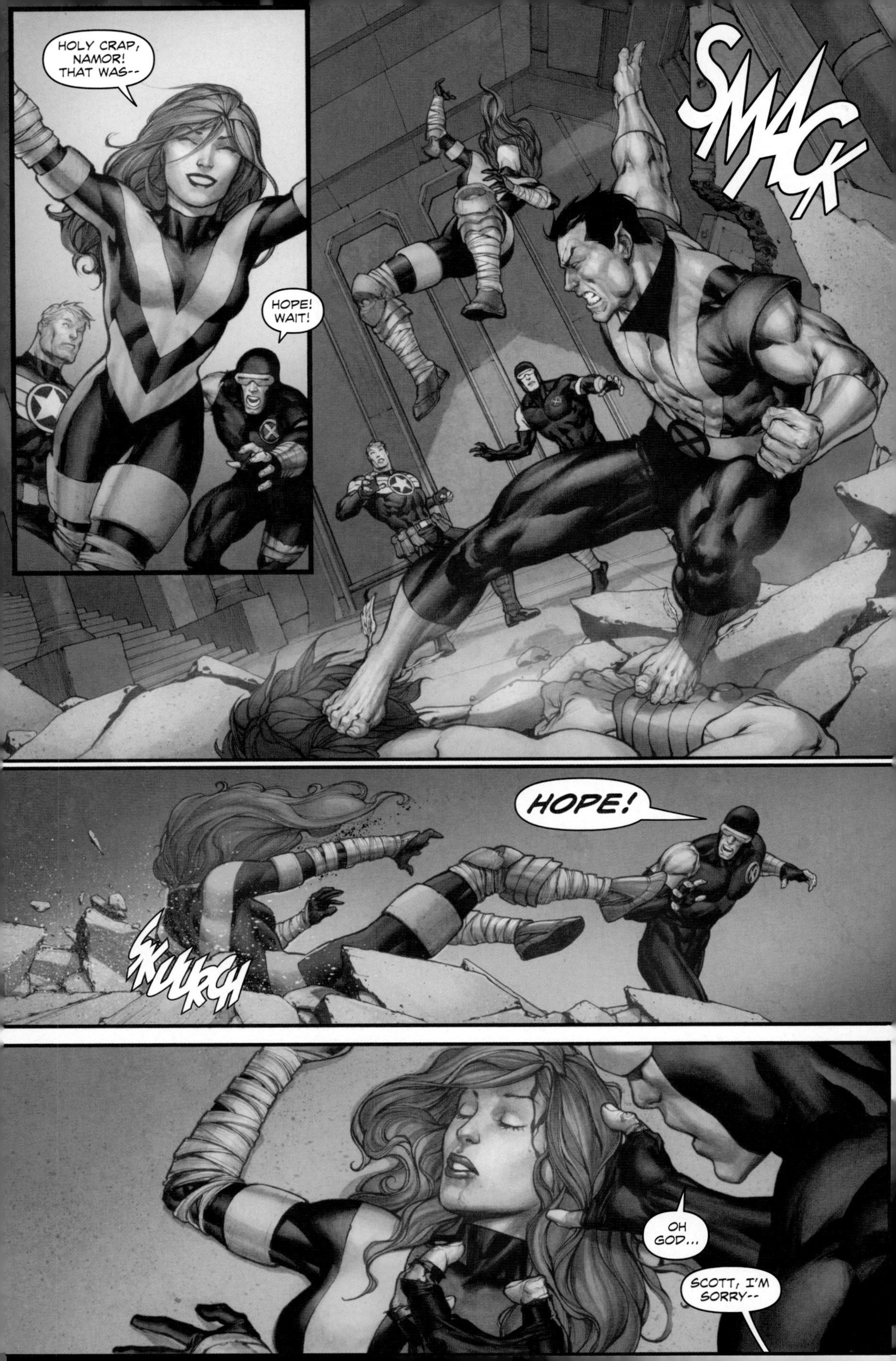
HOLY CRAP, NAMOR! THAT WAS--
HOPE! WAIT!
SMACK
HOPE!
SKUURCH
OH GOD...
SCOTT, I'M SORRY--

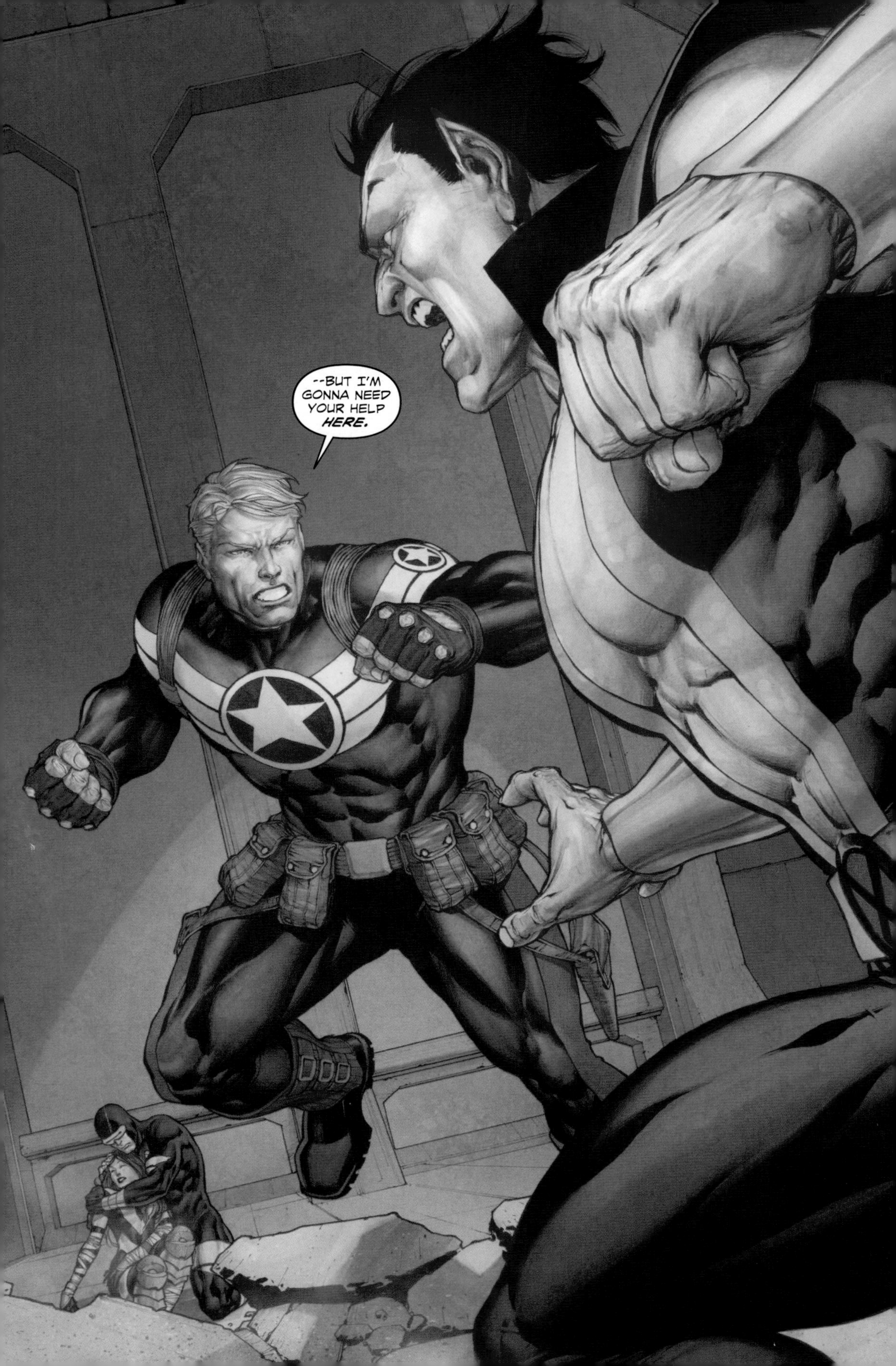
--BUT I'M GONNA NEED YOUR HELP *HERE.*

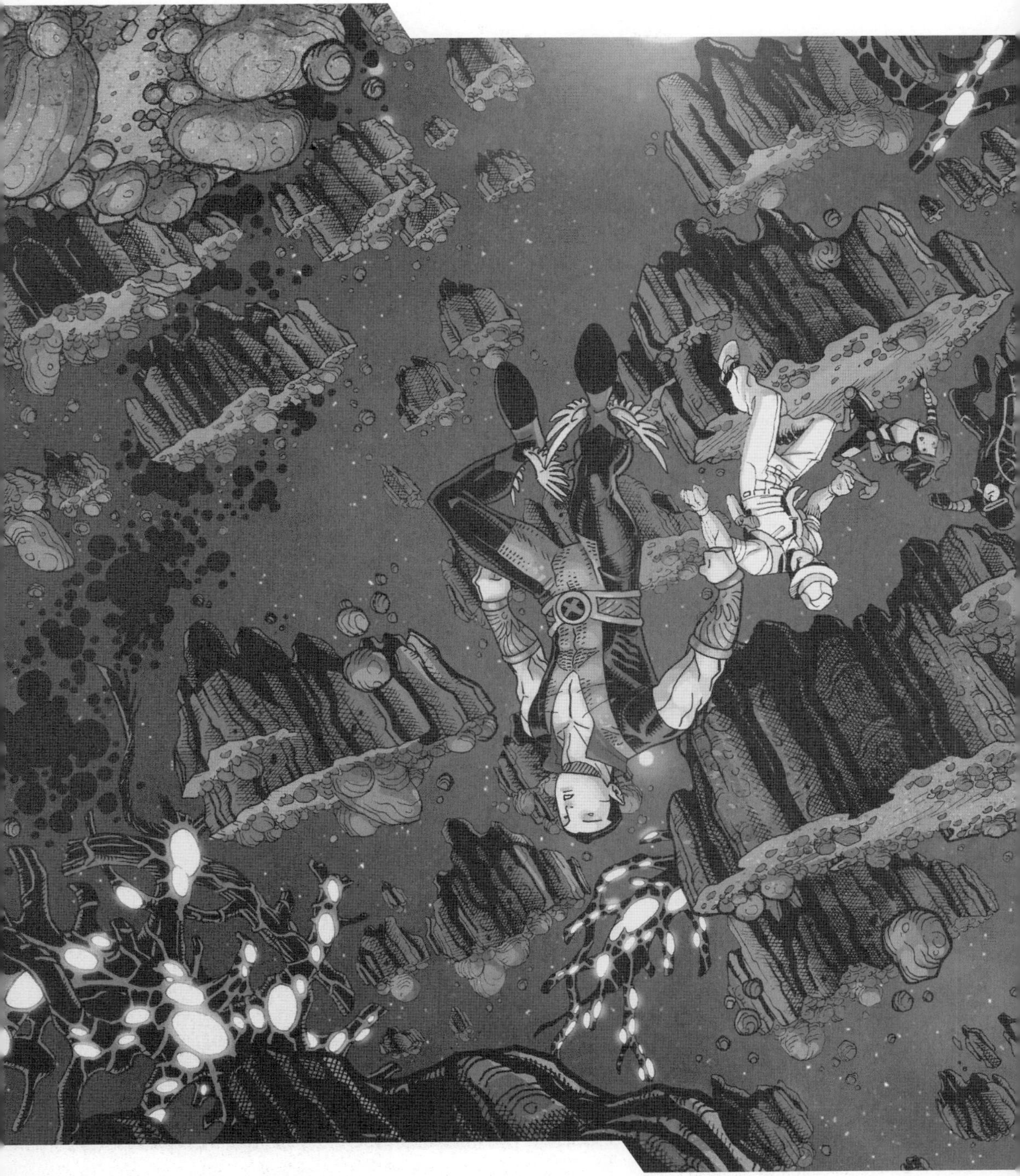

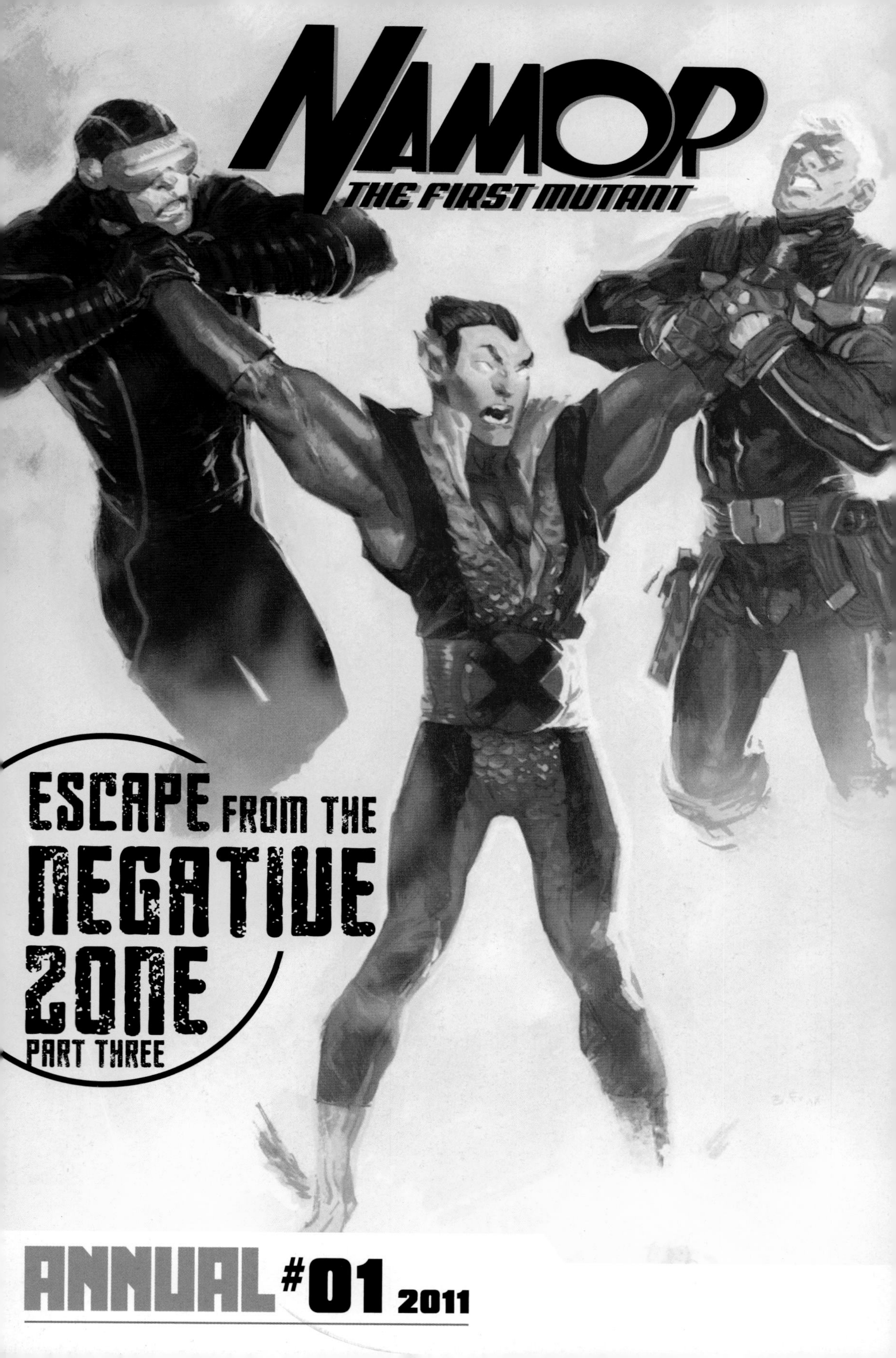
NAMOR
THE FIRST MUTANT
ESCAPE FROM THE NEGATIVE ZONE
PART THREE
ANNUAL #01 2011

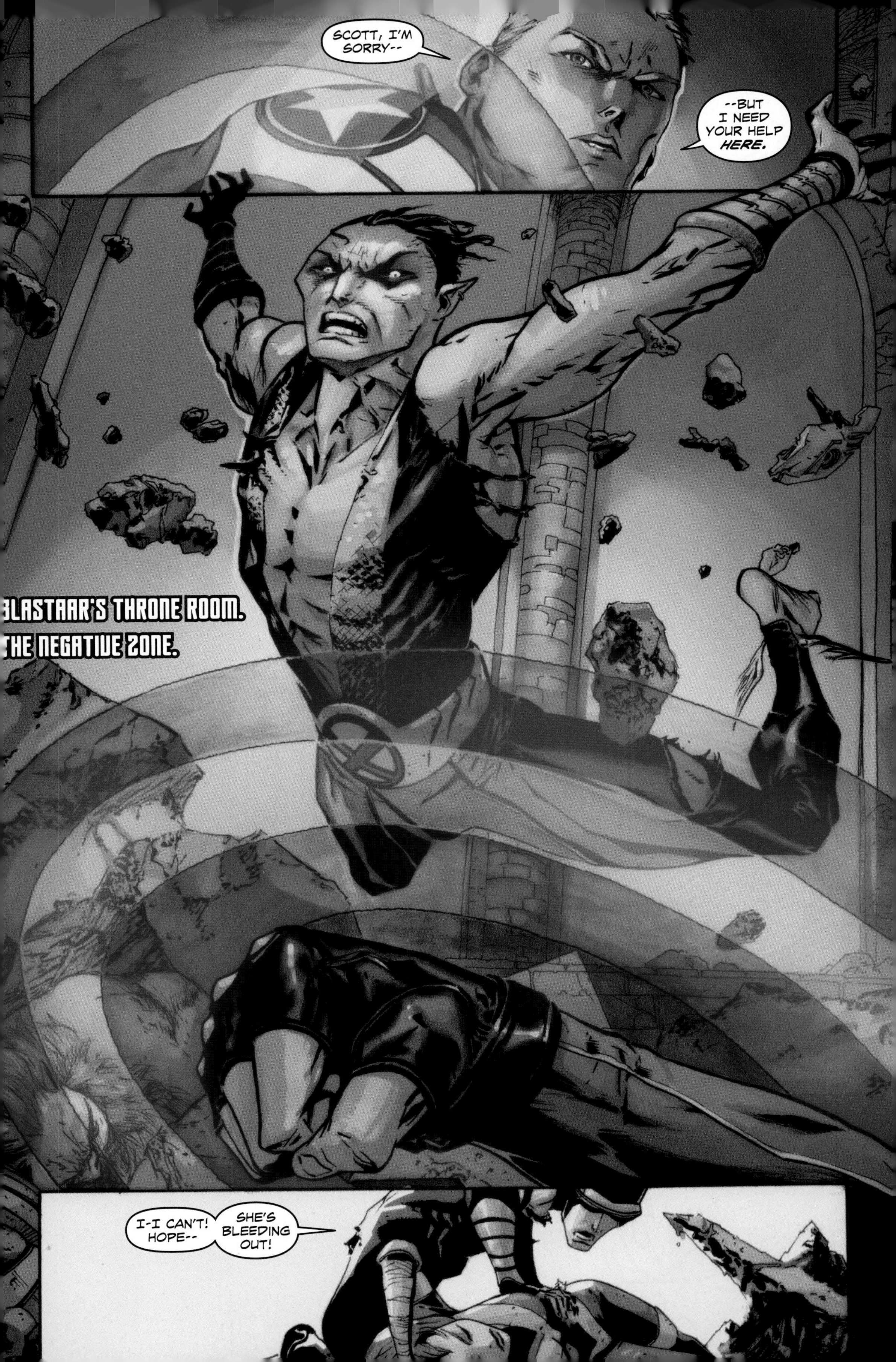
SCOTT, I'M SORRY--
--BUT I NEED YOUR HELP HERE.
LASTAAR'S THRONE ROOM.
THE NEGATIVE ZONE.
I-I CAN'T! HOPE--
SHE'S BLEEDING OUT!

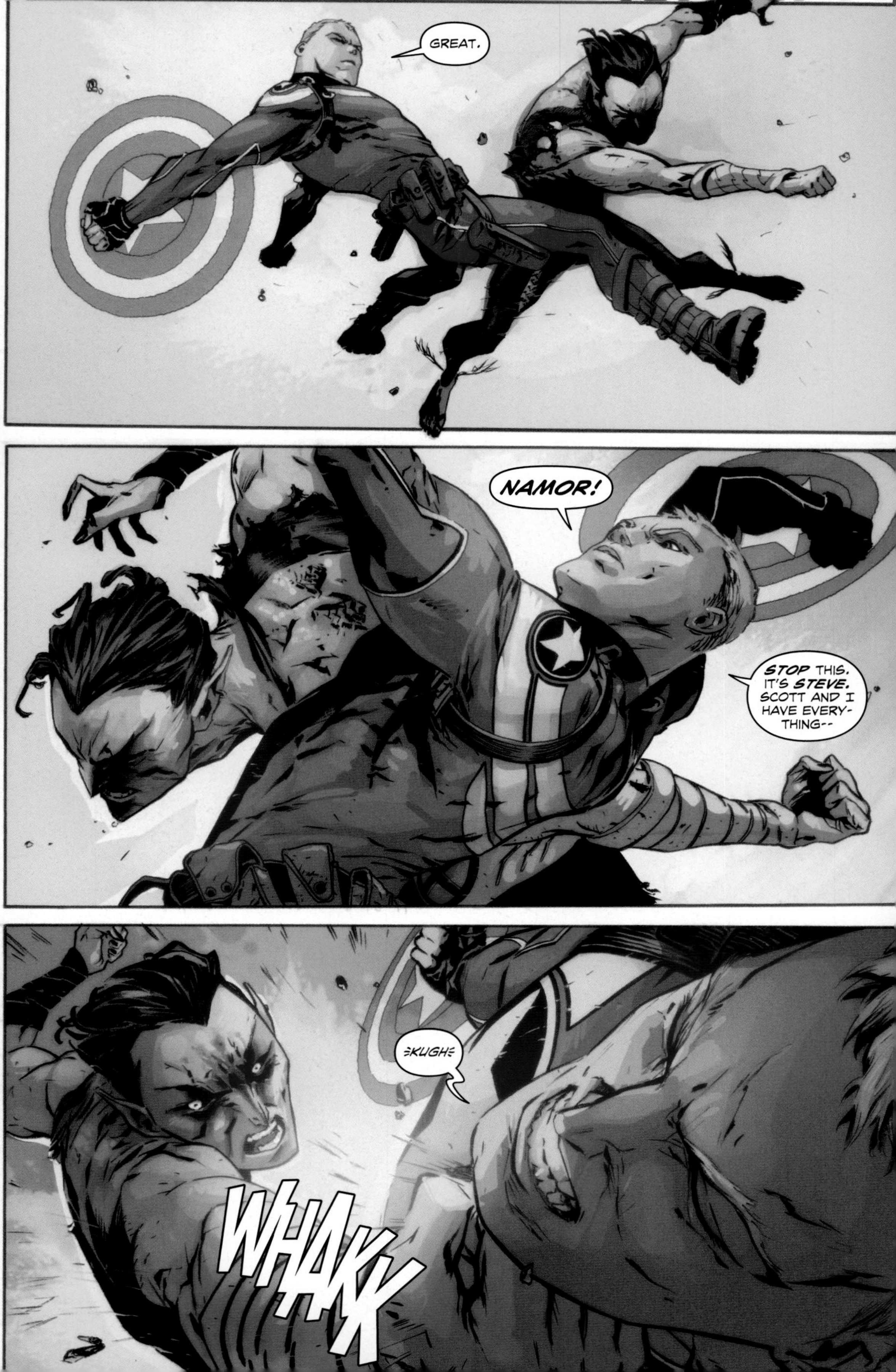
GREAT.
NAMOR!
STOP THIS. IT'S STEVE. SCOTT AND I HAVE EVERY-THING--
KUGH
WHAKK

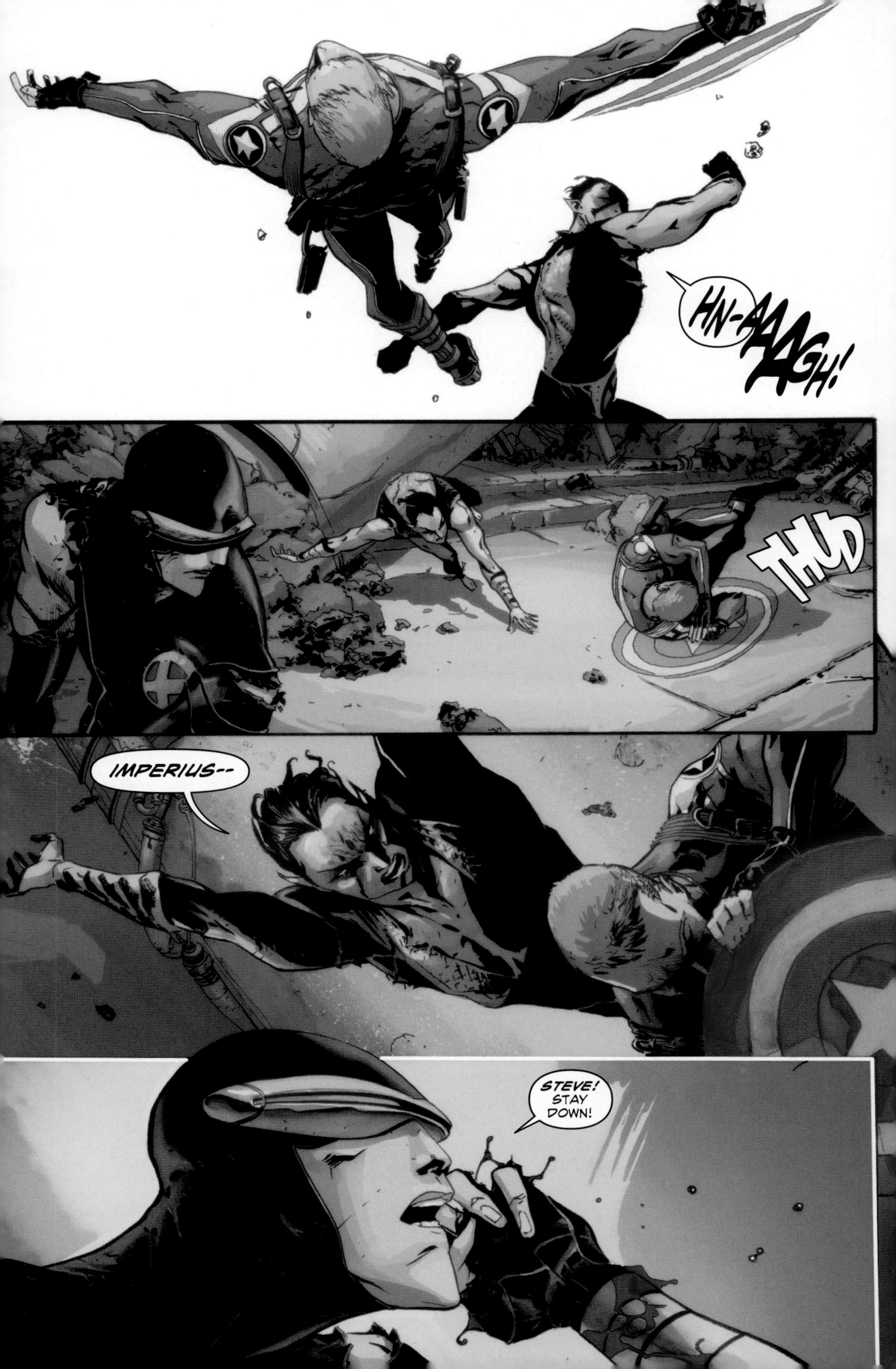
HN-AAAAGH!
THUD
IMPERIUS--
STEVE! STAY DOWN!

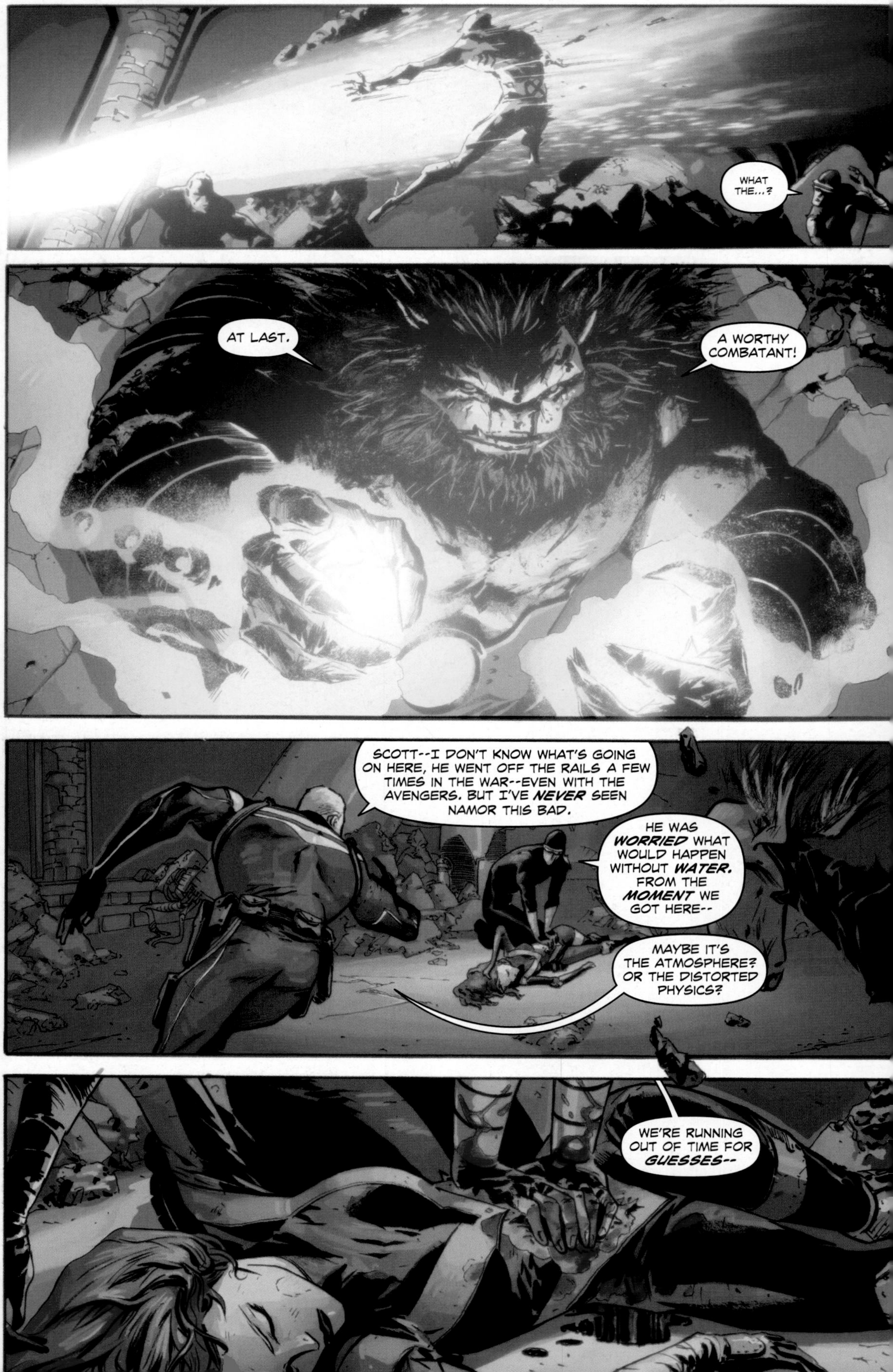
WHAT THE...?
AT LAST.
A WORTHY COMBATANT!
SCOTT--I DON'T KNOW WHAT'S GOING ON HERE, HE WENT OFF THE RAILS A FEW TIMES IN THE WAR--EVEN WITH THE AVENGERS. BUT I'VE NEVER SEEN NAMOR THIS BAD.
HE WAS WORRIED WHAT WOULD HAPPEN WITHOUT WATER. FROM THE MOMENT WE GOT HERE--
MAYBE IT'S THE ATMOSPHERE? OR THE DISTORTED PHYSICS?
WE'RE RUNNING OUT OF TIME FOR GUESSES--

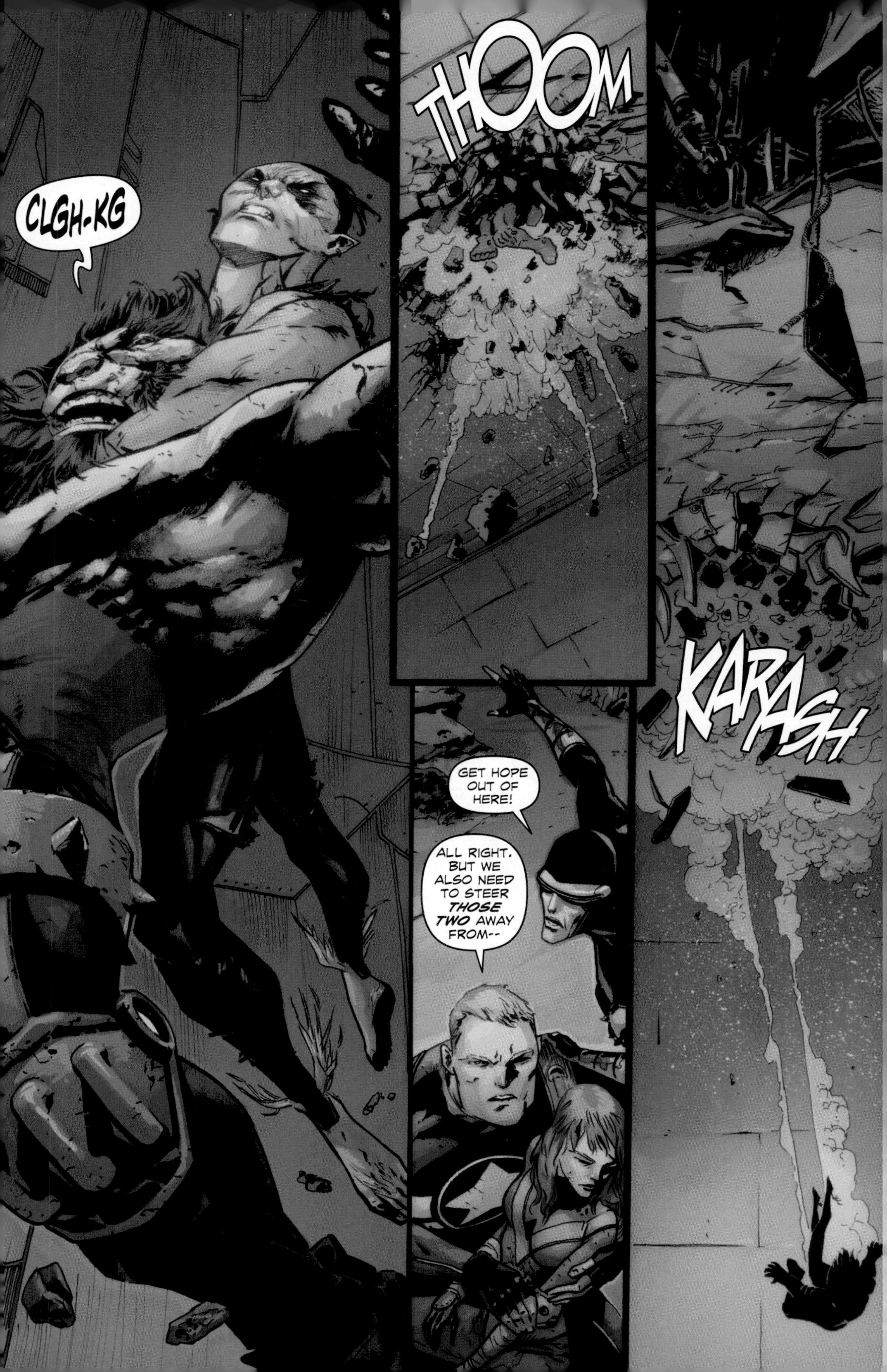
CLGH-KG
THOOM
KARASH
GET HOPE OUT OF HERE!
ALL RIGHT, BUT WE ALSO NEED TO STEER *THOSE TWO* AWAY FROM--

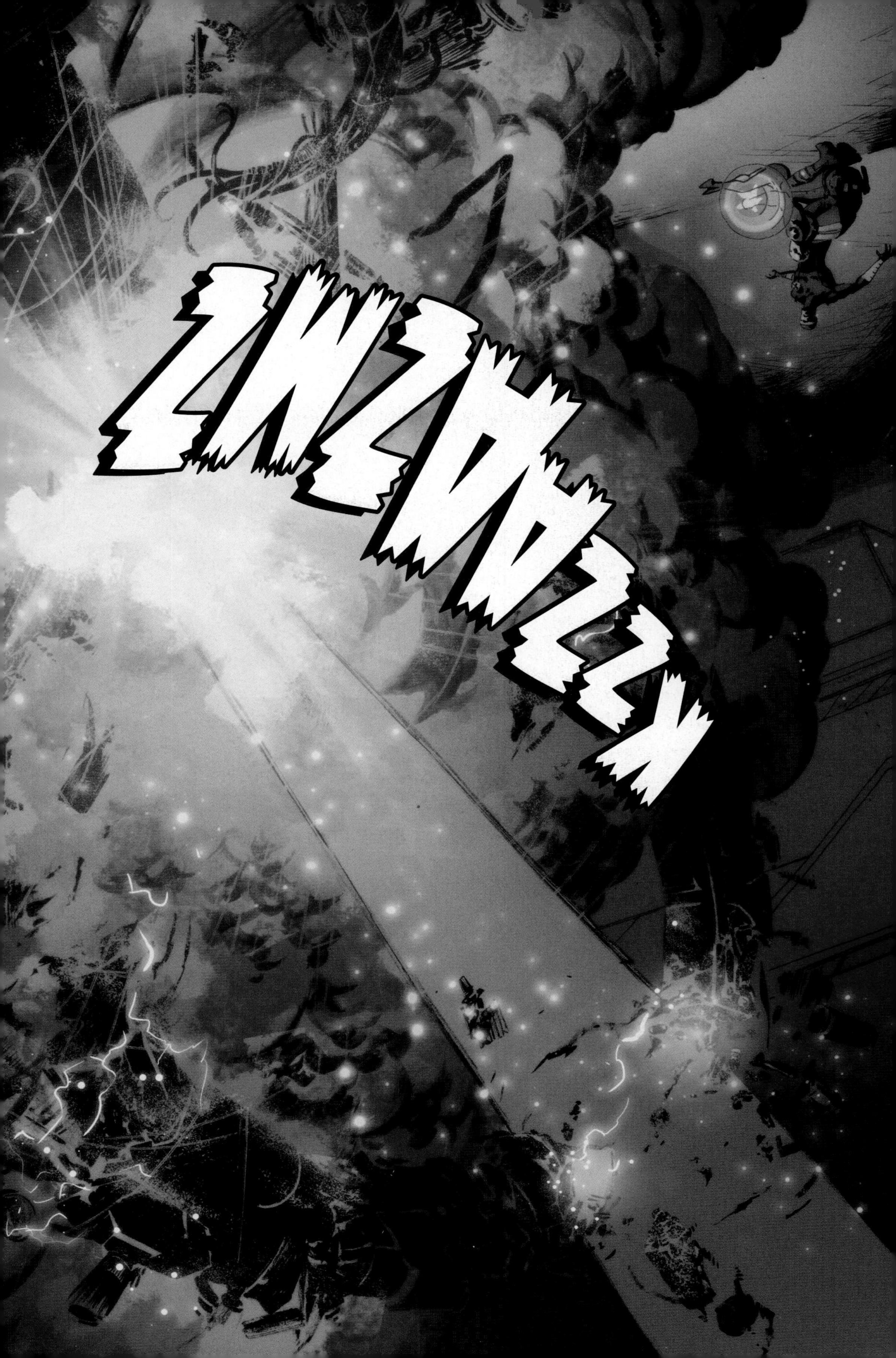

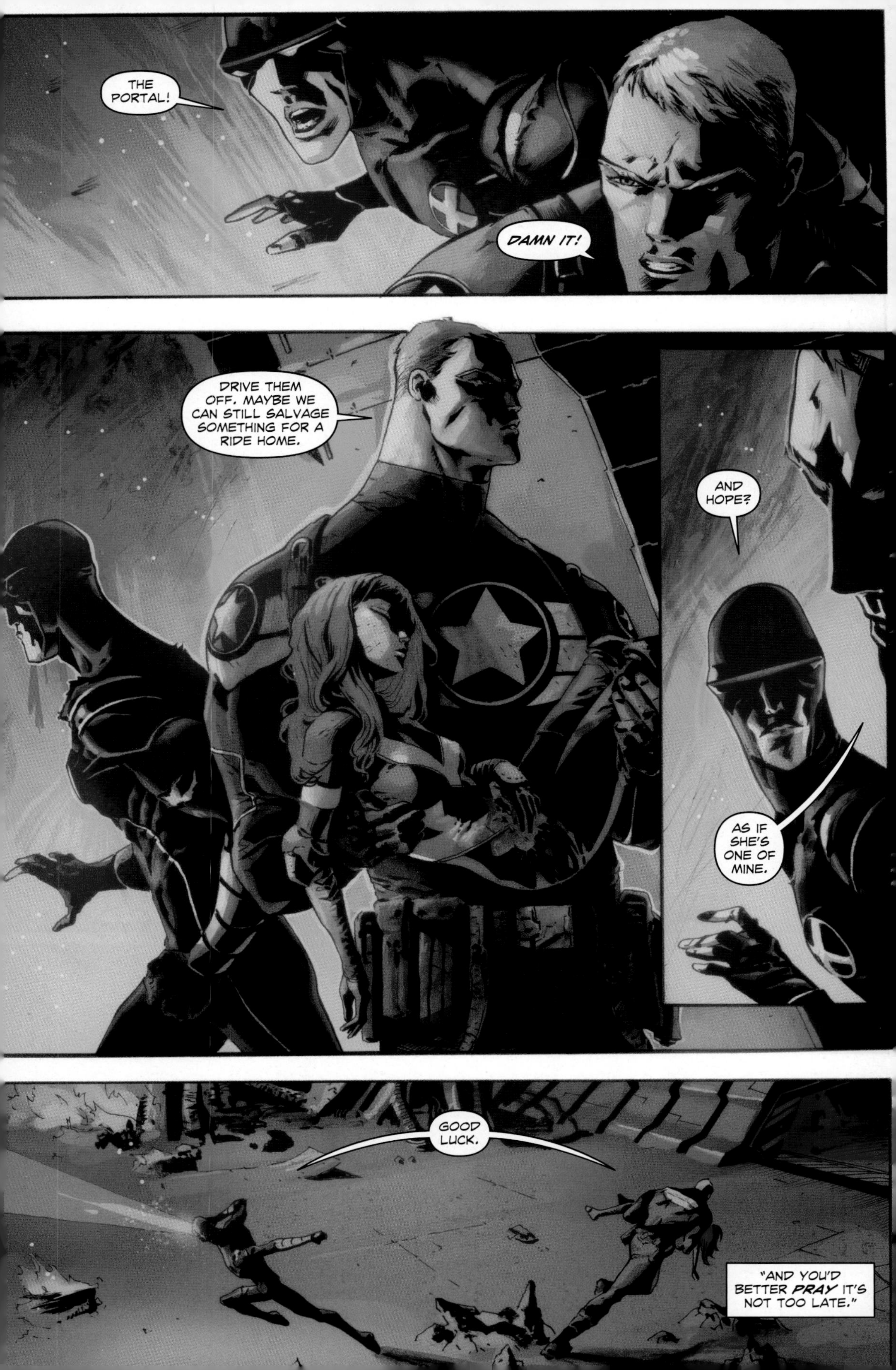
THE PORTAL!
DAMN IT!
DRIVE THEM OFF. MAYBE WE CAN STILL SALVAGE SOMETHING FOR A RIDE HOME.
AND HOPE?
AS IF SHE'S ONE OF MINE.
GOOD LUCK.
"AND YOU'D BETTER PRAY IT'S NOT TOO LATE."

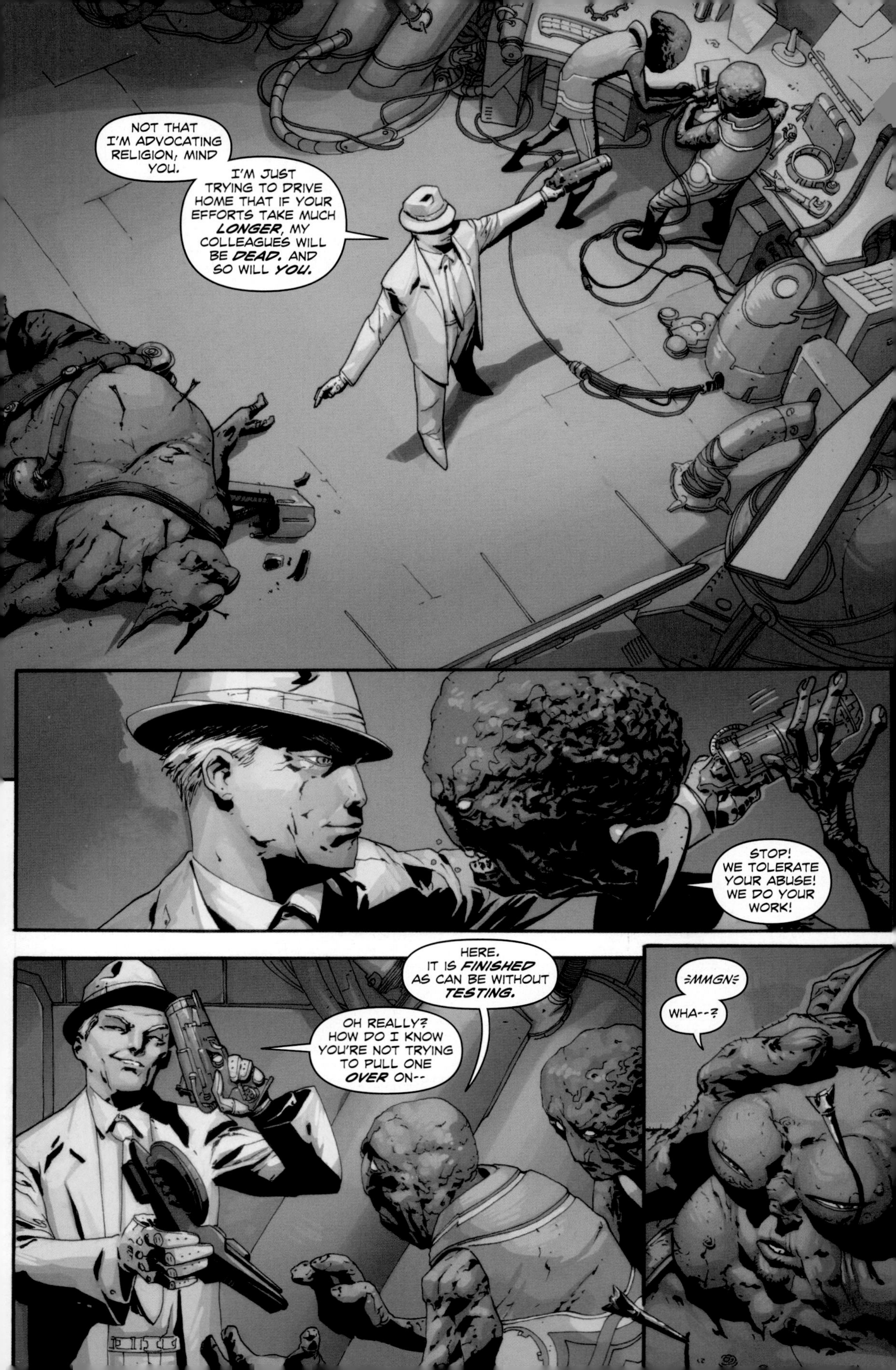
NOT THAT I'M ADVOCATING RELIGION, MIND YOU.
I'M JUST TRYING TO DRIVE HOME THAT IF YOUR EFFORTS TAKE MUCH **LONGER**, MY COLLEAGUES WILL BE **DEAD**. AND SO WILL **YOU**.
STOP! WE TOLERATE YOUR ABUSE! WE DO YOUR WORK!
HERE. IT IS **FINISHED** AS CAN BE WITHOUT **TESTING**.
OH REALLY? HOW DO I KNOW YOU'RE NOT TRYING TO PULL ONE **OVER** ON--
=MMGN=
WHA--?

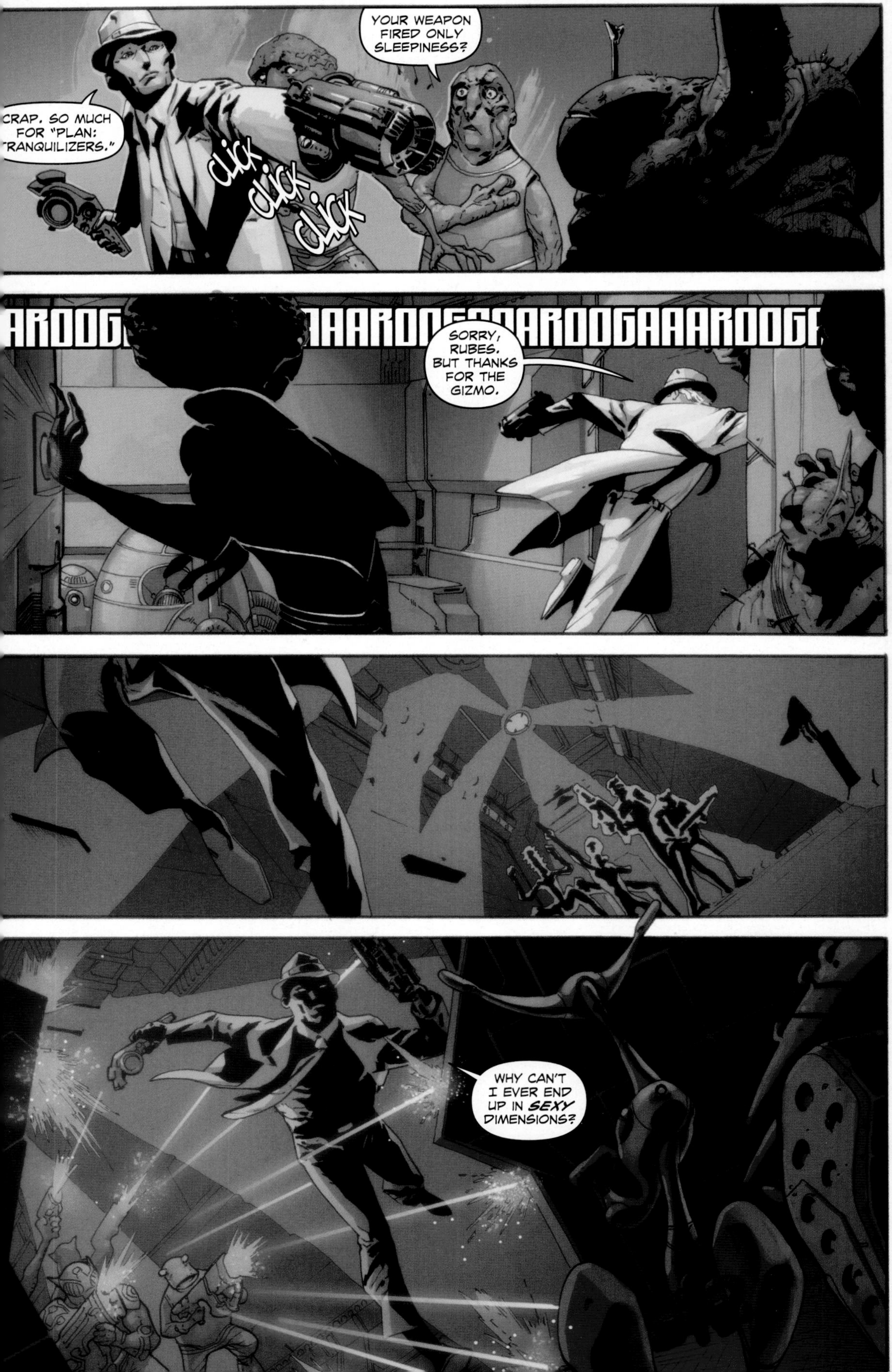
CRAP. SO MUCH FOR "PLAN: TRANQUILIZERS."
CLICK CLICK CLICK
YOUR WEAPON FIRED ONLY SLEEPINESS?
SORRY, RUBES. BUT THANKS FOR THE GIZMO.
WHY CAN'T I EVER END UP IN SEXY DIMENSIONS?

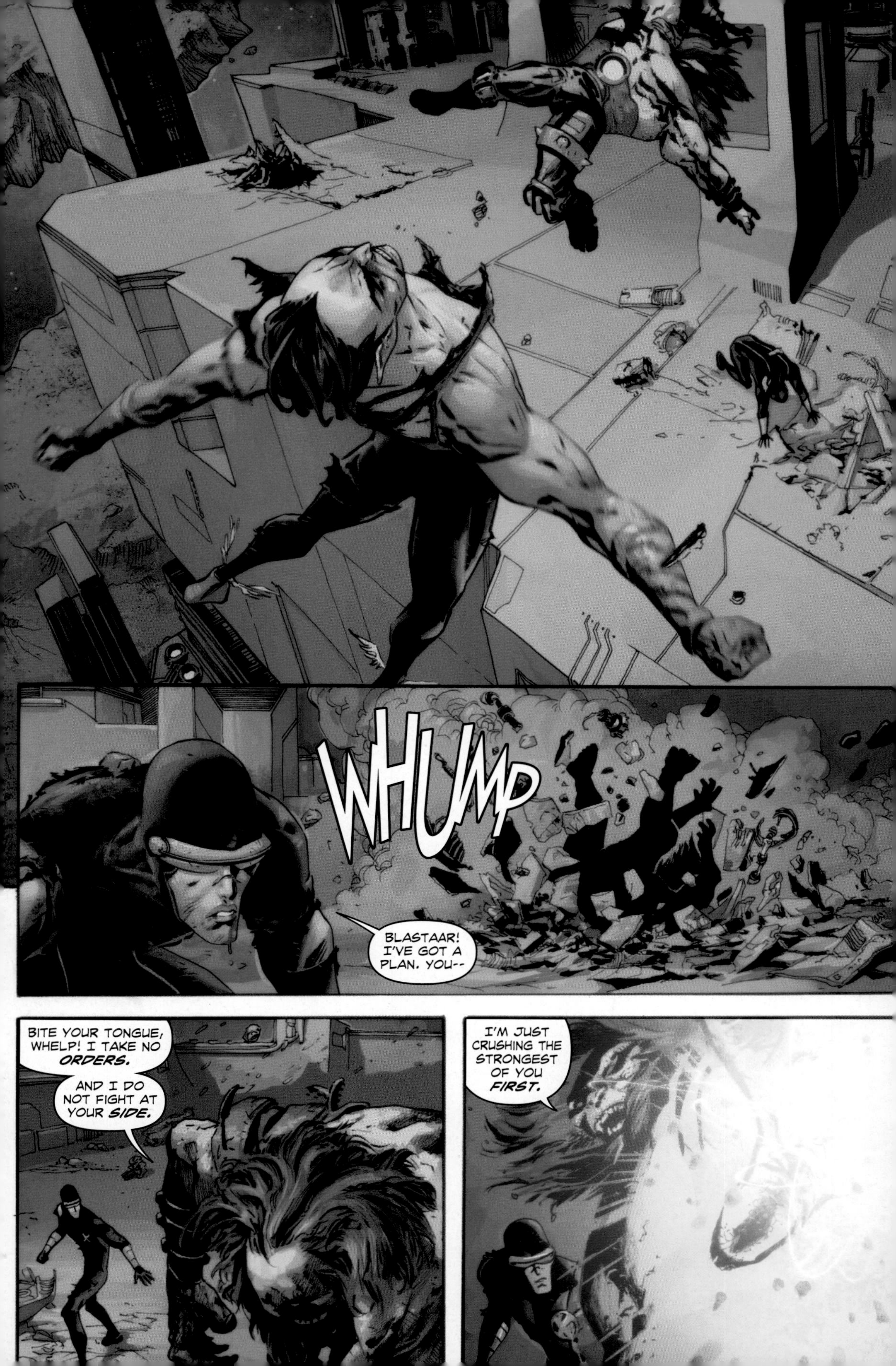
WHUMP
BLASTAAR! I'VE GOT A PLAN. YOU--
BITE YOUR TONGUE, WHELP! I TAKE NO **ORDERS.**
AND I DO NOT FIGHT AT YOUR **SIDE.**
I'M JUST CRUSHING THE STRONGEST OF YOU **FIRST.**

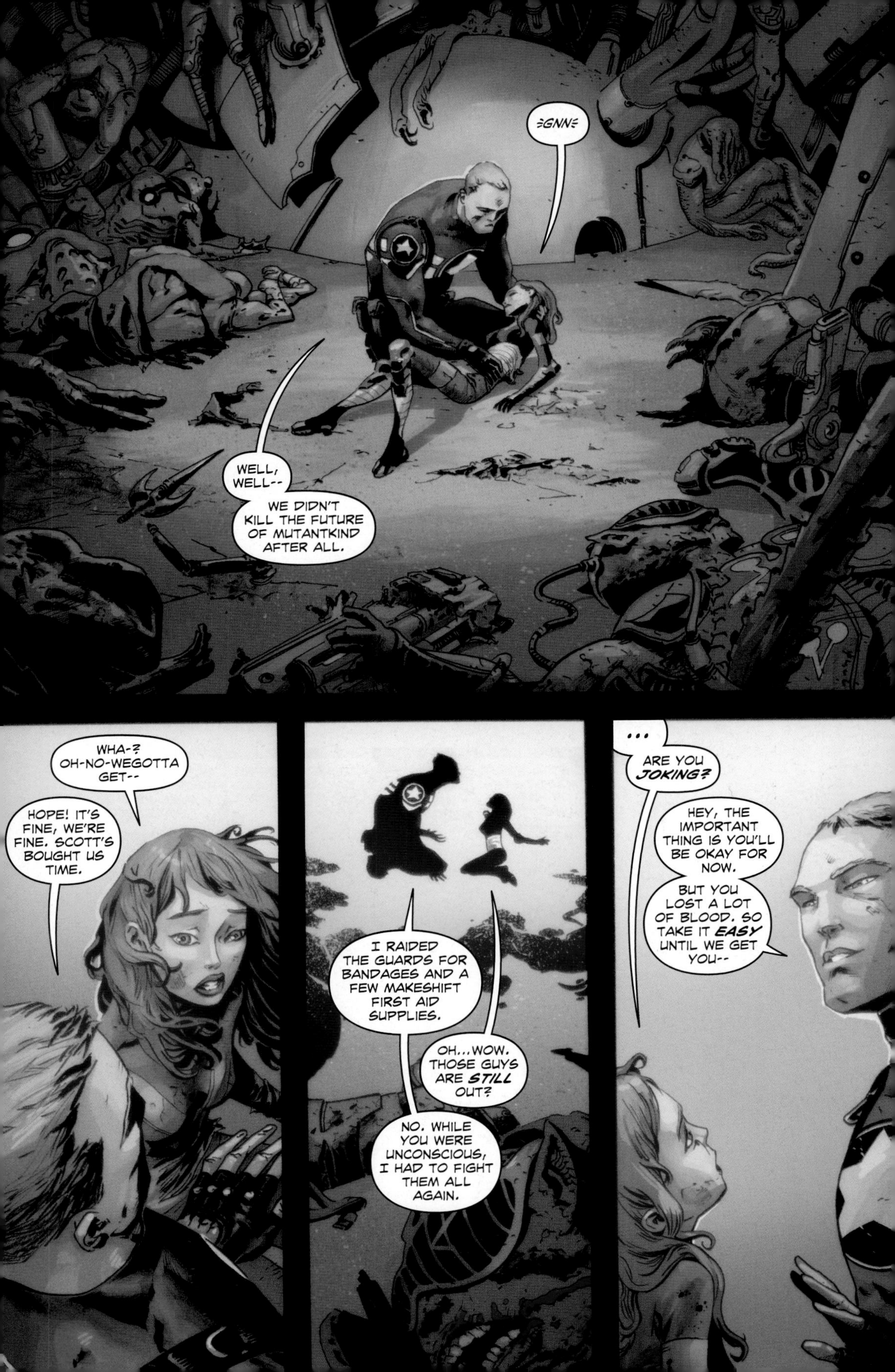
GNN
WELL, WELL--
WE DIDN'T KILL THE FUTURE OF MUTANTKIND AFTER ALL.
WHA-? OH-NO-WEGOTTA GET--
HOPE! IT'S FINE, WE'RE FINE. SCOTT'S BOUGHT US TIME.
I RAIDED THE GUARDS FOR BANDAGES AND A FEW MAKESHIFT FIRST AID SUPPLIES.
OH...WOW. THOSE GUYS ARE STILL OUT?
NO. WHILE YOU WERE UNCONSCIOUS, I HAD TO FIGHT THEM ALL AGAIN.
...
ARE YOU JOKING?
HEY, THE IMPORTANT THING IS YOU'LL BE OKAY FOR NOW.
BUT YOU LOST A LOT OF BLOOD. SO TAKE IT EASY UNTIL WE GET YOU--

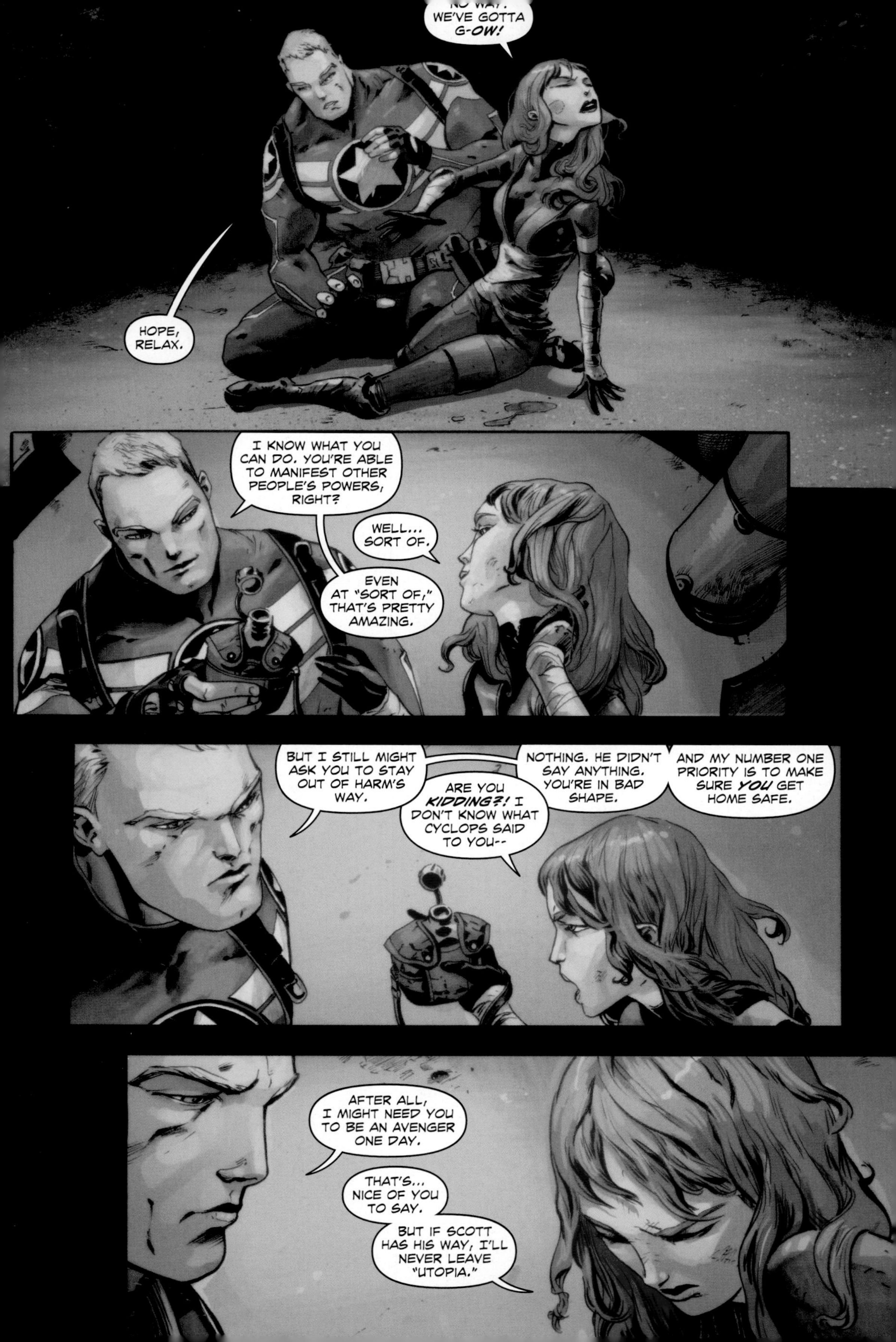
WE'VE GOTTA G-OW!
HOPE, RELAX.
I KNOW WHAT YOU CAN DO. YOU'RE ABLE TO MANIFEST OTHER PEOPLE'S POWERS, RIGHT?
WELL... SORT OF.
EVEN AT "SORT OF," THAT'S PRETTY AMAZING.
BUT I STILL MIGHT ASK YOU TO STAY OUT OF HARM'S WAY.
ARE YOU KIDDING?! I DON'T KNOW WHAT CYCLOPS SAID TO YOU--
NOTHING. HE DIDN'T SAY ANYTHING. YOU'RE IN BAD SHAPE.
AND MY NUMBER ONE PRIORITY IS TO MAKE SURE YOU GET HOME SAFE.
AFTER ALL, I MIGHT NEED YOU TO BE AN AVENGER ONE DAY.
THAT'S... NICE OF YOU TO SAY.
BUT IF SCOTT HAS HIS WAY, I'LL NEVER LEAVE "UTOPIA."

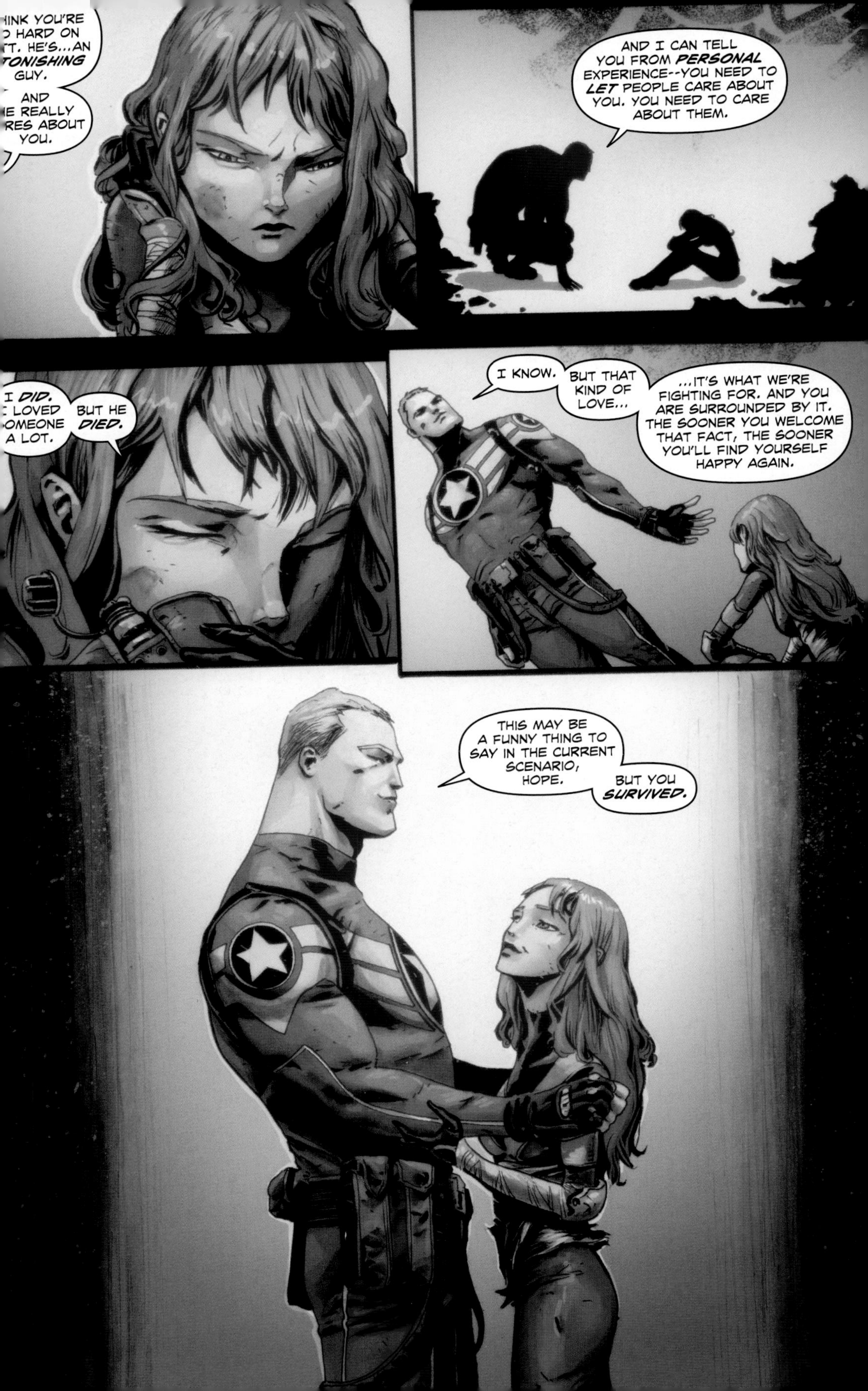
GUY.
AND I CAN TELL YOU FROM PERSONAL EXPERIENCE--YOU NEED TO LET PEOPLE CARE ABOUT YOU. YOU NEED TO CARE ABOUT THEM.
I DID.
A LOT.
BUT HE DIED.
I KNOW.
BUT THAT KIND OF LOVE...
...IT'S WHAT WE'RE FIGHTING FOR. AND YOU ARE SURROUNDED BY IT. THE SOONER YOU WELCOME THAT FACT, THE SOONER YOU'LL FIND YOURSELF HAPPY AGAIN.
THIS MAY BE A FUNNY THING TO SAY IN THE CURRENT SCENARIO, HOPE.
BUT YOU SURVIVED.

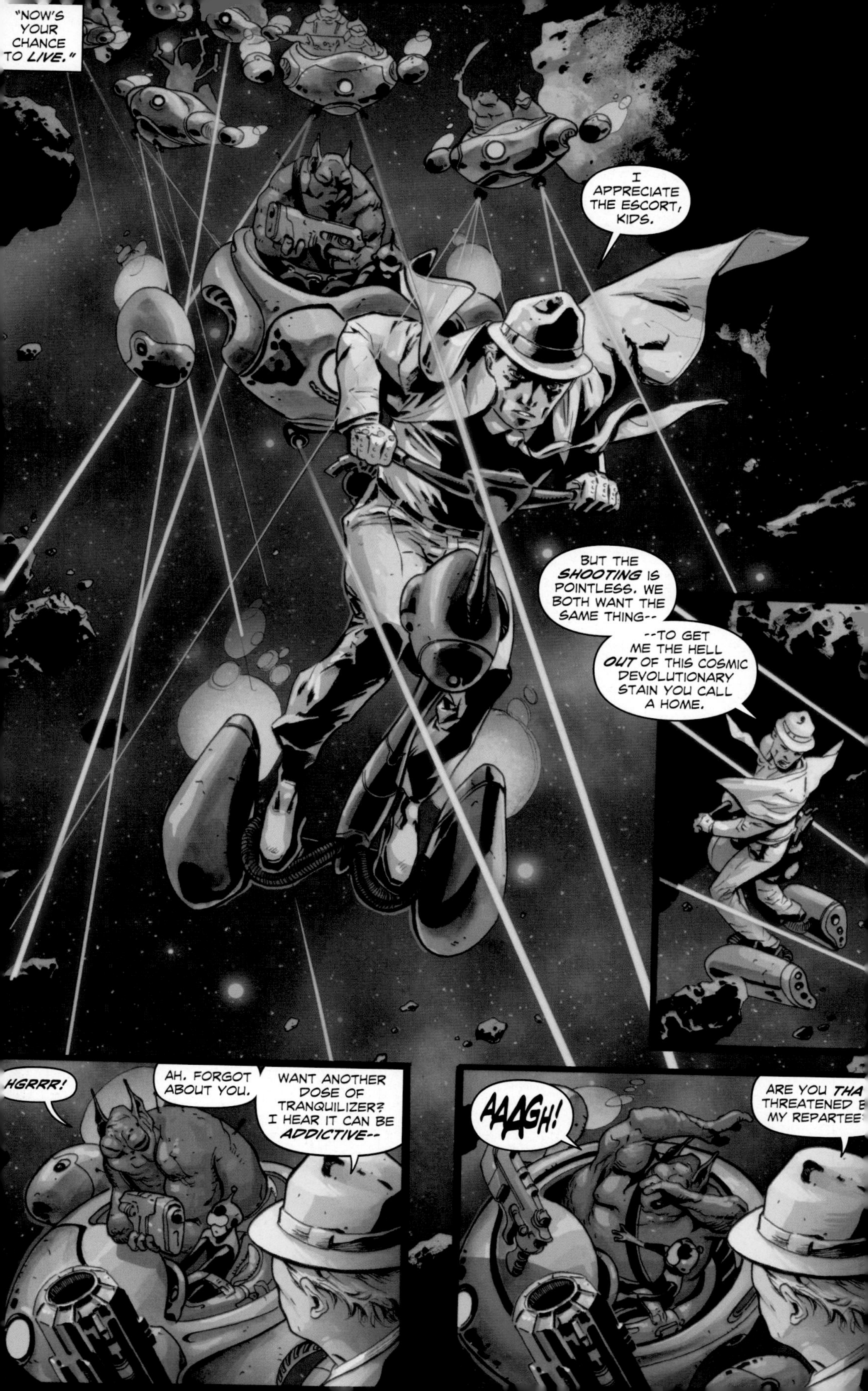
"NOW'S YOUR CHANCE TO *LIVE.*"
I APPRECIATE THE ESCORT, KIDS.
BUT THE ***SHOOTING*** IS POINTLESS. WE BOTH WANT THE SAME THING--
--TO GET ME THE HELL ***OUT*** OF THIS COSMIC DEVOLUTIONARY STAIN YOU CALL A HOME.
HGRRR!
AH. FORGOT ABOUT YOU.
WANT ANOTHER DOSE OF TRANQUILIZER? I HEAR IT CAN BE *ADDICTIVE*--
AAAGH!
ARE YOU ***THA*** THREATENED MY REPARTEE

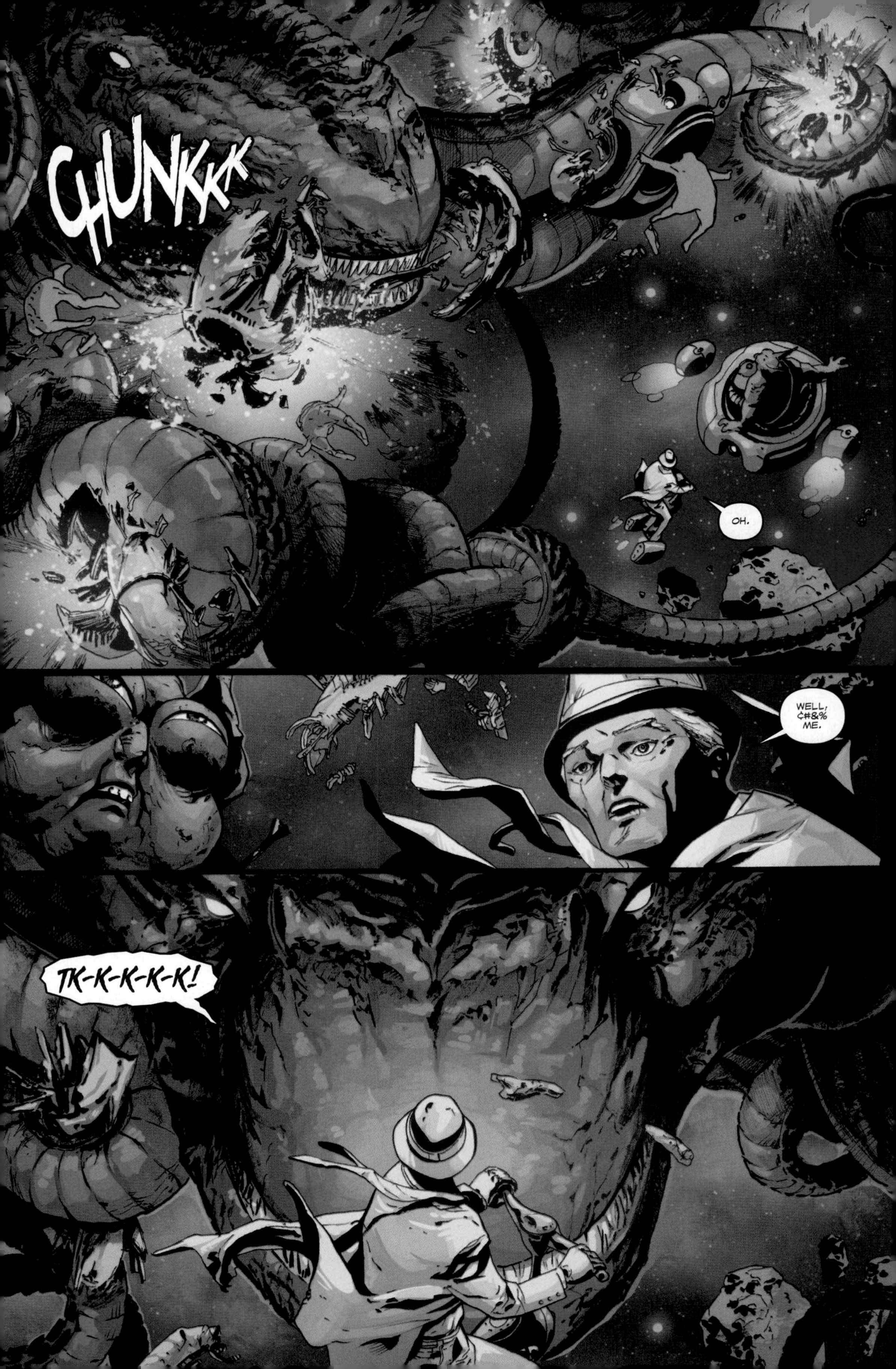
CHUNKKK
OH.
WELL, ¢#&% ME.
TK-K-K-K-K!

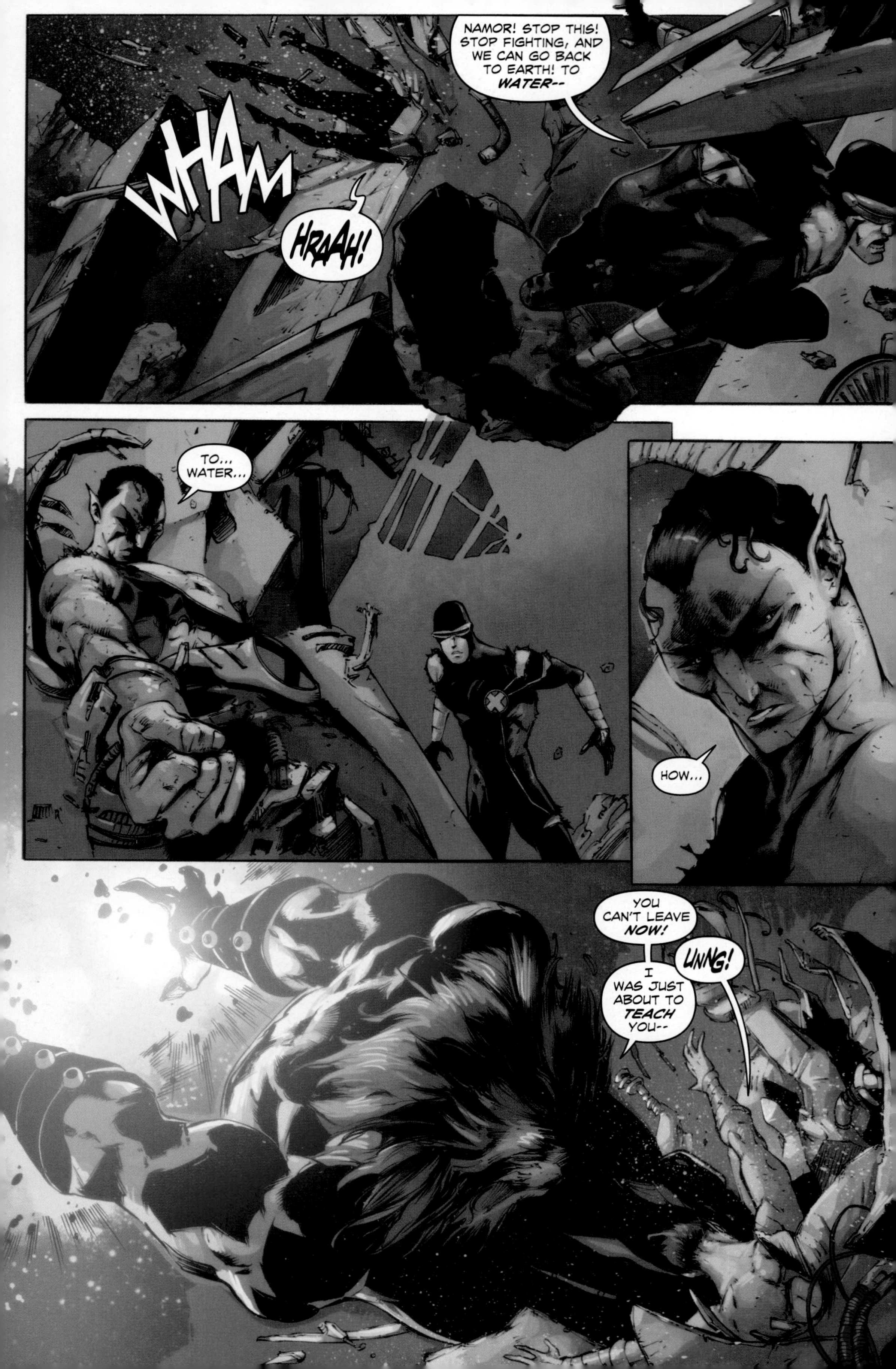
NAMOR! STOP THIS! STOP FIGHTING, AND WE CAN GO BACK TO EARTH! TO *WATER--*
WHAM
HRAAH!
TO... WATER...
HOW...
YOU CAN'T LEAVE *NOW!*
I WAS JUST ABOUT TO *TEACH* YOU--
UNNG!

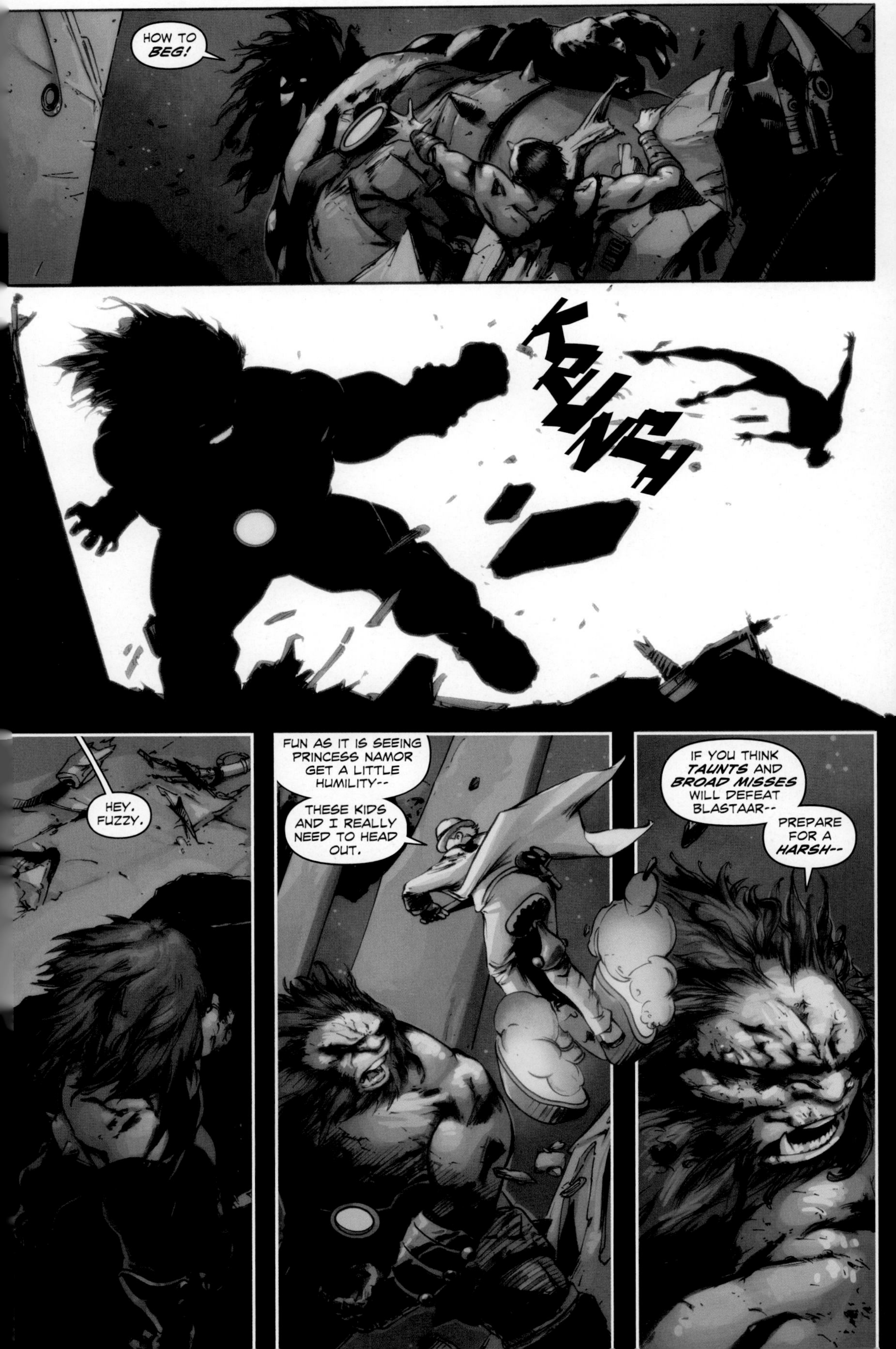
HOW TO BEG!
KRUNCH
HEY. FUZZY.
FUN AS IT IS SEEING PRINCESS NAMOR GET A LITTLE HUMILITY--
THESE KIDS AND I REALLY NEED TO HEAD OUT.
IF YOU THINK TAUNTS AND BROAD MISSES WILL DEFEAT BLASTAAR--
PREPARE FOR A HARSH--

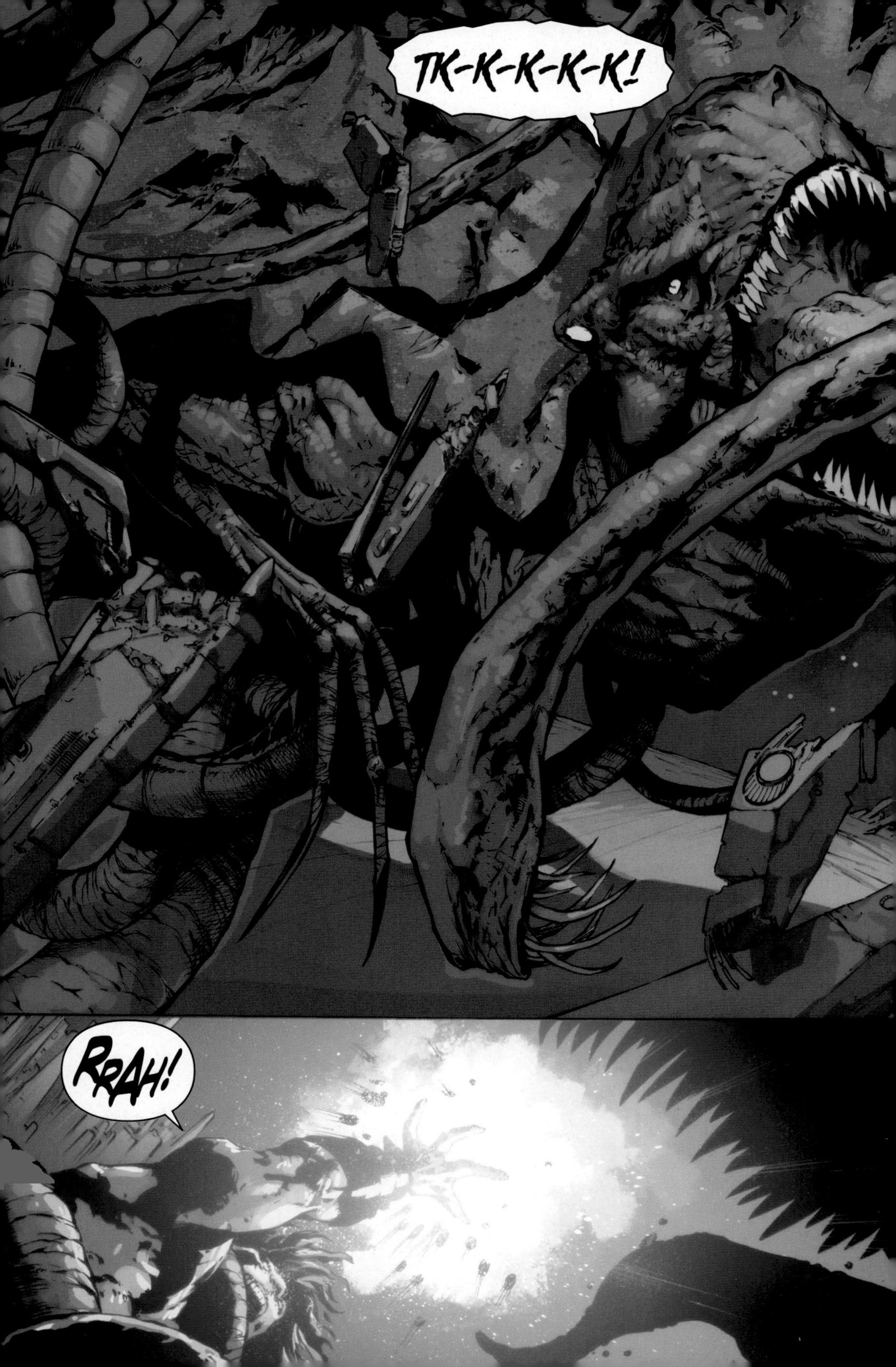
TK-K-K-K-K!
RRAH!

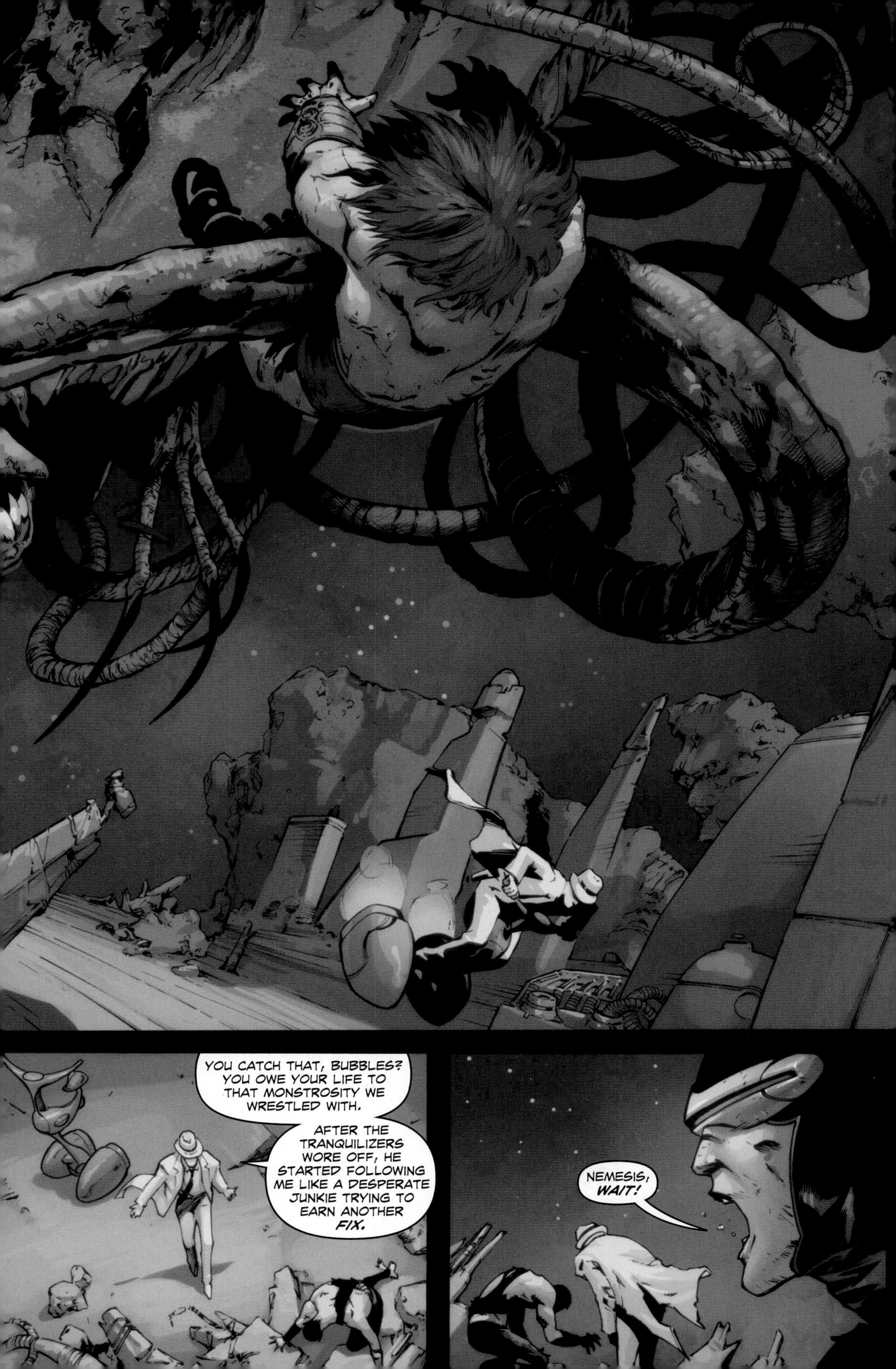
YOU CATCH THAT, BUBBLES? YOU OWE YOUR LIFE TO THAT MONSTROSITY WE WRESTLED WITH.
AFTER THE TRANQUILIZERS WORE OFF, HE STARTED FOLLOWING ME LIKE A DESPERATE JUNKIE TRYING TO EARN ANOTHER ***FIX.***
NEMESIS, ***WAIT!***

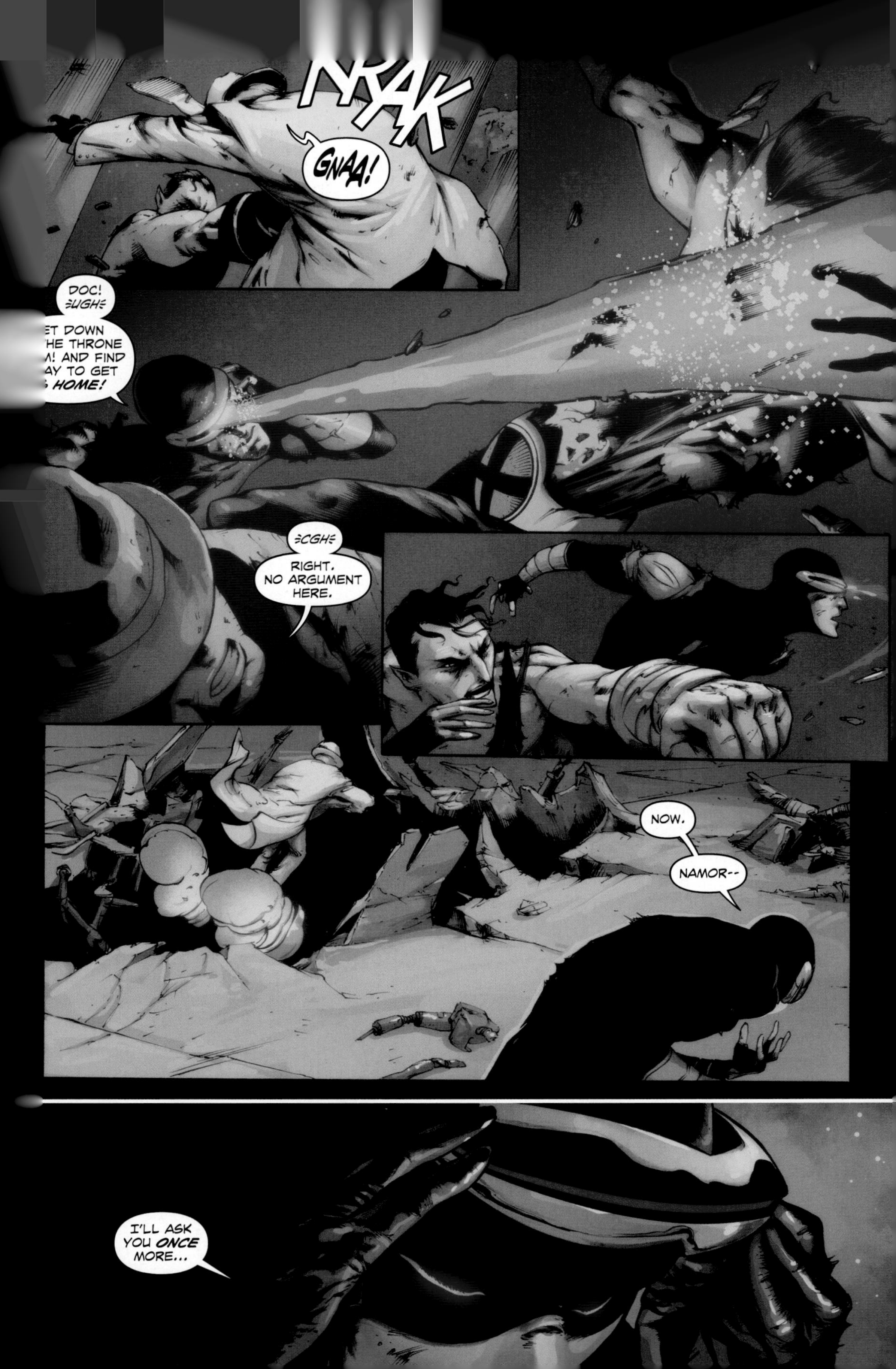
KRAK
GNAA!
DOC!
UGH
ET DOWN
HE THRONE
M! AND FIND
AY TO GET
HOME!
CGH
RIGHT. NO ARGUMENT HERE.
NOW.
NAMOR--
I'LL ASK YOU ONCE MORE...

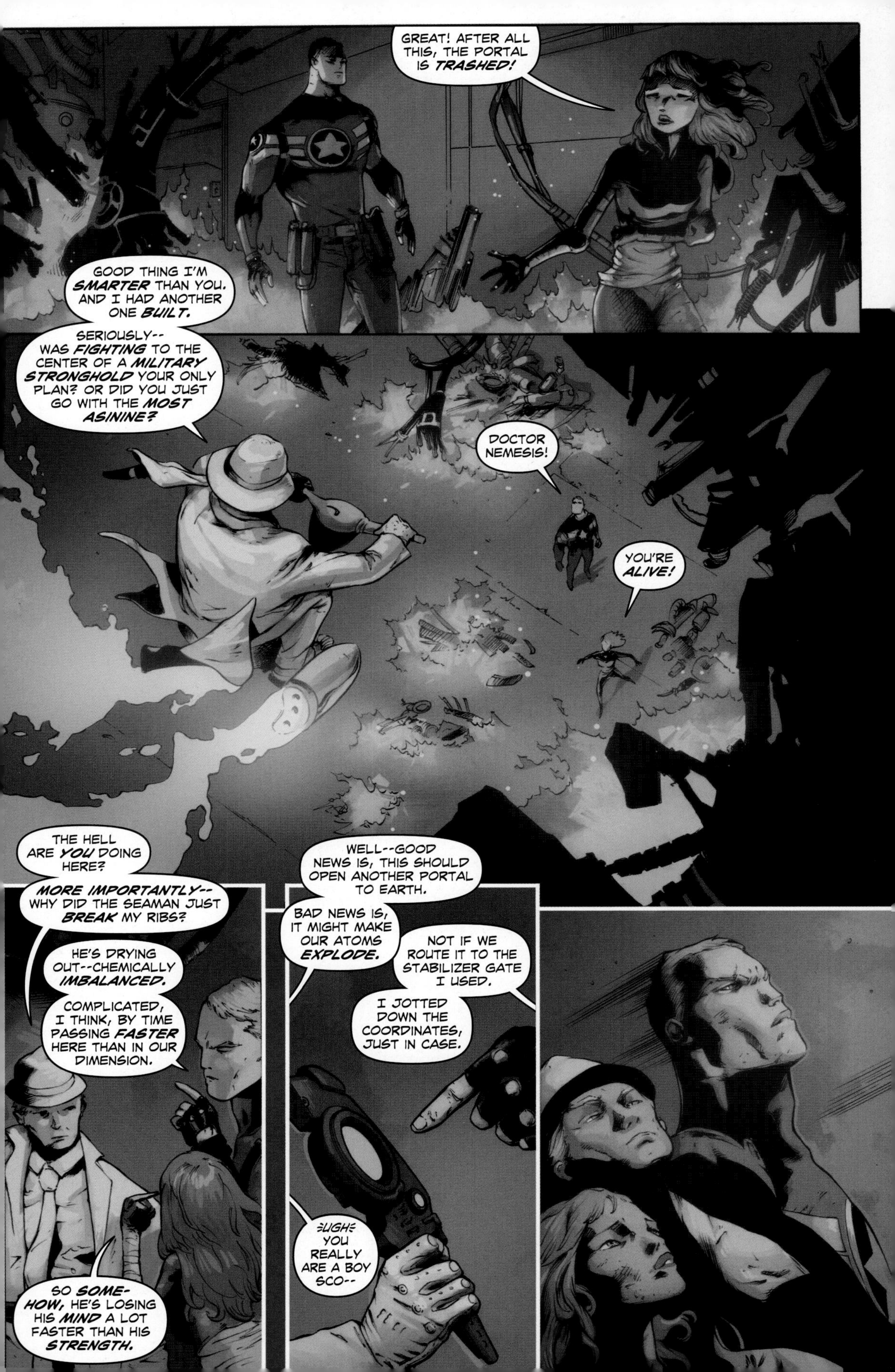
GREAT! AFTER ALL THIS, THE PORTAL IS *TRASHED!*
GOOD THING I'M *SMARTER* THAN YOU. AND I HAD ANOTHER ONE *BUILT.*
SERIOUSLY-- WAS *FIGHTING* TO THE CENTER OF A *MILITARY STRONGHOLD* YOUR ONLY PLAN? OR DID YOU JUST GO WITH THE *MOST ASININE?*
DOCTOR NEMESIS!
YOU'RE *ALIVE!*
THE HELL ARE *YOU* DOING HERE?
MORE IMPORTANTLY-- WHY DID THE SEAMAN JUST *BREAK* MY RIBS?
HE'S DRYING OUT--CHEMICALLY *IMBALANCED.*
COMPLICATED, I THINK, BY TIME PASSING *FASTER* HERE THAN IN OUR DIMENSION.
SO *SOME-HOW,* HE'S LOSING HIS *MIND* A LOT FASTER THAN HIS *STRENGTH.*
WELL--GOOD NEWS IS, THIS SHOULD OPEN ANOTHER PORTAL TO EARTH.
BAD NEWS IS, IT MIGHT MAKE OUR ATOMS *EXPLODE.*
NOT IF WE ROUTE IT TO THE STABILIZER GATE I USED.
I JOTTED DOWN THE COORDINATES, JUST IN CASE.
=UGH= YOU REALLY ARE A BOY SCO--

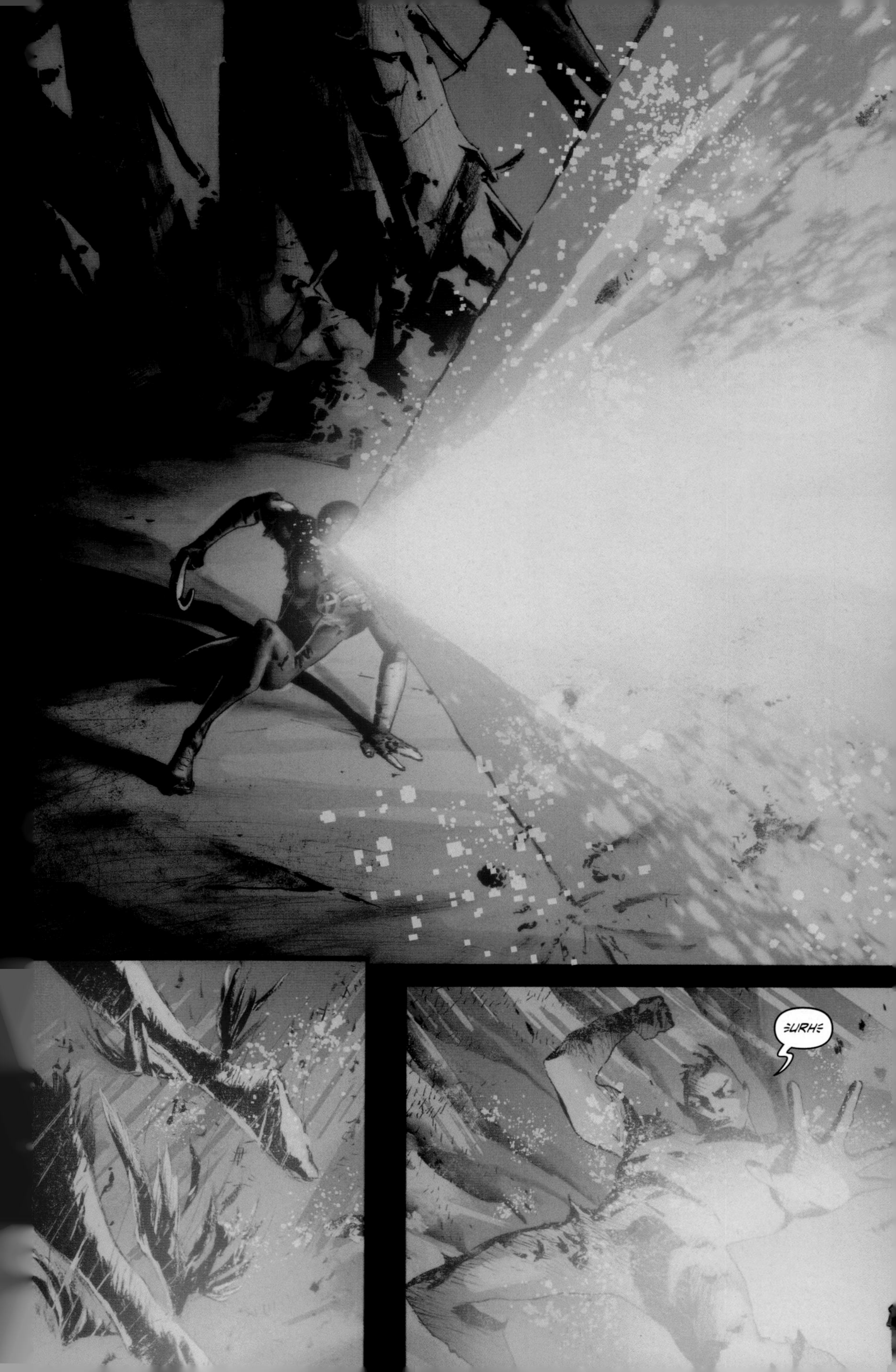
URH

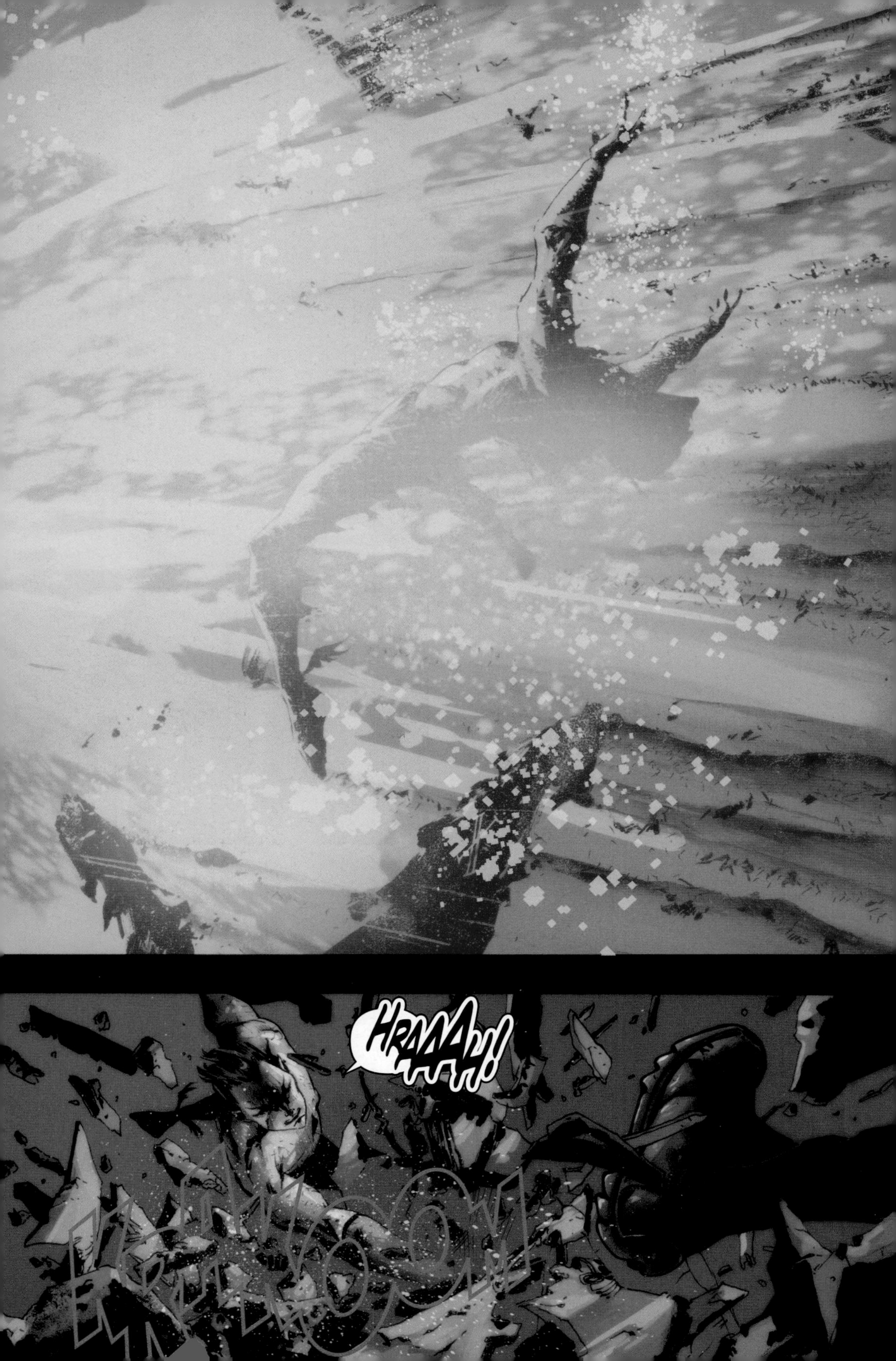
HRAAAAH!

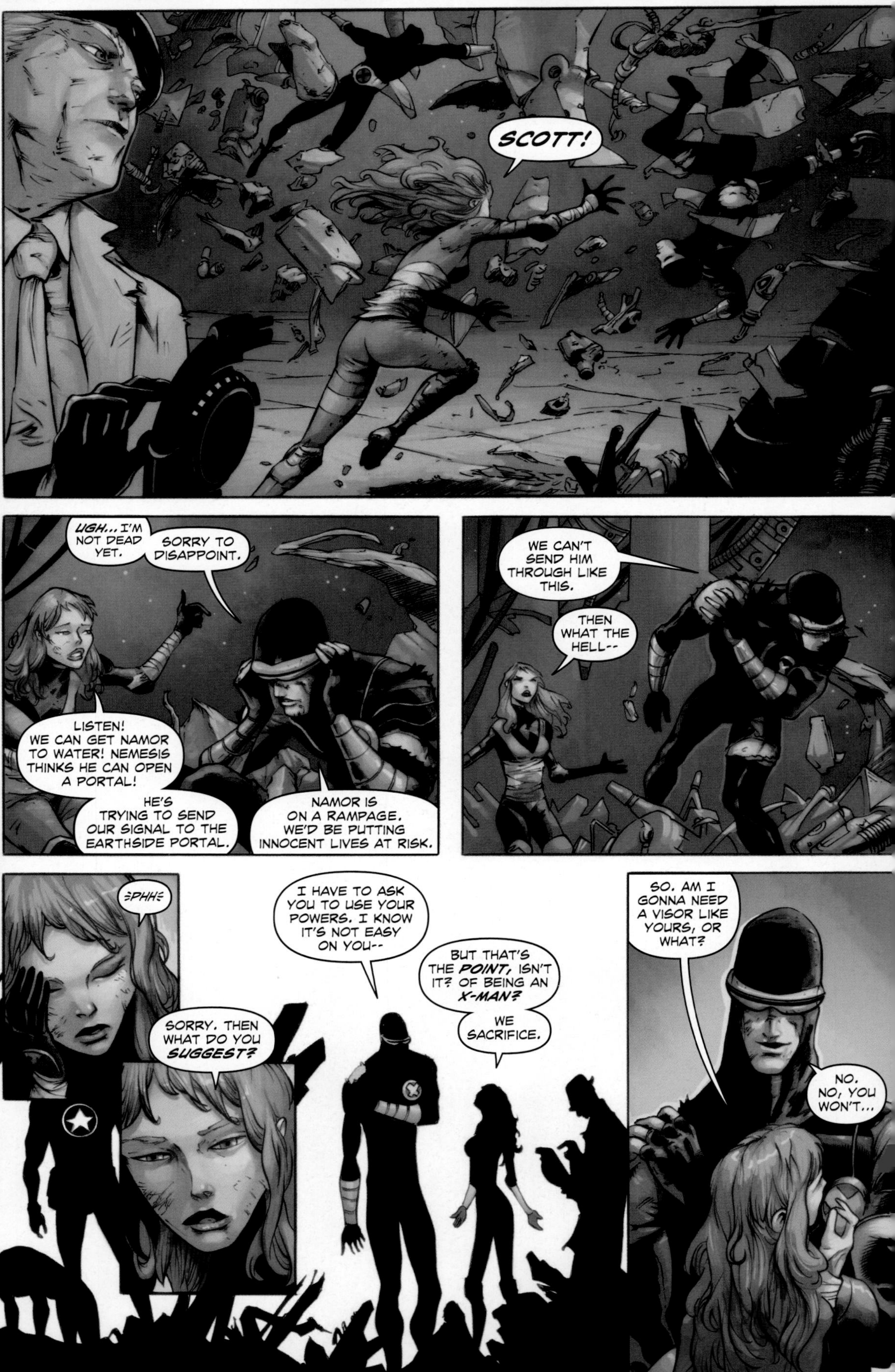
SCOTT!
UGH... I'M NOT DEAD YET.
SORRY TO DISAPPOINT.
LISTEN! WE CAN GET NAMOR TO WATER! NEMESIS THINKS HE CAN OPEN A PORTAL!
HE'S TRYING TO SEND OUR SIGNAL TO THE EARTHSIDE PORTAL.
NAMOR IS ON A RAMPAGE. WE'D BE PUTTING INNOCENT LIVES AT RISK.
WE CAN'T SEND HIM THROUGH LIKE THIS.
THEN WHAT THE HELL--
PHH
SORRY. THEN WHAT DO YOU SUGGEST?
I HAVE TO ASK YOU TO USE YOUR POWERS. I KNOW IT'S NOT EASY ON YOU--
BUT THAT'S THE POINT, ISN'T IT? OF BEING AN X-MAN?
WE SACRIFICE.
SO. AM I GONNA NEED A VISOR LIKE YOURS, OR WHAT?
NO. NO, YOU WON'T...

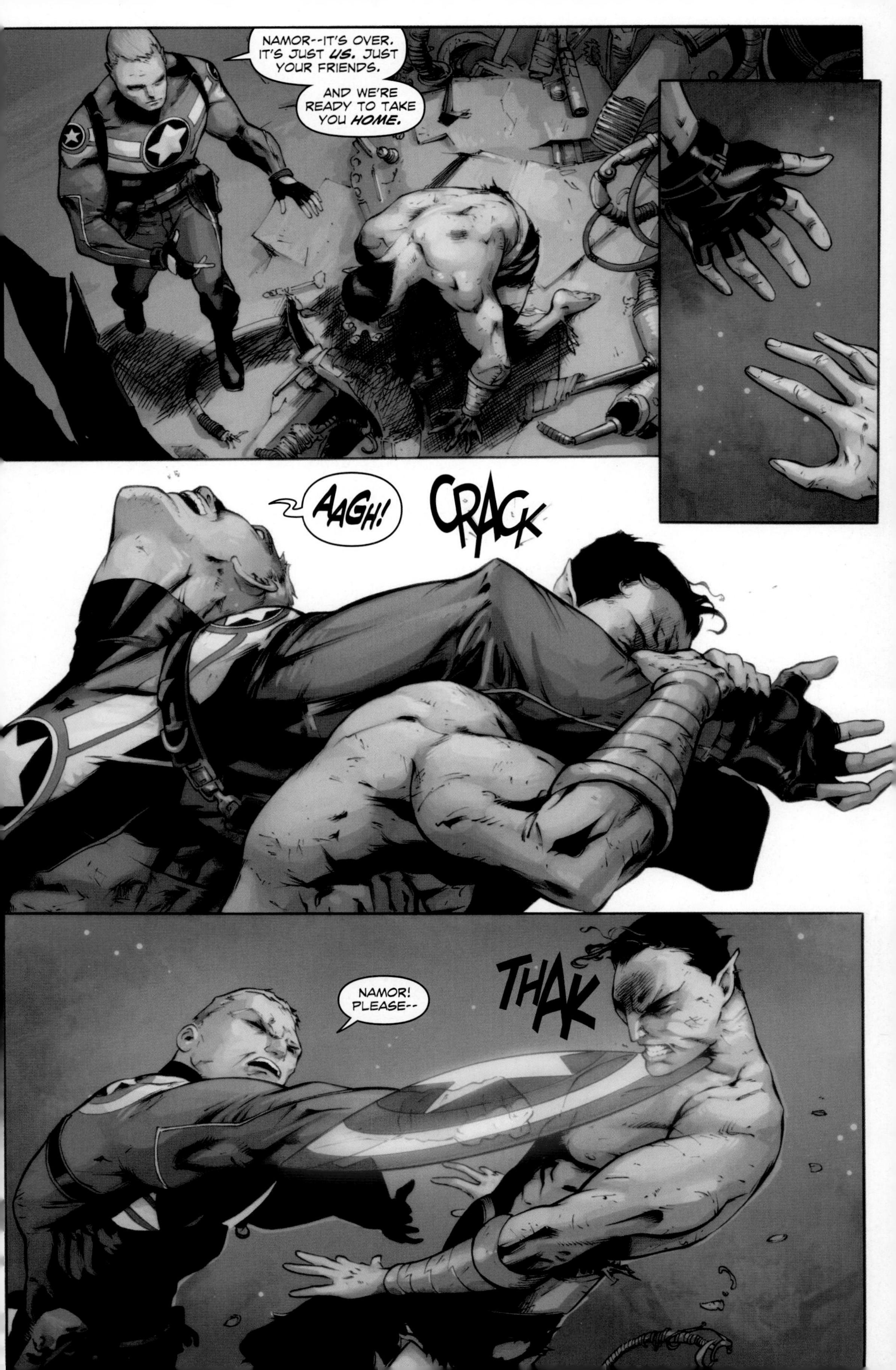
NAMOR--IT'S OVER. IT'S JUST *US.* JUST YOUR FRIENDS.
AND WE'RE READY TO TAKE YOU *HOME.*
AAGH!
CRACK
THAK
NAMOR! PLEASE--

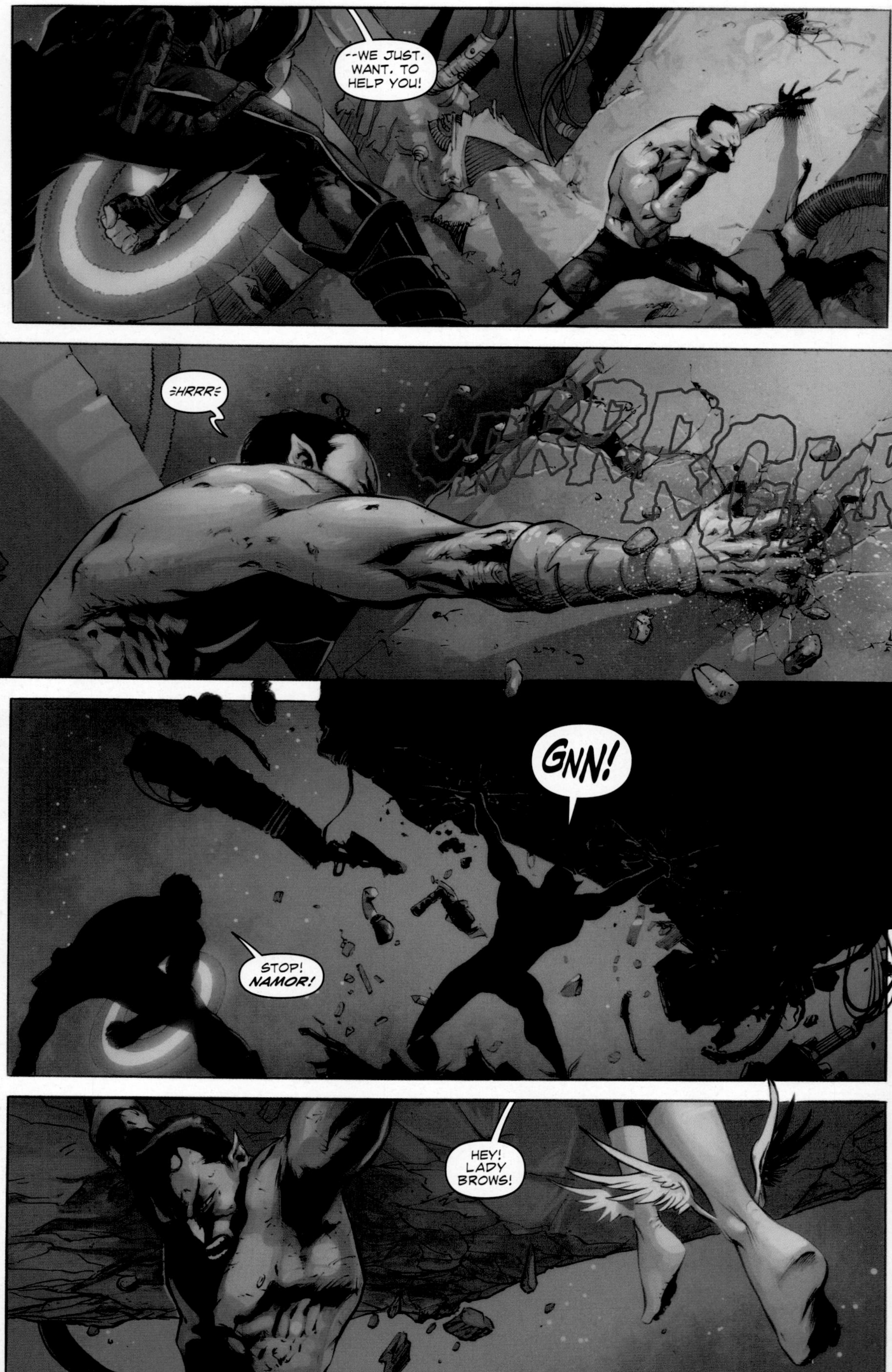
--WE JUST. WANT. TO HELP YOU!
HRRR
GNN!
STOP! NAMOR!
HEY! LADY BROWS!

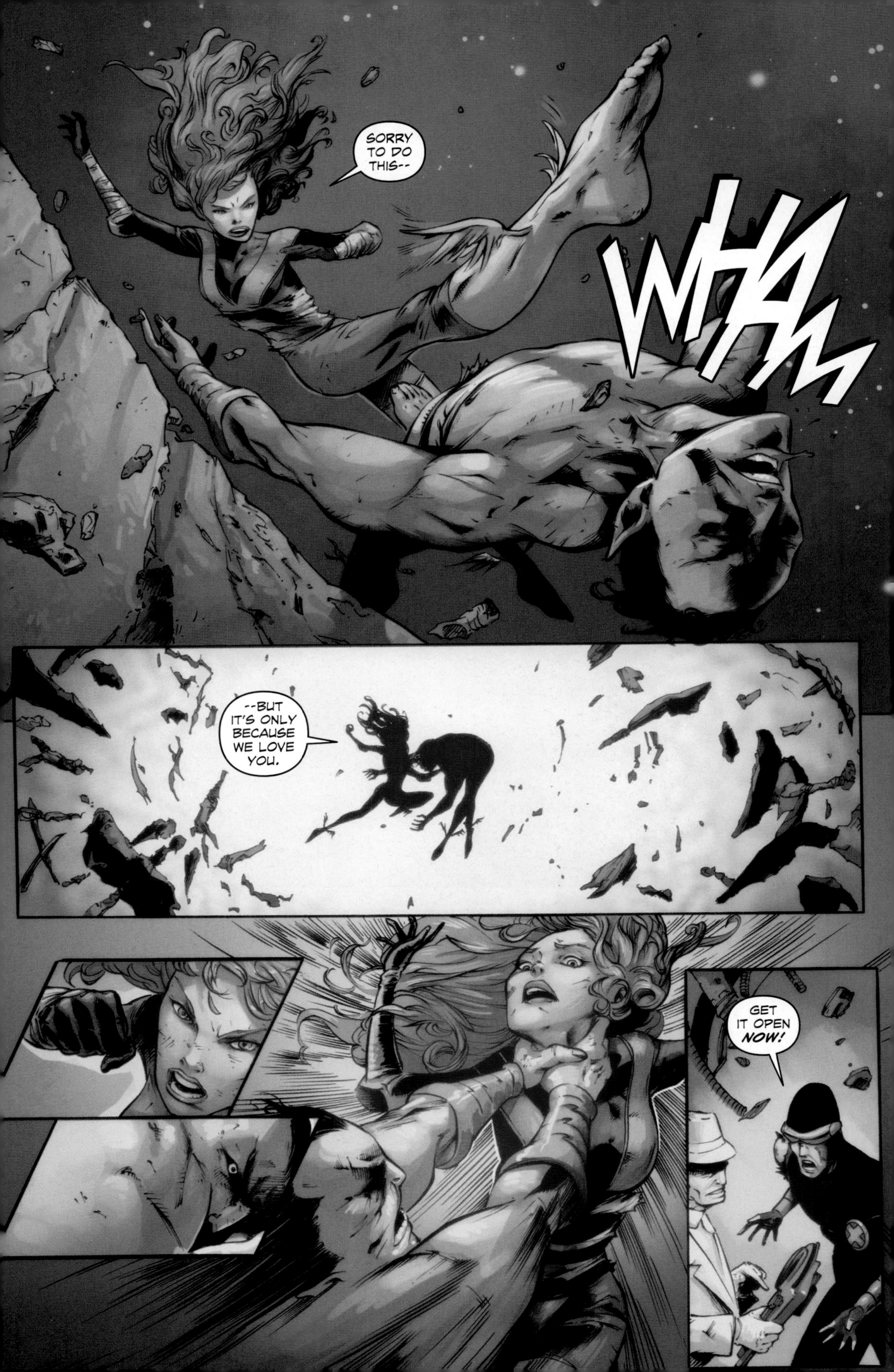
SORRY TO DO THIS--
WHAM
--BUT IT'S ONLY BECAUSE WE LOVE YOU.
GET IT OPEN NOW!

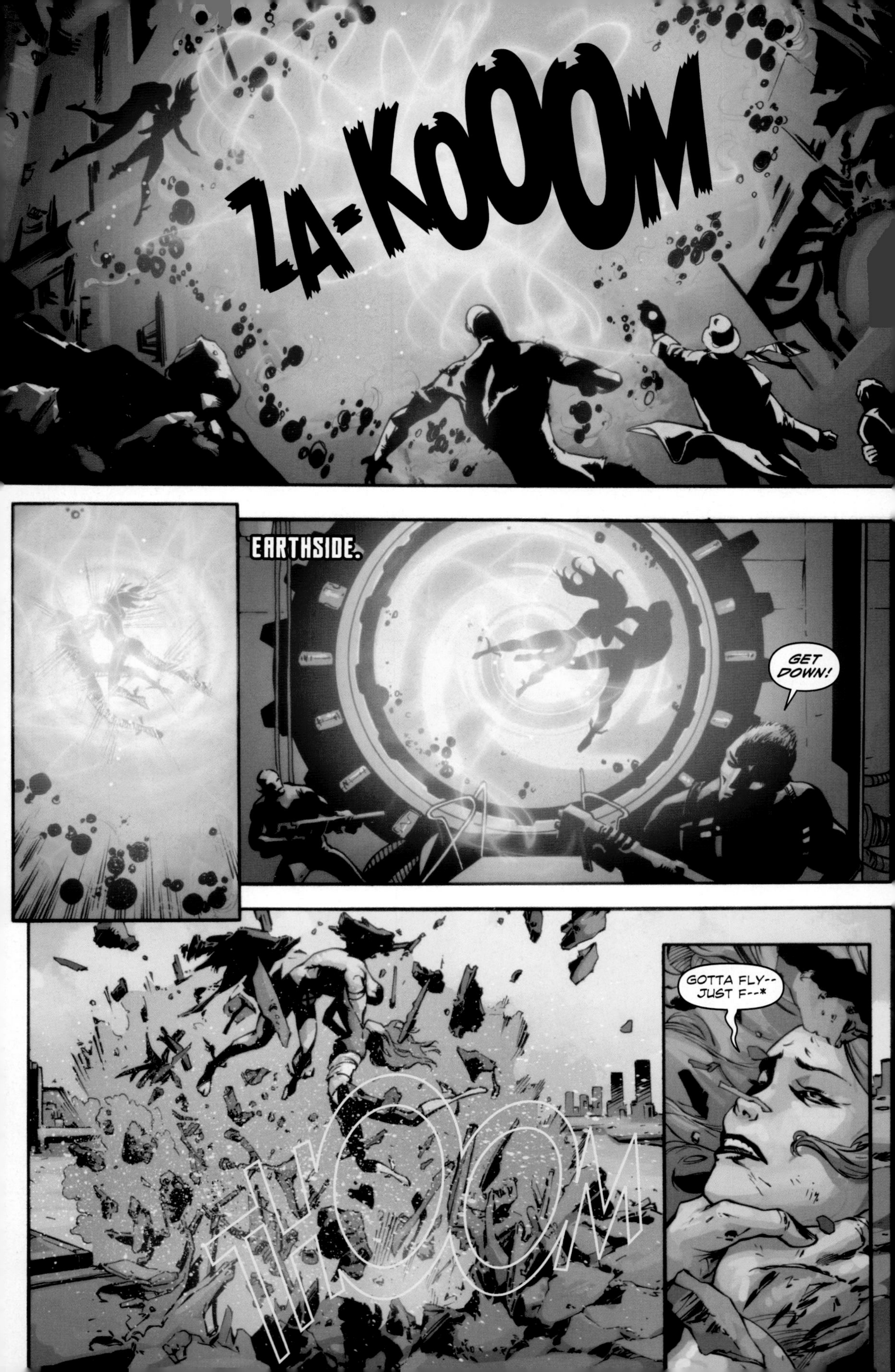
ZA-KOOOM
EARTHSIDE.
GET DOWN!
GOTTA FLY-- JUST F--*
THOOM

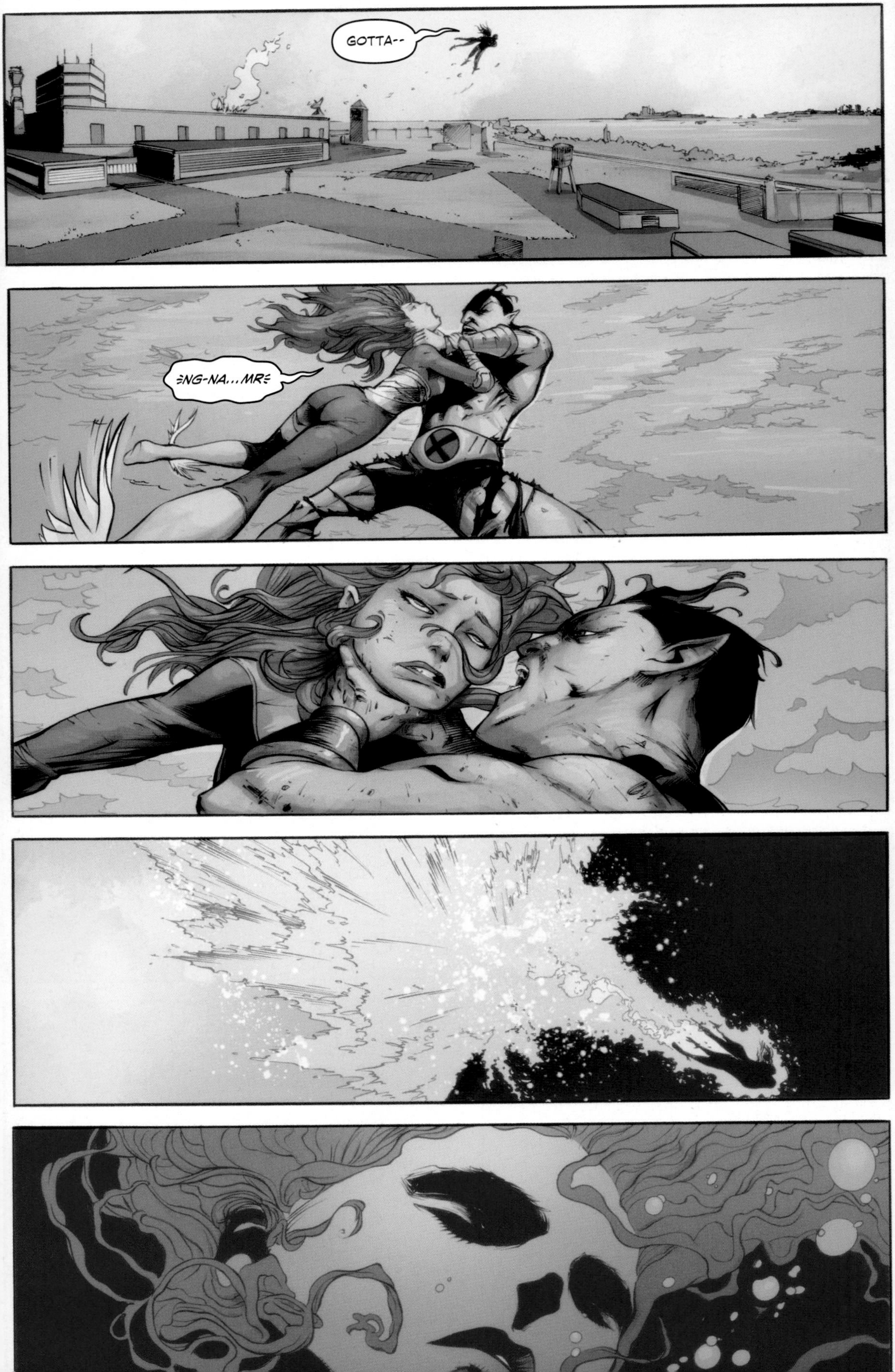
GOTTA--
NG-NA...MR

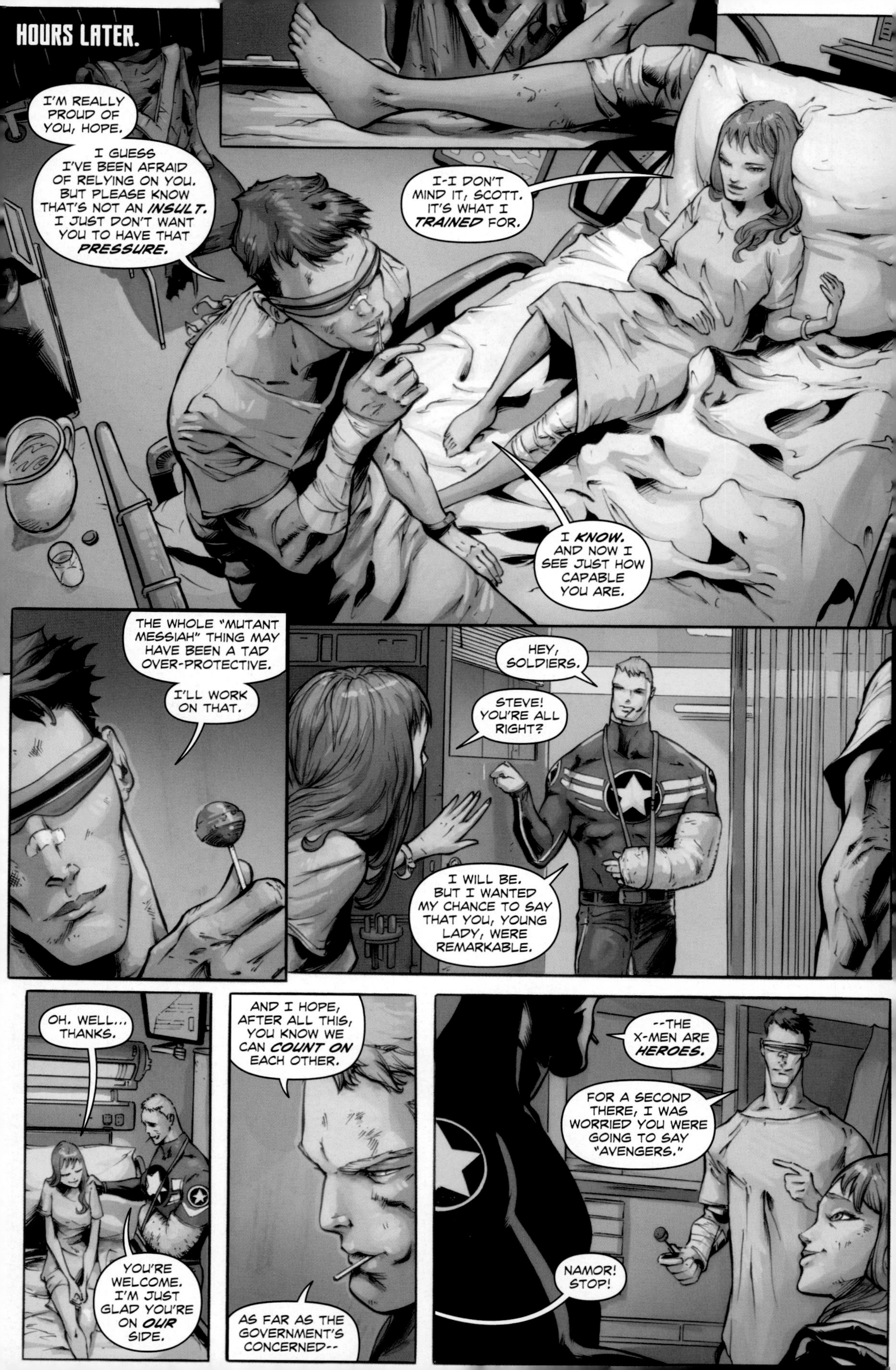
HOURS LATER.
I'M REALLY PROUD OF YOU, HOPE.
I GUESS I'VE BEEN AFRAID OF RELYING ON YOU. BUT PLEASE KNOW THAT'S NOT AN *INSULT.* I JUST DON'T WANT YOU TO HAVE THAT *PRESSURE.*
I-I DON'T MIND IT, SCOTT. IT'S WHAT I *TRAINED* FOR.
I *KNOW.* AND NOW I SEE JUST HOW CAPABLE YOU ARE.
THE WHOLE "MUTANT MESSIAH" THING MAY HAVE BEEN A TAD OVER-PROTECTIVE.
I'LL WORK ON THAT.
HEY, SOLDIERS.
STEVE! YOU'RE ALL RIGHT?
I WILL BE. BUT I WANTED MY CHANCE TO SAY THAT YOU, YOUNG LADY, WERE REMARKABLE.
OH. WELL... THANKS.
YOU'RE WELCOME. I'M JUST GLAD YOU'RE ON *OUR* SIDE.
AND I HOPE, AFTER ALL THIS, YOU KNOW WE CAN *COUNT ON* EACH OTHER.
AS FAR AS THE GOVERNMENT'S CONCERNED--
--THE X-MEN ARE *HEROES.*
FOR A SECOND THERE, I WAS WORRIED YOU WERE GOING TO SAY "AVENGERS."
NAMOR! STOP!

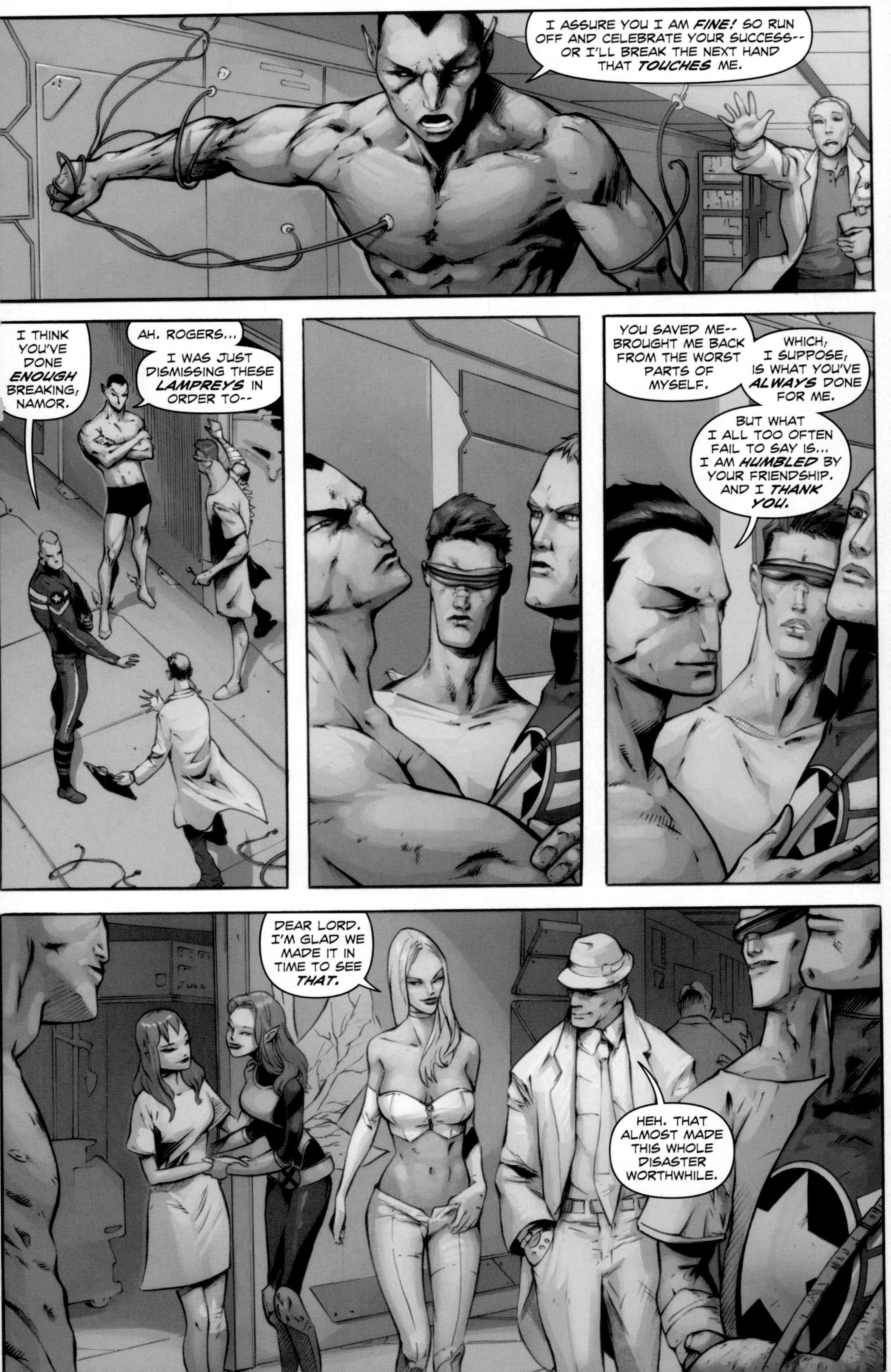
I ASSURE YOU I AM FINE! SO RUN OFF AND CELEBRATE YOUR SUCCESS--OR I'LL BREAK THE NEXT HAND THAT TOUCHES ME.
I THINK YOU'VE DONE ENOUGH BREAKING, NAMOR.
AH. ROGERS...
I WAS JUST DISMISSING THESE LAMPREYS IN ORDER TO--
YOU SAVED ME--BROUGHT ME BACK FROM THE WORST PARTS OF MYSELF.
WHICH, I SUPPOSE, IS WHAT YOU'VE ALWAYS DONE FOR ME.
BUT WHAT I ALL TOO OFTEN FAIL TO SAY IS... I AM HUMBLED BY YOUR FRIENDSHIP. AND I THANK YOU.
DEAR LORD. I'M GLAD WE MADE IT IN TIME TO SEE THAT.
HEH. THAT ALMOST MADE THIS WHOLE DISASTER WORTHWHILE.

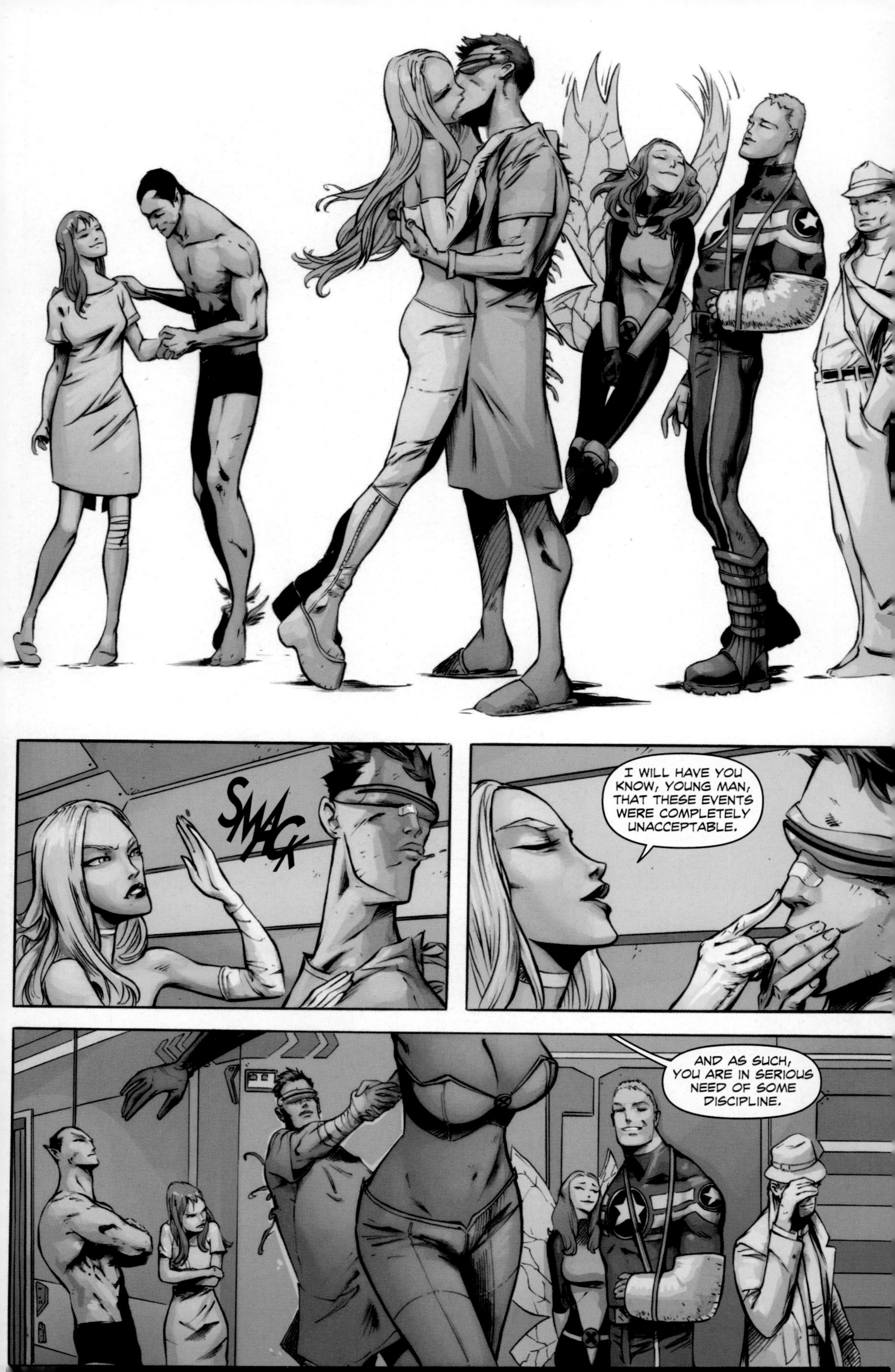
SMACK
I WILL HAVE YOU KNOW, YOUNG MAN, THAT THESE EVENTS WERE COMPLETELY UNACCEPTABLE.
AND AS SUCH, YOU ARE IN SERIOUS NEED OF SOME DISCIPLINE.

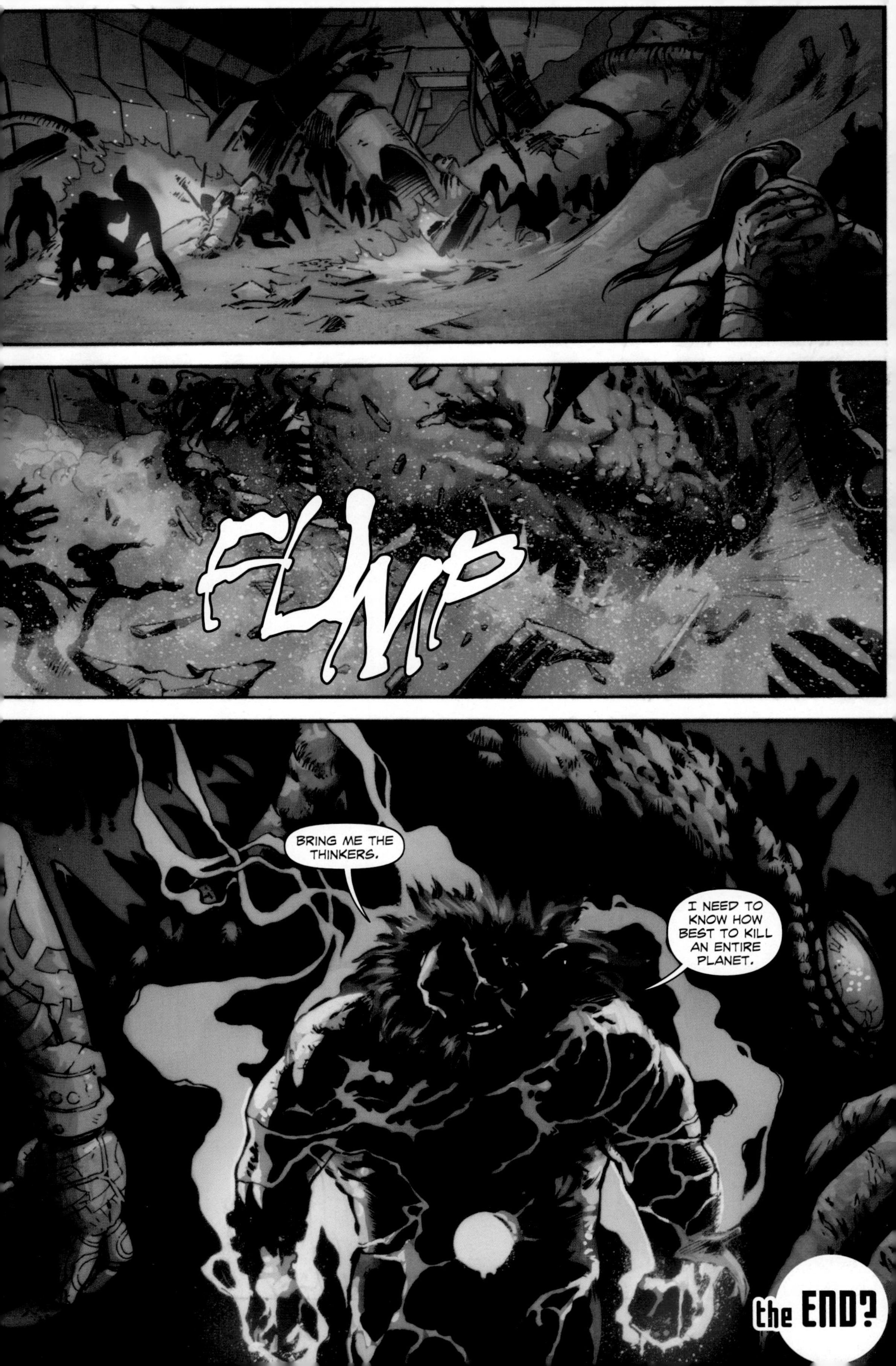
FLMP
BRING ME THE THINKERS.
I NEED TO KNOW HOW BEST TO KILL AN ENTIRE PLANET.
the END?

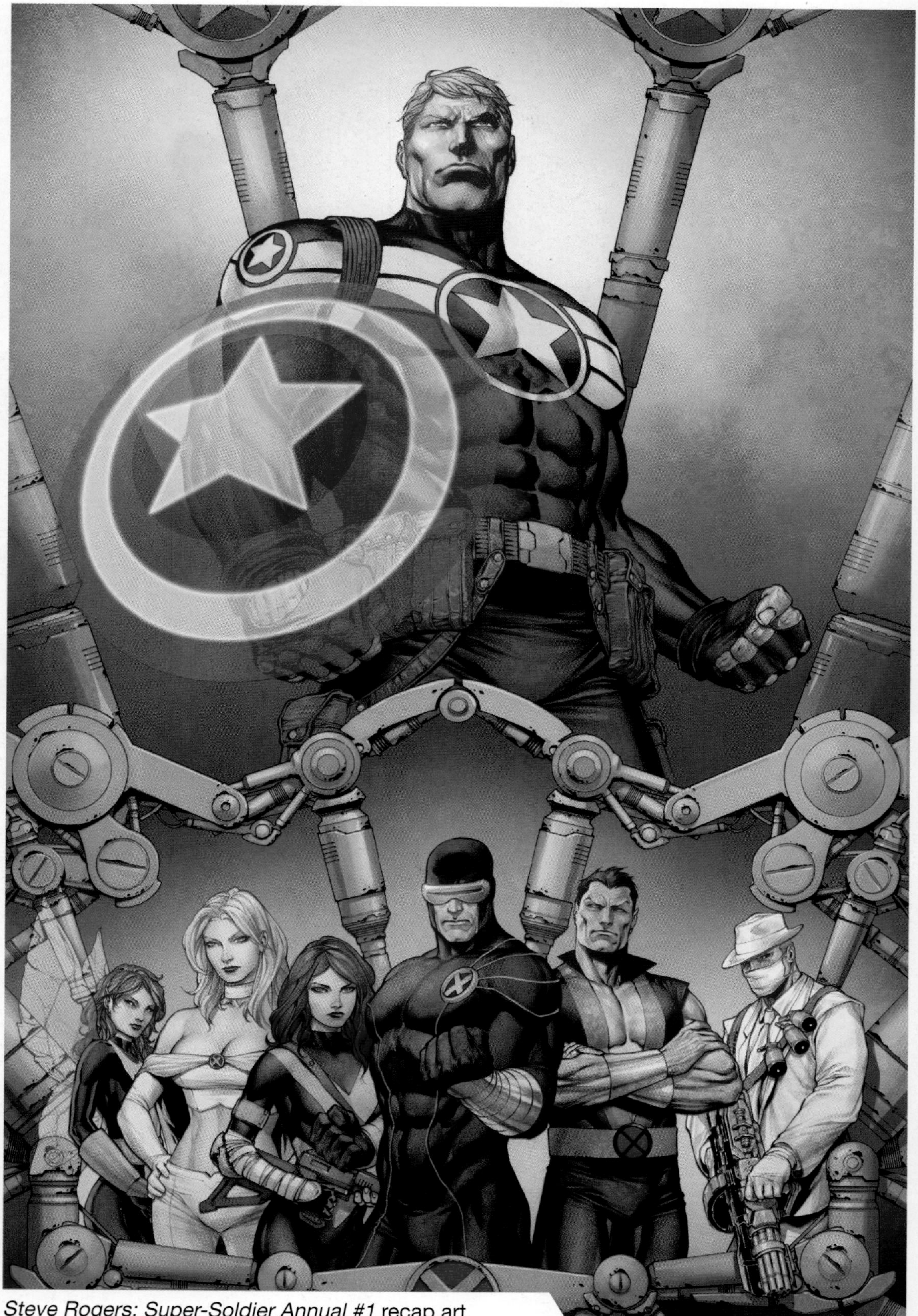

Steve Rogers: Super-Soldier Annual #1 recap art
by **Ibraim Roberson**

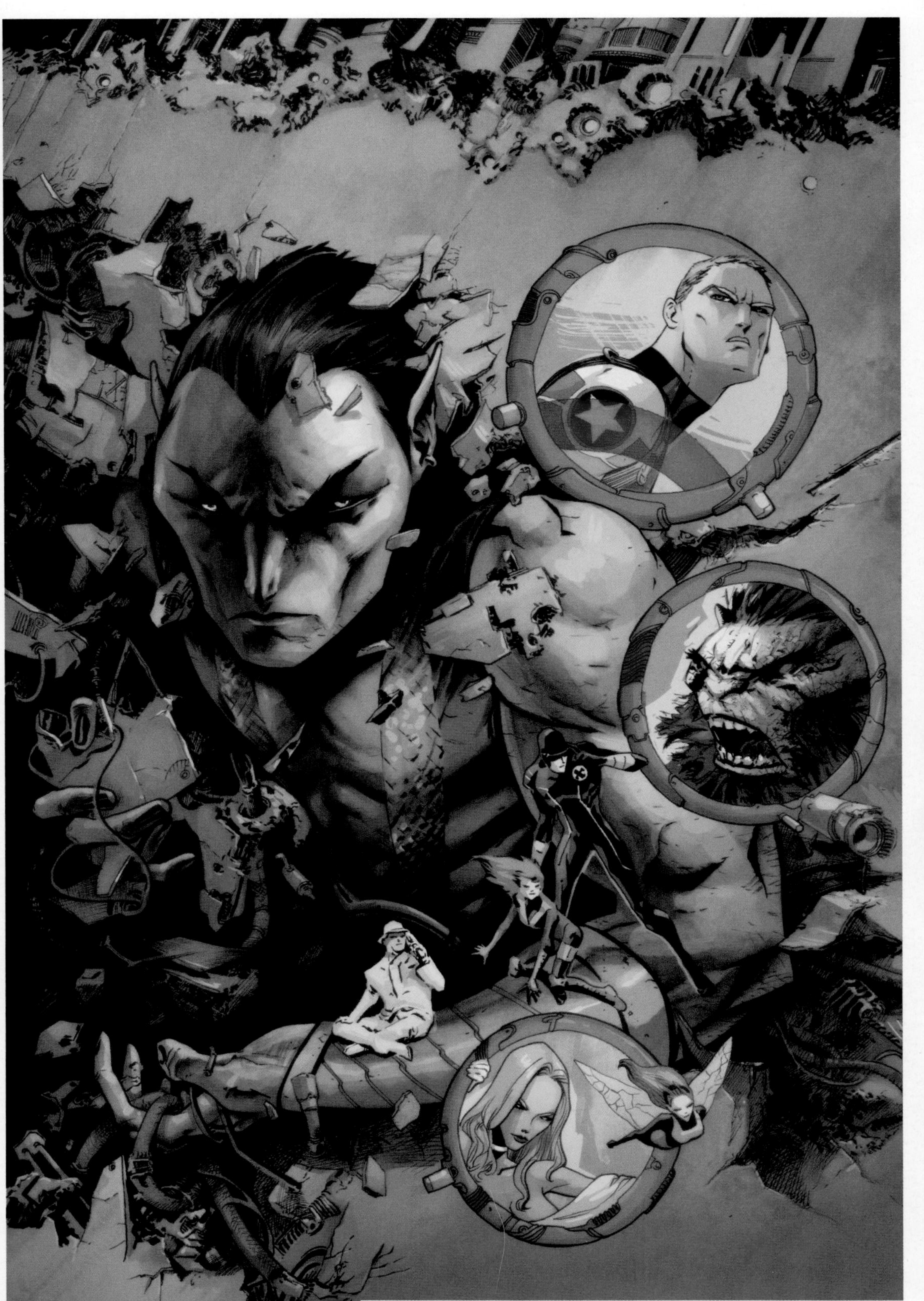

Namor: The First Mutant Annual #1 recap art
by **Max Fiumara**

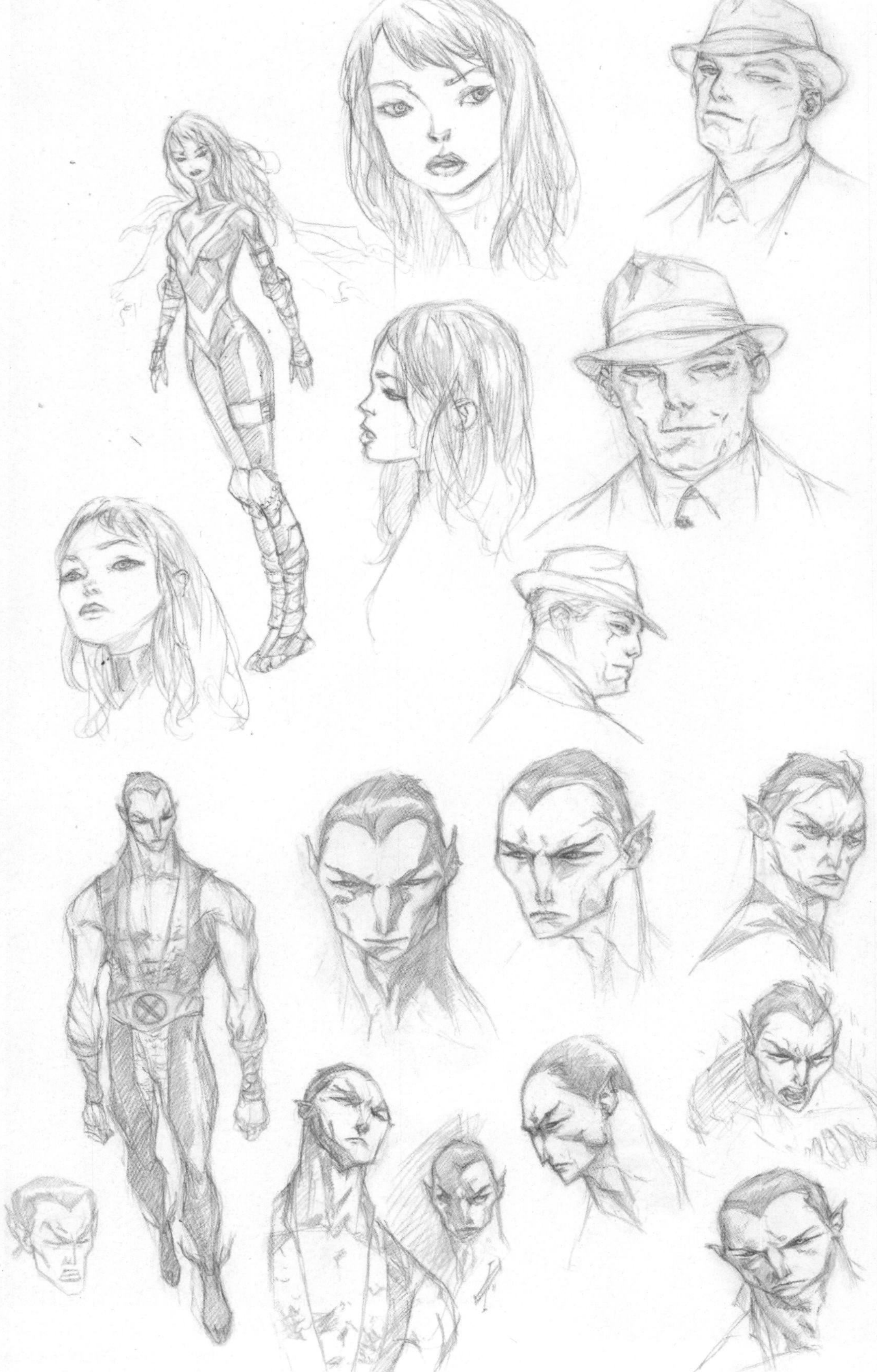

Character studies by **Max Fiumara**

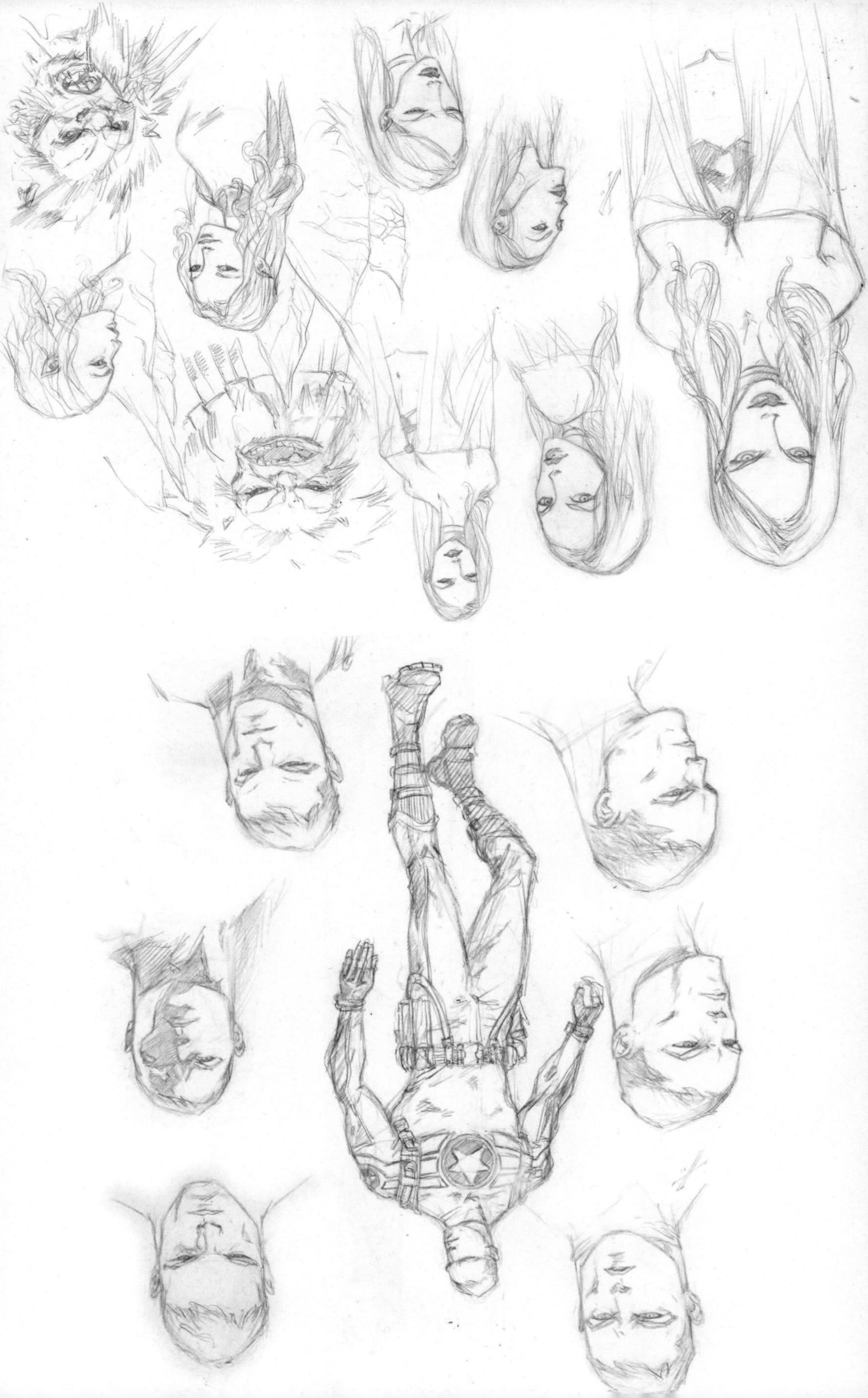

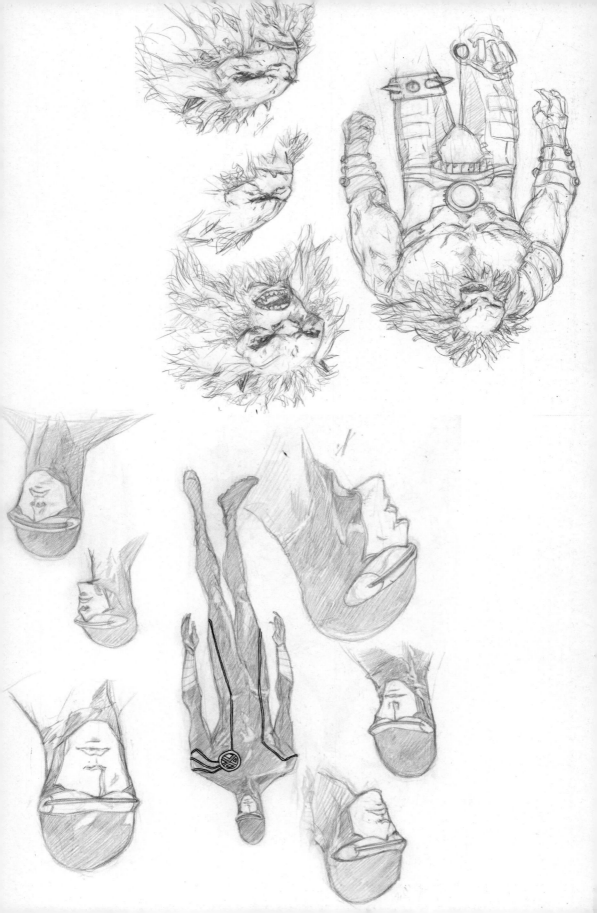